Voices from the Heartland

Voices from the Heartland

Edited by

CAROLYN ANNE TAYLOR

EMILY DIAL-DRIVER

CAROLE BURRAGE

SALLY EMMONS-FEATHERSTON

UNIVERSITY OF OKLAHOMA PRESS : NORMAN

Publication of this book is made possible by a generous grant from Michael Miller in honor of his mother, JoAnne Miller.

Library of Congress Cataloging-in-Publication Data

Voices from the Heartland / edited by Carolyn Anne Taylor . . . [et al.].
   p. cm.
  ISBN 978-0-8061-3858-9 (hardcover : alk. paper)
  ISBN 978-0-8061-4031-5 (paper)
  1. Women—Oklahoma—Social conditions.   2. Women—Oklahoma—
Biography.   I. Taylor, Carolyn Anne, 1957–
  HQ1438.O5V65 2007
  305.4092'2766—dc22
  [B]
                                2007004150

The paper in this book meets the guidelines for permanence and durability of the Committee on Production Guidelines for Book Longevity of the Council on Library Resources. ∞

2 3 4 5 6 7 8 9 10

For all our mothers

Contents

Creations

Education

Legacies

Preface

Oklahoma ranks first in the United States in its percentage of women incarcerated yet near last in its percentage of female legislators. Women in forty other states are more likely to have a college education, and one out of seven women in Oklahoma lives below the poverty line.*

So how do women such as tribal chief Wilma Mankiller, best-selling author Billie Letts, prima ballerina Maria Tallchief, Coach Sherri Coale, and First Lady Kim Henry flourish in such a climate? And how do they rise to be among the most highly regarded women in the country and the world?

And how do other Oklahoma women—those without household names who live their lives outside the glare of the public spotlight—manage to make significant contributions to their families and communities, thriving in spite of Oklahoma's history of devaluing their gender?

Voices from the Heartland is a thought-provoking collection of essays presenting the wisdom of Oklahoma women, a rich natural resource too often hidden by grim statistics. The contributors are from a wide range of professions, lifestyles, backgrounds, and experiences. There are plenty of household names but also some you've never heard before: teachers, artists, mothers, ministers, politicians, and more. From prima ballerina to prisoner, from abuse survivor to Oklahoma City bombing survivor, from national writer to Native success story, women across Oklahoma are speaking in individual voices that resonate for all women.

We did not limit the stories in this collection to one theme or thread, such as family, work, or relationships. The contributors were asked to reflect on the events and encounters that shaped them into who they are now. In response, they have shared remarkably revealing experiences that have amazed or disappointed them and that have had a lasting influence. They

---

* Institute for Women's Policy Research, *The Status of Women in Oklahoma* (Oklahoma City: Oklahoma Commission on the Status of Women, 2004).

have pondered self-discovery and fulfillment and told how their extraordinary lives grew from the seeds of seemingly ordinary girlhoods. Each voice is distinctive, yet most share a stance: unsentimental, reflective, compassionate, and unflinching. Some essays are snapshots of a single moment, while others span the arc of a lifetime. The common thread through these stories is the wisdom of persevering, of nurturing a passion, of paying attention to what brings happiness, and of appreciating that the path from here to there is seldom a straight line.

We believe we are not alone. Women everywhere are hungry for a substantive discussion of the dilemmas that confront us all. Often we hear about what separates us or how one region differs from another—red vs. blue, coastal vs. flyover. We rarely hear about what we have in common. As Susan Glaspell says in her play *Trifles*, "We live close together and we live far apart. We all go through the same things—it's all just a different kind of the same thing."

Voices from the Heartland contains stories that connect. Though written by Oklahoma women, this book transcends place. It tells who we are: proud residents who happen to live in the national crossroads of experiences, values, and culture and who stumble onto wisdom in the most unexpected of places. Our stories reveal what it means to be an American woman today.

· · ·

We give special thanks to our contributors who so generously shared their stories with us. All profits from the sale of this book will be donated to the Women's Foundation of Oklahoma.

Sooner Spirit

Most American

Rilla Askew

> Who knows but that, on the lower frequencies, I speak for you?
> —Ralph Ellison, *Invisible Man*

In 1994 Rand McNally accidentally left Oklahoma out of the index to its national road atlas. That same year, as the winter snows outside my house in upstate New York climbed toward 105 inches and the daytime temperatures sat stubbornly near zero, I began to talk of escaping to Oklahoma. My friends in the frozen Catskills exclaimed, "But isn't it *cold* out there?" They seemed to imagine Oklahoma as existing in an area vaguely north of Nebraska and south of the Dakotas. Americans aren't noted for their geographical acuity, but Oklahoma's elusiveness in the public mind goes beyond lack of knowledge: there has long been an almost mystical anonymity to the place.

Before 1995, Oklahoma kept its invisibility well: we were an indefinable vowel-state located somewhere in the middle of the country, a place recalled, if at all, mainly through the catchy show tune of the same name. Even now, on the Weather Channel, Oklahoma is where reporters stand to discuss the fronts moving through the rest of the United States. Calls for submissions from southwestern writers seldom include Oklahoma—nor do calls coming from the West, or the Midwest, or the South. These regions don't claim us, though Oklahoma borders, and reflects, all of them. It's as if each region shrugs and says to itself, "No, it's no part of us; it must belong to them over there."

This essay first appeared in *Nimrod* 50.1 (Fall/Winter 2006): 102–11.

Growing up in Oklahoma, I silently agreed. My home state seemed to me then a black hole in the center of the country, a literal and figurative No Man's Land. My niece Olivia, when she was a very little girl, would cut her eyes at the rolling grasslands or scraggly blackjacks whipping past our car window, fold her arms, and announce to the family, "We're in the big fat middle of nowhere!" I didn't teach her the phrase, but she had surely translated, decades later, the secret language of my teenage heart. I came of age in Bartlesville, biding my time till I could shake Oklahoma's dust off my heels and make for the coasts—California in my original ambition, and later New York—because I knew very well that the real world was "out there."

This is a common teenage attitude certainly, but it's possible that young people in Oklahoma have it worse than most. Our sense of our state's unimportance, its lack of grandeur or glamour or coolness, is acute—but hardly surprising. We've been molded by a literature created primarily by outsiders; educated to a sanitized, romanticized version of our own past coupled with a half-suppressed history that has been curtailed by our own lawmakers, teachers, civic leaders; and all of this largely unknown to us. No wonder we sometimes seem stuck in a kind of perpetual adolescence, suffering that youthful combination of overweening self-consciousness and low self-esteem. We don't understand the strength and ferocity of our own story. We don't know ourselves. How can we? We've only been told a part of the truth.

What I've come to understand, and what I wish I'd been told as a girl growing up here, is that, far from being a blank spot in the middle of the nation, Oklahoma *is* America: we are its microcosm; our story is America's story, intensified to the hundredth power. For a time after the 1995 bombing of the Murrah Federal Building, it seemed the rest of the country understood this. The name *Oklahoma City*—like *Ruby Ridge* and *Waco* before it, and *Columbine* to follow—came to represent far more than a place; it came to stand in the mind of the nation as an elliptical shorthand for the awful event of the bombing itself, for domestic terrorism, the rise of American right-wing militias, and, because of the behavior of Oklahomans in the aftermath, one of the nation's last, best opportunities to be proud of itself. For many weeks after the bombing, the Oklahoma character—or that portion of it available to the camera's eye, witnessed on television screens in living rooms and airports and sports bars around the country—was claimed by the whole of the United States.

To be swept from near-invisibility to the public stage within seconds by a single act of psychopathic violence is an iconic American story, as the entire drama of the Oklahoma City bombing, from the most horrid detail to the noblest action, is a distinctly American story—as Oklahoma itself is America's story. The media sensed this; they tried to put a face to it, an identity, a name. They called us America's Heartland, and I think most Americans—and most Oklahomans—believed it. In my view, they got the idea right but the anatomy wrong. This state that has long been a cipher and mystery and, like an illegitimate child, unclaimed by any region, is not the heartland; it is the viscera, the underbelly, the very gut of the nation.

An acquaintance of mine, who originates from Long Island and has traveled widely, found herself living for a time in a small town in southeastern Oklahoma; she told me it was the most foreign country she'd ever been in. And that is true too. In language and history and culture, Oklahoma is such an extreme distillation of what has taken place on this continent over the last five hundred years that it is nearly unrecognizable to the rest of the nation. Too southern to be midwestern, too western to be southern, too midwestern to be purely southwest, Oklahoma has kept the secret of its identity as a chameleon does. To the degree we've been seen by outsiders at all, it's been in stereotype—Curly and Laurie, the Joads, tornadoes and trailer trash, cowboys and Indians, dust: worn, one-dimensional sketches which we ourselves have been too willing to adopt. But like Thomas Wolfe's Brooklyn that only the dead can know, Oklahoma is an enigma, a will-o'-the-wisp which can be recognized only slantwise, in relation to its mystery; it is never, I think, what it seems to be.

This is the land that gave birth to the twentieth century's premier American athlete, a Sac and Fox Indian, Jim Thorpe; its definitive white workingman's hero, Woody Guthrie; its finest black novelist, Ralph Ellison; and deadliest pogrom, the Tulsa Race Riot, all within a few dozen years and a hundred miles of one another. Oklahoma is the only place, anywhere, that ever spawned a committed struggle to create an all-black-and-Indian state, and yet the first laws enacted by our virgin legislature after statehood were Jim Crow. Still we have more incorporated black towns than any other state in the nation. Still more Native tribes survive and thrive here than anywhere on the continent—but with the added irony that in Oklahoma they don't live on reservations: in the Land of Red People, Indian people have lost most of their land.

Oklahoma's history is a compressed, ironically inverted miniature of the national narrative, unfolding in a matter of days and weeks and months—sometimes hours—rather than decades, beginning with the Trail of Tears. Our schoolchildren receive a sanitized version of that history, one that is justifiably eloquent about the heroic survival of the Cherokee people but seldom mentions the other tribal nations that suffered equally in being forced to come here and survived just as nobly. The Trail of Tears is never named in our history books for what it was: the country's largest-scale government-sanctioned, bureaucratically administered program of ethnic cleansing. Native people died by the thousands during the Removals, and some of the histories tell us that; but they seldom tell how, within only a few decades after that suffering, this new "Indian Territory" was legislated out of Indian hands. We celebrate again and again the dramatic reenactment of the land runs but aren't told what those runs meant to tribal people already settled here. We learn about Oklahoma's oil boom but not the Osage Reign of Terror, when dozens of Indian people were assassinated for the sake of oil greed.

By numbers and attitude and collective forgetfulness, Oklahoma is, like the rest of the nation, still predominantly white; it is profoundly religious, politically conservative, inextricably rooted to the land. And this land, a vast skyscape of mountains and lakes and prairies, is peopled with descendants of pioneers and mountain folk, slaves and Indians, entrepreneurs and oil barons, coal miners, immigrants, farmers, cowboys, and outlaws—an inheritance that is like the rest of the country's, except that, in Oklahoma, we're hardly a generation removed from those roots. Like the South's, our language remains richly accented and idiomatic, and like the Midwest we still hold the prairie habit of neighbor helping neighbor, even as we carry a ferocious Western notion of independence that makes us suspicious of federal control and any lawmakers' interference. Some of America's most superb fine artists, from ballerina Maria Tallchief to sculptor Willard Stone, come from this state where children die at the hands of their parents at twice the rate of the rest of the nation. Good-natured friendliness is the dominant trait of a people who were among the first to enact a law allowing private citizens to carry concealed handguns.

Paradox and dichotomy dominate Oklahoma's character, and this is part of what accounts for our mystery, for why we cannot be classified, categorized. Paradox doesn't lend itself readily to sound bites or to easy history lessons. Our story is a study in self-contradiction: unity and division, widespread socialism and reactionary politics, Christian faith and outlaw culture, neighborly helpfulness and murderous greed. If one tries to capture who we are simplistically, from a single cohesive viewpoint, looking only at what is best in us, the effort is doomed to failure. Yet it seems that this is exactly what was handed down to me, a one-dimensional understanding of who we are. I had very good teachers in the public schools in Bartlesville, but they told a half-truth version of Oklahoma's story, when they spoke at all of our history. And half the truth, of course, is no truth at all.

I wish I'd been told that ethnic cleansing was the founding condition of my state, or about the conflagration that took place in Tulsa in 1921. I wish someone had told me that Woody Guthrie was a worthy native son, as worthy of honor as our other famous native son, Will Rogers. I would have liked to have grown up knowing that Woody was a genuine folk hero—not just Oklahoma's but the nation's. I knew he was from Okemah; I had an aunt and uncle who lived there and we visited often, but I thought we were supposed to be ashamed that Woody Guthrie came from Oklahoma because he was supposedly a Communist, although we sang "This Land Is Your Land" in our school.

I wish I'd been told about Oklahoma's Progressive past, our Socialist past, as well as the facts about the sudden rise and almost as sudden disappearance of the Ku Klux Klan here, or that there were more female Klan members in Oklahoma than any other state, or that one of our early governors was impeached in part because of his opposition to the Klan. I wish I'd known about the Green Corn Rebellion, the ill-fated, courageous, perhaps foolish rebellion of Native, black, and white Oklahomans who resisted the draft, the jingoism and false patriotism that led the country into the First World War.

Growing up Baptist in this deeply segregated state, I wish someone had told me that the very first Baptist church here was founded by two African

Americans, one Native American, and one Anglo American—a blending of the races that is distinctively Oklahoma's story just as it is fundamentally the American story. Scott Malcolmsen, in his study of race in America, *One Drop of Blood*, writes of the great experiment of race in Oklahoma; he speaks of the three founding races—black, white, and red—and returns many times to Oklahoma in order to examine race in America; but, as a young person growing up here, I had no idea how dramatic, how singular, that story was. I grew up knowing nothing about Oklahoma's black towns or the proposed state of Sequoyah or the post-Reconstruction expectation among African Americans that Oklahoma might finally be the Promised Land. It was not until I came to adulthood and read the essays of Ralph Ellison that I learned that "the Territory" toward which Huckleberry Finn lit out at the end of his adventures was *our* Indian Territory—that is, Oklahoma. No educator or parent or preacher told me that.

I wish someone had taught me about Miss Ruth Brown, the Bartlesville librarian who tried to create freedom of access for people of all races during the climate of fear and repression of the early 1950s and who lost her job in the process. She was an authentic Oklahoma hero, one of the very first whites to strive for integration here; but, as a child visiting the Bartlesville Public Library, I had no knowledge of the struggle that had taken place there a decade earlier. All hint of that story had been silenced, as the memory of the Tulsa Race Riot had been silenced in the years of my growing up. For a time, in the late 1990s, it seemed we were becoming ready to own what had happened in the Greenwood area of Tulsa in 1921, to look clearly and honestly at that violence, even atone for it, perhaps, but the brief opening of our minds to the whole truth seems to have passed.

It's not surprising that we teach only part of our history. To look at one's own transgressions requires great spiritual and emotional maturity, and this is as true for a people or a nation as it is for the individual. Our natural impulse is to open our eyes only to what's best in us, to own that part and no other. In the same way that the nation remembers the three thousand victims of the September 11th attacks—a necessary remembrance, but one which says these attacks on civilians were an exception, an unforgivable atrocity, a new kind of warfare—while choosing, at the same time, to forget the hundreds of thousands of civilians who died at the hands of America in

Dresden and Tokyo, at Hiroshima and Nagasaki; just so do we in Oklahoma memorialize the 168 innocents who died in the Murrah Building, while carefully, consciously, legislatively choosing not to acknowledge the unnamed, uncounted citizens who died in Tulsa in 1921—at the hands of Oklahomans.

. . .

I drove to Oklahoma City a few days after the bombing. My purpose, like that of thousands of others who came, was to try, in my pain and grief and bafflement, to do something to help, though I had only a dim idea what that might be. When I pulled off I-35 in the late afternoon I was deeply uneasy, fearful of intruding, disquieted by the surreal aspect of downtown. The streets were nearly empty. There were no rubberneckers, no gawkers, no hustlers or hawkers trying to con a buck from the merely curious, none of the opportunistic hustling my years in New York had taught me to expect. Nor were there as yet the grieving witnesses who would come later, to stand outside the fence and look on in silence, to lay wreaths and notes and teddy bears. On that April afternoon, at what should have been nearly rush hour, the whole of Oklahoma City seemed abandoned. There was almost no traffic. I saw no pedestrians, no cops. Yes, there were blue sawhorses and yellow strips of police tape lining the perimeter of the bomb site; there were people in uniforms and bright slickers scattered along the approaches to the Murrah Building, but the other streets were empty; and, although I expected at any moment to be directed away, to be told, "If you have no official capacity here, ma'am, you're going to have to leave"—in fact, no one told me I had no right to be there. As I drove the quiet streets; located the gutted, too-small semiloaf of the Murrah Building in the distance; parked my car and walked in that peculiar engineless silence toward City Church, where I'd heard I might help to feed rescue workers, I was struck by the incredible forbearance of Oklahomans to stave their curiosity and anger; to come to help, if they might; or to stay away out of respect and a profound sense of decency, if they could not.

One legacy of the Murrah bombing is that no event since the Second World War—and none so rooted in place, so tied to America's idea of itself, so heedless of race and class and our other unnamed divisions—had done for America what the actions of the people of Oklahoma City did: allowed us to remember what is right about us. In a terrible way it made us glad—not for the destruction or the unspeakable grief of the victims' families or to understand for the first time how vulnerable we are—but to remember that we can be willing to risk our lives to save the life of another; to believe that, at the moment of highest duress, we will behave with honor, we'll forget race, forget fear; that the American character retains the capacity for dignity, willingness, self-sacrifice.

That evening I watched trays of food pour into City Church, sent by individuals, civic groups, businesses, till the church's kitchen counters were filled to overflowing and we had to throw much of the food away. I saw the too-many willing hands reaching to do the too-little work, people struggling to find a way to contribute, in the same way thousands had stood in line for hours on the day of the bombing, waiting to give blood, though there would be tragically too few survivors to receive it. I was moved by these people—my people—even as I couldn't help but be aware of a kind of unspoken hierarchy among the volunteers, defined by who traveled inside the perimeter and who did not. I listened to a young society matron enthuse about having met the governor at one of her volunteer efforts. I saw young men swagger as they drove the empty streets in their humming golf carts, decked officially in Day-Glo slickers, holding walkie-talkies to their lips to report on the coffee needs of the rescue workers. I saw the self-conscious nature of the people's giving, their secret pride in themselves. In an age where no tragedy is too sacred for the camera's eye, even the best must suffer the postmodern curse of self watching self.

At dawn the next day, seated at a typewriter in a featureless, florescent-lit room in an undamaged building a few blocks from the bomb site, typing up name tags for workers who would go inside the perimeter, I watched the solemn faces of men and women just coming off the graveyard shift at their jobs—telephone workers, Tinker Air Field workers, postal workers, including a bunch from the U.S. post office in Edmond, where a similar, smaller-scale tragedy had played out years before—and I saw, not that unconscious pride, but grief and a deeply unassuming humility. They stood in line patiently, these weary, determined, sorrowing men and women, waiting to be cleared by FBI security, to have their names and tiny Polaroid photos laminated and pinned to their jackets before they turned to walk

out into the thin daylight after having worked a full night's shift, to labor
the whole day among the mangled remains. They came to work tirelessly
in a hopeless endeavor because the thing had been so terrible, so horrifi-
cally wrong, and they had to work to fix it right. In this way, too, they proved
to be quintessentially American.

Oklahomans reflect the whole of the American paradox—our selfless-
ness and keen self-absorption, our conservatism and revolutionary impulses,
our modernity and deep ingrainment in the past. We are a generous people,
compassionate, hardworking, self sacrificing, capable of great heroism,
decent. Violent. Filled with prejudice. Profoundly and pridefully independent. Sentimental.

In the days immediately following the September 11th attacks, I walked
my Catskills country road under jeweled autumn skies with a familiar pain
and fear and bafflement in my chest, a déjà vu–like sense of already having
lived through this. In lower Manhattan the rescue efforts continued, the
victims' families waited and hoped and prayed, but I knew there would be
no more survivors pulled from the rubble. I knew how quickly the unthink-
able would become the new reality, how the nation's mind would open to
accept the unacceptable, and close around it. That the pain and bafflement
would soon turn to a cry for vengeance for many, and, for the few, to the prin-
ciple of forgiveness, a seeking for peace. I knew that the site of the destruction would become both sacred ground and a source of division and
controversy. This sense of familiarity is one I believe most Oklahomans shared.
It seemed to me then, seems to me now, that 9/11 was one more way our
story is the nation's story. As a writer I can't help but see connections between
events, the narrative through line that runs beneath coincidence. In that sense
it seems to me now unsurprising that Oklahoma would have been the site
of the horrific explosion that was prelude to our current age of terrorism, but
with the added twist that, in Oklahoma City, it wasn't foreign terrorists who
killed Americans, but the nation's own turning against her own.

The bomb that destroyed the Murrah Building was composed of fertil-
izer and diesel fuel, two substances woven into Oklahoma's story, reflecting
both the farming and oil industries that have shaped us. The men who
conceived each of those terrorist assaults—the Oklahoma City bombing
and the 9/11 attacks—had become radicalized by the same event, in the

same time period: the 1991 Gulf War. Osama bin Laden developed his supreme hatred for the United States because of American military stationed in Saudi Arabia in the time of the Gulf War—the very war in which Timothy McVeigh learned the unleashing of violence, learned terms like *collateral damage*, which he used to describe the children who died in the Murrah bombing. And that first Gulf War, although it had other named justifications, was finally a war about the struggle to control oil—a world-sized reflection of one portion of Oklahoma's story we'd like not to remember: the shameful, terrorizing, often murderous theft of oil rights from our own Freedmen and Native people.

The blueprint McVeigh used for the bombing was a white-supremacist polemic, *The Turner Diaries*, which outlined a terrorist act very like the Murrah bombing, and what was the goal of that fictional terrorist action and, implicitly, McVeigh's goal? An American race war. And in fact the nearest thing to an American race war did take place in Oklahoma, in Tulsa, in 1921. That event has been called different names, the Tulsa Race Riot, the Burning, the Tulsa Disaster, but it bears many of the worst characteristics of ethnic war: armed conflict, wild rumor, the imputation to the other side of one's own worst acts, a profound silence and collective forgetfulness that follows. Still, one of the most enduring images of the Oklahoma City bombing, preserved in photographs of the victims and survivors, the children and adults, grieving family members, rescue workers is how completely and harmoniously racially mixed the people are. And so the circles go, the twists and inversions, the connections and parallels.

And yet, when I look at the story, I see at the heart of it perhaps the greatest paradox of all: since 1995 Oklahoma has been idealized as what's best in America—the "Oklahoma standard," it is called—and yet we continue to be anonymous in the mind of the nation. Seen and not seen. Mythologized and virtually invisible. April 19, 1995, is understood as a watershed date like December 7, 1941; and November 22, 1963; and September 11, 2001: a cataclysmic turning point at which America lost her innocence. Except of course we were never innocent, merely cocooned from half our history. The truths of theft, slavery, genocide, the nation's founding core of violence remain in our soil and blood and memory, whether we choose to look at them or not.

But why look at these buried sorrows? What does it matter that we teach our children only part of our story? We don't, as a state or a nation, do such things anymore—or at least so we want to tell ourselves. Part of the American paradox is that, on the one hand, we delight in stories of redemption, tales that reflect "the triumph of the human spirit," that remind us of the old verities William Faulkner spoke about—love and honor and pity and pride and compassion and sacrifice. On the other hand, we subscribe to a pitiless, senseless Western myth of redemption through violence. Both impulses are simplistic, romantic, sentimental. Sentiment, in its subtlety, can be a grave enemy. It looks at one side only, hides its face from unpleasantness, from responsibility. To surrender to it is to forget that redemption is earned. It cannot be won without repentance, and *repentance*, in the old Hebrew understanding, means to turn away from *with knowledge*. One cannot repent what one will not own. This is as true spiritually for a nation or a people as it is for the individual soul.

I hunger for the old verities as Faulkner outlined them; I believe them to be the dominant traits that characterize us as Americans, as Oklahomans, but I believe, too, that there is a spiritual law which says we cannot be forgiven until we are willing to forgive, and that we will not find in our hearts forgiveness for those who have wronged us until we have owned our own part.

Oklahoma's story has always been the American story. Our pain of April 19, 1995, presaged the nation's pain on September 11, 2001, in the same way our past encapsulates, exaggerates, intensifies America's past. Just so, I believe Oklahoma's spiritual future could guide America's future. If we as a people should turn from sentiment to the task of owning our whole history; if we were to begin to make amends for past wrongs, first of all by owning them and then by turning away from them with knowledge; if we were to teach our children the whole truth of who we are and who we have been, Oklahoma could become the conscience of the nation. It would hardly matter then whether the rest of the country recognized us. In fact, it's not good to become too conscious of one's conscience, is it? The still, small voice, we call it. And we are, after all, the nation's underbelly, the source of the lower frequencies Ralph Ellison wrote about.

No Guarantees

Sherri Coale

"Be careful what you ask for—you just might get it" was what the backs of the T-shirts said. Our high school's student body printed them up and they sold like hotcakes. Kids bought them. Parents bought them. Fans bought them.

Our biggest basketball rival had said they wanted us in the play-offs. They got us, and we won by thirty.

Hence the T-shirts.

Then, when the whole town of Norman descended on Tulsa's Mabee Center wearing the cocky mantra for our state semifinal rematch, the ball went square, and we were the ones who got it. We were supposed to give it. Final score: Choctaw 39, Norman 36. It wasn't pretty—the game or the aftermath. I will never, as long as I live, forget the hollow sorrow of that group of girls.

Our talented squad regrouped that spring. We locked arms and attacked summer league with a vengeance, destroying everyone who came in our path, without ever seeming to try very hard to do it. Our jaws were set. There wasn't much celebrating when we won. We just dove in, sort of surgically, wiped a team out, and then went on our way in search of another means of purging.

Summer soon gave way to fall, and our posturing crew tiptoed into preseason workouts, faking out everyone in sight. Well, almost everyone. A few weeks in, I asked my assistant coach what he thought was wrong. He said, "What are you talking about?"

And I told him. "Something's not right. Something's missing."

He said, "It's a long time until March, Coach. They know the part that matters. Give them time."

So I did. Two weeks was an eternity for me. That's how long it took until my dam just burst.

I blew the whistle in the middle of practice, sending everyone to the locker room. They hadn't messed up a drill; they hadn't loafed; no one had talked back. Everything was good, but nothing was right. I couldn't stand the incongruity of it all. Into the locker room they filed, a bunch of scabbed-over dreamers who were scared to death that the proverbial pot at the end of the rainbow had a hole in it. The silence in that concrete den was deafening.

"What's the deal?" I asked, to the tops of fifteen heads. Fifteen pairs of eyes stared at the floor. Pregnant pause. "Somebody want to tell me what's going on?" Surprise to none: the brazen summer goddesses had gone mute. They had no opinions. No one shuffled her feet, no one hemmed or hawed. My women on a mission scarcely even breathed. And so I asked, through fear so thick you would need a machete to carve your way out, "What is it you are afraid of?" And fifteen sets of eyes the size of silver dollars rose to look at me as if I'd found the Holy Grail.

"Let me guess," I said, enjoying the perspective that a summer of soul-searching had afforded me. "You are scared to go all out again. You are afraid to go after this thing with all of your being, like you did before, because you have no guarantees that you can make it happen and you don't ever want to feel again like you felt last spring." Bingo. Fifteen heads nodded in unison, and I ached for their terror—shared it to a degree—but knew it was my job to grab this moment, the "teachable one" that comes when it's ready, rarely when you are.

I told them, my voice quivering, that things of real value never come with a guarantee. I told them we were talented enough that we might be able to go through the motions and win the whole darn thing. That was a fact. But I also told them that going all out and pursuing it with all of our being promised us nothing in return.

Then I told them what I prayed was true, "Life gives you no guarantees. But I know this one thing: if you go all out but lose, it will mean more to you than if you just go through the motions and win. It's not about what you get at the end. It's about how you choose to live the pursuit." Then, growing bold from my own words, I added, "I have news for you. I only know one way to go about a thing and that's full out. So if you want to tiptoe hopefully toward an end, you're going to have to do it without me."

And I left that tomb of a locker room to the fifteen sets of silver-dollar eyes staring at the fork in the road.

The next day was a frenzy, a typical high school day by definition. I'll never forget running through the tiled hallways to the old south gym where our practice was to be. It was a defining day and activities beyond my control had caused me to be a little late. I reached down for the old iron handle on the swollen double doors, my heart in my throat, not having any idea where the previous day's conversation had taken my team. When I opened the door, I knew. You could smell it. You could taste it. You could hear it. You could feel it. My kids had decided to dive in. They weren't going to tiptoe around. They weren't going to close their eyes and back down. My guys were going for it—no guarantees, no promises, no safety net. They were in, come what may. It was 110 degrees in that sweatbox, but there wasn't one square inch of my body that didn't have a goose bump on it. No other team had a chance come March. I knew that in my bones. And it was only September.

Seven months later our team ran out of the tunnel at the Mabee Center on the campus of Oral Roberts University. We were ushered onto the state championship stage in grand fashion with smoke and strobe lights and a booming spot that locked on our team as the girls lined up along the baseline like paper dolls. The bright lights made them appear invincible, but the tears down their cheeks made them real. The game announcer introduced each team member, then the starting five, and what I had to say in the huddle that followed made absolutely no difference whatsoever. Hearts were bound, and stakes had long been pulled.

We took the floor and our first defensive stand was the finest I've seen in seventeen years of coaching. We were rabid. Unlike the surgical summer-league squad we had been just months before, we reveled in every single play. I had never seen before, and I've yet to see since, a squad so united in the joy of competition. The poetry of our fight landed us a 17 to 6 first-quarter lead and a performance that had cajoled the opposing coach into utilizing all of her time-outs with twenty-one minutes left to play. And the madness grew from there. We took a 22-point lead into halftime and opened the third quarter with a three from my point guard. The margin never lessened from that point on.

As the game wound down, I had the unique opportunity of taking my seniors out one at a time. They left their high school careers to thunderous applause, tear-stained hugs, and a resilience that is born only from immersion. The powers-that-be handed us the gold ball at center court; and, while I know there were people everywhere, I don't remember any of them. I don't remember the noise, and I can't recall the handshakes, but I will never forget the joy.

Reporters afterward wanted to talk about redemption and comebacks and the obvious justification we must feel from replacing failure with record-setting success. They all sounded drunk to us as they droned on inside our locker room. Our players showered, I conducted obligatory interviews, and we boarded that big yellow bus for home. We were twenty miles outside of Tulsa before we discovered we'd left the trophy behind.

It had *so* never been about what you get at the end.

I kept that T-shirt, the one with the caution label on the back. It is my reminder that we must be bold in our aspirations and that we must be willing to put our arms around whatever comes toward us along the way. I wish sometimes that all my teams could learn what that one did. Those fifteen saucer-eyed kids know now what something feels like when it is right. They will forever recognize it when they see it, and they will abhor a thing that isn't, even when they're not sure why. They will be different employees, different spouses, different parents, better friends because of what they learned together as they slew dragons—real and imaginary—on a 94-foot hardwood stage.

That ragged old T-shirt is my badge. It's my "risk-to-chance-reward" trophy that reminds me of the cave that pain can carve—and the capacity for joy that can be unleashed to fill it. "Be careful what you ask for—you just might get it." And then some. I'll keep my fingers crossed that you do.

Living in Paradox

Susan Urbach

One morning I went to work.

That doesn't sound like a defining moment, does it? I've gone to work on thousands of days in my lifetime, as perhaps you have. Yet one beautiful spring morning—April 19, 1995—I went to work, and life literally exploded. My office window directly faced the Alfred E. Murrah Federal Building in downtown Oklahoma City.

For many in Oklahoma City, we begin at the same point in time from the same event; yet as the years go on, we are scattered on the spectrum of healing. Some are at the one end of the scale: healed, which is where I place myself. Some are still healing, and some will never heal. I give one story.

I am the director of the Oklahoma Small Business Development Center with the University of Central Oklahoma (UCO). We are an off-campus site of UCO, and we were excited when we moved to the Journal Record Building in downtown Oklahoma City in the spring of 1993. I love downtown Oklahoma City. I had worked in the Federal Building in the mid-1980s, so I leapt at the chance to relocate our office there.

Once I stepped out of my house in the morning, so much of my life revolved around the downtown area. My job, my church, the credit union, the YMCA, the public library, the dry cleaners, the post office, my favorite restaurants, all were right there within a several-block area. I grew up in a small town; and, for me, downtown Oklahoma City is like my town square. It's not a huge, faceless, or anonymous place, but a place of great joy and comfort.

When the blast happened, my office was destroyed. I was hauled off to the hospital for several days. If you totaled up the stitching (which the doctor and I did because Workers' Comp wanted the information), it was about 3 1/2 feet worth of stitches on my left side from the cheek on my face to the other kind of cheek. I knew seven people who died, and I had other friends who were injured. All of those beloved places that were part of my personal life were either heavily damaged or destroyed. We had no office, and I had traumatized employees.

My home was a mess as well. I owned an old house, and I had just finished gutting and Sheetrocking the living room. When I was brought home, friends had to move the tarps and ladders out, move furniture in, and hook up outlets and lights. I lived in that makeshift setup for months until I was ready to deal with the chaos. My car, damaged in the bombing, was fixed, only to be damaged again when a man made a wrong turn and wrecked it, giving me yet another injury on top of all my other ones. One of my cats died unexpectedly three months after the blast, and another came down with a chronic illness that was with him for ten more years until he died. So in home or out, all was turmoil. I felt like Job.

Until one is part of such a wounding event, it's difficult to have even a clue as to how long the trauma continues to grip those involved. With the issue of terror, of malicious intent, there was also the legal system to contend with: trials, appeals, an execution, a state trial ... these have gone on for six to ten years. Even the building of the memorial kept the event front and center for the five to six years it took to complete.

From an emotional and internal standpoint, the time frame for healing takes much longer than one would ever think. Terror comes like a huge tornado that whips your life away, quick and hard and devastating. We all want healing to come that same way, but it's totally different. Healing is much slower, like the way the earth itself recovers from devastation. There are shoots of new life that emerge and grow, little by little, until at long last restoration has occurred. It's different, though, because it can never be the same as it was.

Though the bombing was a very public trauma, it was different for those directly involved than for those who were farther removed. On the one hand, there were well-meaning people who were totally clueless as to the utter chaos that my life was thrown into. A few weeks after the bombing, I ran into an old friend. She asked me about what had happened to me with the bombing, and I went through my litany of losses. Then she cheerily chirped, "Okay. Now tell me what's *really* going on in your life." I couldn't even respond because this ... *thing* was the only reality. Whatever life path I had been on abruptly ended at this cliff of April 19.

On the other hand, there were people who for years afterwards would grasp my hand, look searchingly into my eyes, and say, "How are you doing? Are you okay?" What I saw in those searching looks was a mixture of both hope and fear. With something as random as the bombing, people know it could just as easily have been them as me, simply going to work one morning. Sometimes people told me they admired my courage. I certainly didn't feel courageous. In the early days, I just felt like I was slogging through to get from one place to another, one day to the next.

There are so many facets to having been part of the bombing, and literally years of processing to get to the point where I could say, "Yes, I am healed," and say that without feeling guilty that I could say it when I knew others dear to me who couldn't. Some will never be able to say it. There are several things that started me on that path to healing early, and I'd like to share those.

The Lonely Walk Only You Can Walk

The bombing was such a huge trauma; I doubt I will ever have to face anything quite so huge again. At least, I hope not. Because it's been such an enormous thing to deal with, I have come to the observation that you don't stay the same after such deeply distressing experiences. Who you were before will help determine who you will be afterwards. You will either become stronger, or you will find more sorrow than ever in your life. Before the bombing, I was a resilient, optimistic person, full of mental and physical energy, and I am again. I had faced many challenges and adversities. But even for me, I had months when I could hardly drag myself out of bed. I went to counseling for several years. So if the hardy get depressed, the more vulnerable have an even harder time coping.

Two parts of my background taught me lessons that came in handy: I am a classically trained musician, and I have restored an old house. They actually teach some of the same lessons. No matter what teacher you study with, even the best, you can't get better without practice. While the teacher can coach you along, ultimately it is your work, practicing in the alone times, that makes the difference. While practicing can be fun, there's a lot of monotony, especially for instrumentalists. Your teacher can always tell if you have been practicing or not. Music is called a discipline, and sometimes you have to make yourself spend the time, by yourself, regularly, so that you get better and are right on, every time.

With an old house, there's always some unpleasant surprise and generally a lot of tedium. Doing the final paint job is what everyone likes to do and see. Unfortunately, there is a lot of slogging through the prep part before you get to the fun part.

My alone part lasted for three years and consisted of a great deal of pondering and writing. I tussled with what was happening with me, and I tussled with all sorts of unanswerable questions that other people, philosophers, and theologians have struggled with, like tragedy, (un)fairness, life, death, justice, punishment, and mercy, just to mention a few. Though I didn't come up with answers to those unanswerable questions (they *are* unanswerable after all), the struggling helped immensely. I look back at hundreds of pages of writing, and I can read through my journey from darkness to light. Nobody could take that walk for me.

The Wounding and the Healing

A few weeks after the bombing, I received a call from a BMX bicycle magazine editor. He was doing an article on Mat Hoffman of Hoffman Bikes, and since Mat and I had been working on some things together, he asked the editor to call me. Ultimately we got around to talking about the bombing.

"Mat told me you had been injured pretty badly," said the editor. "You're probably going to have a bunch of scars, aren't you?"

"Yes. I probably am," I admitted.

"Cool!" he said. "That's really cool, because scars tell stories."

That was not the kind of response I had gotten from anyone else! I was then a woman in my thirties, with stitches all over my body, especially on my face, including even the tip of my nose. I was under doctor's orders not to wash my face, which meant having dried blood on it for six weeks. I didn't feel very attractive. Yet here was this guy all excited that I was probably going to have scars. I knew from Mat that the guys who do BMX stunts really know about injury and pain. In fact, Mat can probably find it easier to tell you what he hasn't broken on his body than what he has. So why was this guy, who understands pain and injury, so excited that I was going to have scars? I really had to ponder that. This is my conclusion:

A scar tells the story of *both* a wounding and a healing. The more you are wounded, the more healing that needs to come your way in order for you to get your scar. You can't get that scar if the wound is festering. You can't just cover it over. But a scar bookmarks your body to a place of importance.

Because that was one of my earlier ponderings, I made it a point to look for the healing coming my way, not only for the woundedness and the losses. Healing came in strange, often very humbling ways for this very independent woman. I had to accept help. I had spent much of my adult life avoiding dependency, so it was sometimes a difficult lesson to learn. I heard it clearly from Don, a neighbor from several blocks away whom I did not know at the time but who showed up at my door and told me he would be taking care of my lawn all summer. Oh no, I told him, that was way too much. I would be happy with one time, but no, no, I couldn't let him do that. "You have to let me do this," he said. "I need to do this and you need to let me. There's nothing that I can do for the bombing, but I can do this. You need to let me give." He was right.

The Role of Faith

I am an Episcopalian-flavored Christian. In the United States, and certainly in Oklahoma, our numbers are not huge, yet it was a wonderful perspective to have after the bombing. The biggest lesson I learned from the bombing was that of paradox—of the blessing and curse, the wounding and healing, that in every joy there is a loss and in every loss there can be an unexpected joy. My church, St. Paul's Episcopal Cathedral, was two blocks from the Murrah Building. On the morning of the bombing when I lay in the street waiting to be taken to the hospital, I could look to my left and see a friend who seemed to be bleeding to death. If I looked to my right while hell was breaking loose, I saw that my church still stood.

I didn't see that the roof had been lifted up and slammed down, that the dormers on the building had fallen off. I didn't see the damage. All I knew was that it was there, and that it gave me hope.

George Back, the dean of the cathedral, is a wise and spiritual man. In his spirituality, he engages his intellect at a very high level. He modeled for us how to walk as a congregation in a damaged place that took four years to rebuild. The physical aspect looks very much the same today, yet it's radically different from what it was before the bombing, and as a congregation we have emerged as deeper people.

One day I was walking through the courtyard at church, and I met the dean. I was basically whining about how, after four months, we were still in our long-term temporary places. Long-term temporary office, long-term temporary church setup, long-term temporary Y, long-term temporary this and that. Who knew when we would ever be in our really permanent places?

He paused and characteristically, thoughtfully looked up to the side and said, "Well. Life is temporary."

Oh. That stopped me. I knew early on that Life as It Was Before was gone with the bombing. But it was a real revelation to look at *all* things as temporary. We think of some things as permanent because they are as they are for years, decades, centuries, and more. But all is temporary. And if you shift to thinking that everything is temporary, some things just lasting longer than others, then change and responding to change is less frightening.

To be comfortable living in paradox, you need to know and tell both sides. The time after the bombing was, to quote Dickens, "the best of times and the worst of times." It was the worst trauma most of us have had to deal with, and yet it was a time that brought out the best in people. It was a time when the normal masks that we all wear were ripped off our faces and we were all nakedly authentic. I experienced deep love and connectedness with others who were reeling from incredible losses. There is a balance to life somehow; and, with every gain, there is a loss of something else, and with every loss there is also a gain. By being able to accept the nature of paradox, I have lived life more deeply, and more faithfully.

We sometimes talk about the cathedral as being restored. The dean says that it is "re-storied." The one side of the paradox is the story of an act of evil intent that caused the loss of so many and the destruction of so much. To re-story is to tell the other side of that story, which is the story of recovery, of healing, and, hopefully, of overcoming.

As you look at the physical part of downtown Oklahoma City around the bombing area, you see a place that is re-storied in both remembrance and renewal. For many family members, survivors, and the countless others affected in so many ways, they, too, are re-storied. As am I.

Family

Family Plots

Louisa McCune-Elmore

In the spring of 2004, when the *Daily Oklahoman* uploaded more than a century's worth of its articles onto a searchable database, the first thing I did was search my own name. The second search, my mother's marriage to my father in 1960. Then it occurred to me to look up her first marriage to a man who was, by all accounts, a scoundrel. In fact, the same newspaper reported his son's arrest last week for soliciting a prostitute. Naturally, we are happy my mother divorced him not long after their wedding, a brave act for a debutante in the 1950s and a gift to our subsequent family gene pool. Then, of course, it hit me. I needed to see the article about Sallie, my mother's little sister.

Sallie Rucks was hit and killed by a fire truck in November 1946. She was seven or eight years old, I never can remember which. She was walking home from school with a friend and darted into the street at the corner of Twentieth and Hudson, a block away from her home on Nineteenth Street and three blocks from where I'm raising a family of my own.

It was front-page news that November 8, and the *Daily Oklahoman* even showed a diagram with the silhouette of a little girl in the middle of a street, depicting the intersection of impact in gruesome detail for all its readers. I'd never known the name of the driver. I don't think my mother even knew, or perhaps she just blocked it out of her head. But the paper included his name.

Noble Edgar McDonald was scarred for life, I'm sure. At thirty-nine, he was four years older than I am now when he accidentally killed this red-haired beauty, Louise and Bill Rucks' baby girl who reputedly brought spark into every room. I've occasionally wondered how it affected McDonald, how his life continued, what kind of man he was. I've half-envisioned him drunk each night in the corner booth at a corner bar, unable to cope with the guilt of knowing he'd emotionally devastated a family now remembered for this horrific tragedy. My mother never allowed herself the luxury of wondering about Mr. McDonald. Her parents, her brother, my mother—none ever quite recovered from the accident; and today, just a year shy of that sixtieth anniversary, Sallie's death still quietly, subtly affects us all.

It's safe to say that my mother's mother, Louise, my namesake and a writer, too, was saved from her despondency over Sallie's death by three dogs: Bogie, named for Bougainville, the island my grandfather served on during the war; Pete; and Cassandra. A cocker spaniel, technically my uncle's dog, Cassie was from good stock. Bogie and Pete were her offspring. I've been able to piece together that it was the dog-show circuit, starting with these dogs, that inch by inch resurrected Little Gram. That, her "Hound Hill" column in the *Daily Oklahoman,* and a few drinks each night.

My mother, however, saved herself by becoming busy, to this day preferring sweeping and mulling over her Netflix queue than delving into the nether world of her subconscious. I remember, as a child, pointing out to her that when I pushed my belly button a certain way, it was painful. "If it hurts to push it, don't push it," she said.

Death in the days after World War II must have required stoicism. So many women had lost sons and husbands, killed by the machine of war. Everyone suffered, so no one's suffering could be deemed greater than another's. While all of Oklahoma City seemed to mourn Sallie's untimely death—the whole fire department turned out for the funeral—the emotional complex of my mother's family was suppressed. Seven years after Freud's death, talk therapy was reserved for the academic world—to seek help would be as foreign to my grandparents' generation as the Internet. They picked up the pieces, they moved on, but they would never be whole again. A little piece of their lives was buried north of town in the vast Memorial Park Cemetery, a 150-acre plat populated by two generations of pioneers and surrounded by a distinctly eerie brick-on-brick fence.

. . .

Precisely nineteen days ago, my father died. I'm still barely able to comprehend the idea. I still half expect him to stop by my office for a visit before his banjo practice in Midwest City. Occasionally though, something brings me to the reality of it all, like yesterday when I received two items in the mail: a condolence card from Betty Price, the state's arts council director who knew and appreciated my dad from their teenage years in Muskogee, and a form letter from the Oklahoma Medical Research Foundation. Three people had made donations in my father's name. Edward Allison McCune. I wince to see his name so nakedly in print, to know my relationship with him as I knew it—matured and meaningful—is over.

That first round of sympathy cards felt like birthday wishes or Christmas greetings. The senders read the obituary in the paper or heard through the grapevine. How nice of them to support us, me, them, as we endure this loss, I thought. Those first few cards were touching, but also a novelty, a lesson on how to treat others who are enduring the same. It was Betty's card and the letter from OMRF—those were the announcements that something had happened. Your father has died, they seemed to say.

My mother, a woman whose lifetime of decision making has been marred by that one call she made in 1946—to give Sallie permission to walk home from school with friends, without her—spent the last two years tending to the requirements of my dad's illness. His final ten weeks were lived in the hospital he knew so well as a surgeon. She was there, sitting at his bedside, reading book after book and an occasional magazine. Like the past two years, those final days were marked by determined hope and shaded by tendrils of fear.

She was once a hospice volunteer, at another time a Contact Crisis worker, and a longtime Meals on Wheels driver; and though she's never been much on group participation, she has never been afraid of the sick and dying. Daddy fought hard and clung to life, only at the very end acknowledging his imminent death. She, too, stood by, staying focused on the present and never the endgame. My mother, witness and escort to death's gate, shone in the darkness of those moments. She didn't falter. She didn't ponder either. She just responded.

It's in her daily life that she falls prey to regret, agonizing and berating herself for decisions over wallpaper in the entryway and fabric on the couch—the large overstuffed couch. She recounts an endless parade of what she's done wrong in decorating her home, cutting her hair, or buying a wrong-sized Calvin Klein suit. Each "mistake" is a metaphor, a symbol of the responsibility she felt for Sallie's death. This woman, who shows up at the moment it matters most, when most people are afraid of the view, frets over a long-ago color scheme. It's an incongruous image. She's as twin-natured as her astrological sign, Gemini.

. . .

I wasn't born or raised in Oklahoma City, so when I moved back here eight years ago into the neighborhood of my mother's childhood, she was both elated and reflective. Driving past Wilson Elementary, though, nearly always caused her some flinching, and I encouraged my dad to drive into the neighborhood another way. Still, she loved that I lived here, so when I bought my house on Nineteenth Street, a mere three blocks west of her childhood home, she was pleased with my choice but less so that I would be living, unmarried, with my boyfriend.

Now my husband and the father of our two-year-old son, Chad has found a different house on Nineteenth Street he wants us to buy. After walking past it daily these last few weeks and visiting it twice with a Realtor, we're about to make an offer, today actually, which could mean leaving the house we've toiled over, scraped layers of wallpaper off of, and brought our baby home to. It means leaving the home my father knew me in, the one he saw us work so hard to decorate, and the one he so determinedly visited eighteen days after our son was born, his illness so pervasive that he couldn't make it to the hospital and his pride so strong that he wouldn't have the baby brought to him.

"Dammit," he said, it was his duty to come to us, to see that child on our grounds. He would drive himself to the city as soon as he could find the strength. "Dammit, he's a Jim Dandy," he said when he first held the baby, and then came the tears. I took photos, wiping away my own.

This new house, like ours built in 1917, is a block and a half from where Mama and Sallie grew up, and I've been cursed with worries that by living there something tragic might befall my own children. I called my mother and insisted that she tour the house before we committed to an offer. I needed not only her approval but also her sense that it would be safe for Mac and our future children.

"I love it," she said, after we walked through the house with a small entourage composed of two colleagues and our babysitter. She and I hung back on the sidewalk as the others walked ahead. "I can really see you and Chad there, raising a family. And best of all, it's finished. You wouldn't have to do a thing."

"But," I said.

"But what?"

"But what if something happens here?"

"Like what, honey?"

"What if something happens like a baby drowns in the bathtub? What if something like that happens?" I said with intensity, urgency.

"Honey, you can't live your life like that. What if something happens at your present house? A house doesn't have that kind of power. You've got to stop worrying about things like that. It's an unnecessary stress. Besides, you would never leave your baby alone in the bathtub."

"So you feel good about this house?" I asked, wondering if I might someday accidentally leave the baby in the bathtub.

"I feel great about the house," she said. "I can just *see* you there. It is much nicer than I expected. I really can see you there."

· · ·

A few days ago, when my husband and I were driving back from Home Depot, I asked him what his motto was. He said he didn't know, only because heretofore he hadn't given it much thought. Fact is, he has so many standards he lives by and has pondered so many thousands of variations of the human condition that he would be the most likely to have a motto. Right on cue, he asked if I had one, and I shared it with him. Goethe once wrote, "Just trust yourself; then you will know how to live." That is my motto.

My mother is the one who taught me about "that inner voice," to listen to the gut instinct. Yet since Sallie's death so many decades ago, my mother has had a conflicted relationship with this kind of trust, this inner knowing. My dad taught me to be superstitious and safe, and they both demanded in their passive way that we never take anything for granted. No motorcycles, horses, four-wheelers, and no enduring family feuds. Bitterly ironic, then, that my dad, who'd operated on the colon many hundreds of times, died of the very disease he knew most about, never once having had a colon check. For every bit of wood knocked on and black cat avoided, he died ten, maybe twenty years prematurely. So, too, my mother's own irony— she who reminded me dozens of times to listen to that inner voice doubted herself at so many turns.

I am their daughter. I trust myself but not before asking my husband and best friend three times each if I'm making the right decision, not that their opinions matter much. Truth is, I trust myself; I already know my own mind. It's their reassurance, validation, and support I'm seeking. I'll knock on wood from now until the end of my days, but none of my attempts to neutralize tragic events will keep me from that first colonoscopy on my fortieth birthday or from checking my baby's breath at every passing instance.

Yes, trust yourself, and the answers will come. But never close on a house on the thirteenth day of the month.

The Most Beautiful Frog

Julie Carson

I came into the world late one night in October 1970, a unique being in all the world, created by God in his image—well, sort of. My dad thought I looked like a frog. My mom thought I was the most beautiful thing she had ever seen. Regardless of initial impression, both of them have loved me to pieces every moment of my thirty-six years on this earth, a blessing unsurpassed by any level of success, money, or fame a person could ever achieve. It is only by the grace of God that I was born to such a wonderful, loving family, and I am so very grateful. Likewise, it is by God's design that I have my mom's smile but not her beautiful blue eyes; that I have my dad's shiny dark hair and eyes but not his aptitude for all things mechanical. And as God does with all His children, he created in me a uniqueness that is something more than simply a mix of my mom and dad—something just me.

I have no remarkable physical uniqueness that is obviously apparent: I have all the right appendages located in all the right places that all work pretty much as they should. And I look like a pretty even mix of my mom's and my dad's features. Yet in one fundamental trait, one that goes to the core of my being, I am terribly different from not only my parents, but from nearly 90 percent of the human beings on this planet.

I have always known I was different—at least since I was conscious of myself as a person. My parents always knew this too. I had a tendency that was very different from other people, even though everything I saw modeled growing up, by my parents, by my teachers, by society, was to the contrary. I am at a loss to explain how I came to this tendency. I didn't want to be this way; I didn't try to be this way; I don't have anyone in my family who is this way. I just am this way.

At the turn of the century, there was virtually no one like me at all, at least in normal society. True, there were a few famous or infamous characters who are reported to have had the trait I have, but it was mostly viewed as odd or unnatural. In fact, at the time of the Salem witch trials and the height of puritanical fervor, being like me was a clear indication of witchcraft. Thank goodness I wasn't born then! And when I look to the Bible for solace in my uniqueness, I find that not only is my trait considered quite unfavorable, but that the devil himself is nearly always portrayed as being this way! I guess that is where the historical persecution and association with witchcraft come from. Fortunately, we are much wiser now, and people don't still hold such provincial ideas.

As I reflect upon my journey through life, I recall that my parents tried to do what they could to change me, but it wouldn't take. To be sure, their encouragement wasn't narrow-minded or malicious; it was loving, based on the understanding that I would be different from other people and that a number of things in my life would be more difficult. Yet I didn't change: I couldn't. I could fake it. I could imitate others, but it wasn't me. It was unnatural and uncomfortable. This was obvious to my family who, happily, loved me just as I am once they realized this.

In school I never knew anyone else like me. I always felt like the odd one. I went through a phase as a kid where I did try to change, particularly in my early teens when fitting in meant everything. I got really tired of being "different" and wanted to be exactly like everyone else. I tried and tried, but I just couldn't do it because I was so strongly inclined the other way. As I grew older, I found that there were other people like me, though not a lot. There always seemed to be an instant connection when I found someone like me. As a teenager, I even discovered a national organization for people like me. I was excited to join it and finally take pride in my uniqueness.

Now, as a thirty-something with more life experience and education to draw upon, I know and take comfort that science can explain what makes me different. It is part of the hard-wiring in my brain that I cannot control. And while science may be able to decode and decipher the wildly compli-cated interactions of neurons, synapses, and chemicals firing in my brain, and the genes that cause these precise interactions, only God can answer why. I am quite content to leave that in His hands—and accept all of my traits as blessings.

God gave me the rare blessing of being left-handed, a trait that affects everything I do in my life. Playing sports, or tying my shoes, or using a ruler, or writing, or which side of my brain dominates the other—this trait influences everything. I could learn to use my right hand, but I can never change what it is in my brain that makes me instinctively reach for an object or break a fall with my left. Yes, being a southpaw makes some things in my life more difficult or challenging, but it makes some things easier too. Most importantly to me, it makes me who God intended me to be—and who can resist that?

Storming

Joy Harjo

Storms: tornados, hurricanes, and general thunderstorms are what come to mind when I look back at my growing up years in Oklahoma. The weather was always a major topic and the appearance of storms was often sudden, unpredictable.

We lined up in the halls on our knees for tornado drills at school, and at home we were at the mercy of whatever came our way. I was afraid because I knew that houses could be tossed around like toys, but I was also attracted by lightning and thunder. I was elated by the smell of ozone and the urgent response of the earth and was mesmerized by the light show. I felt intimately aware of the communication between earth and sky. My mother warned me away from the doors and windows because the lightning would take me. But the stunning strikes of lightning dancing all around and the terrible roll and slap of thunder spoke to me.

My mother's mother was obsessed with disaster, and her warnings were always followed by the recitation of a catalogue of stories of children who had been struck by lightning, like the baby who was whirled away from her mother's arms by a tornado and found miles away in the crook of a tree. Or the girl pierced exactly through the heart by a broom straw; she disobeyed when she was told to move back from the door, to hide from the storm. See what can happen?

Once my grandmother got started telling these stories she didn't know how to stop. The world was a treacherous vale of danger. You had to be alert to trick death as it rode close to your shoulder, taking everyone around you. By the time I was hearing these tales, she'd lost the scope and depth of the imaginative stories that had kept her children entertained years before. Each episode of her ongoing epic had been a thriller of adventure and drama. My grandfather often left for months to work for the railroad or to take any other work he could find. My grandmother was then left alone with seven children—six boys and my mother—with no resources other than what they could dig up in a depressed community. They were often hungry. Stories were all they had. In my grandmother's stories there was no hunger; there were beautiful homes in which to live and adventures to keep the children's minds off their grumbling bellies and the haunting taunts of the other children at school.

The instinct for good storytelling can be inborn, but the techniques were honed by my grandmother's upbringing in a full-blood Cherokee community near the Oklahoma-Arkansas border in which stories were the libraries of knowledge and storytelling was the school or university.

For some in Oklahoma it's still that way.

I was intrigued by my grandmother's forecasts of disaster, but frightened because I'd seen trees stripped by lightning and uprooted by fierce winds. I'd waded through receding floodwaters at Fort Gibson Lake after yet another famous storm, seen poisonous snakes dangling from tree branches where they'd been caught in rising, rushing waters.

People still talk about the Easter storm in Oklahoma that took place in the 1950s. My parents were working at a bar they briefly owned on the north side of Tulsa. They'd stay out until 2 or 3 in the morning to close it out. (That bar didn't last long. My father and his friends slammed into it with a truck one night after partying up, not long after the Easter storm.) We were left with Mary, our elderly babysitter who lived with us for a while until she became disgusted with my father's drinking and left. She's the first person I ever saw wear house slippers.

That night, as the storm started, Mary walked around the house sprinkling water from a little jar and praying. I followed her, asking questions, intrigued with this ritual. It was because she was Catholic and the water had been prayed over by the priest, she told me. All of this was new to me. She whispered prayers to Mary, Jesus' mother, for whom she was named. In our church Mary was meek and incidental. Women had no place in the power circle.

The storm worsened. Lightning made daylight. Winds shook the house. I wasn't afraid. I climbed onto the top bunk in the children's bedroom and went to sleep. The storm was oddly comforting. I rode into the dream world on waves of thunder booms.

The next morning, when we all got up to look for our Easter baskets, we were greeted with the damage of one of the worst tornadoes to ever hit northeastern Oklahoma. The window sashes had been torn off our house, trees were uprooted, and some neighbors' houses had been destroyed. I had slept through it.

When the heart of the storm hit, Mary took the other three children to my parents' bedroom to huddle with her under the big bed for protection. I was left behind, she told everyone, because I'd kicked and punched her when she tried to wake me.

I remained impressed with Mary's holy water and questioned myself as to its influence in our house's relatively small amount of damage.

Later as I grew up I witnessed a few tornadoes as they skip-jumped through the neighborhood, flew over our house and the city, slamming houses and tossing cars on the way. What is touched and what is left alone is always a story of miracles and disasters. There appeared to be a strange, perverted sense of humor to the logic of a tornado's mind. A cow would be left standing on a roof a mile away calmly chewing grass, and next to it a whole farm would be turned into timber.

I questioned myself about this, too, and catalogued it in the same section as holy water, snakes hanging from trees, and a father who was drinking for a vision.

But for all this potential danger from the weather it was the human storms in our house that did the most damage. When I was eight the culmination of emotional drama blew through our home, and it took my father away from us. I missed my father terribly, though I was confused at the relief I also felt at his departure. His drinking, carousing, incoherent moods were difficult to negotiate. The house was broken either way.

I could not construct a story to hold anything together. I could not invent a story to bring back my father to us, a healed man. At the root of the storm was the sickness of racism. Being Indian in Oklahoma was never easy, even in a time in which many people claimed Indian blood. My father couldn't make peace with being a Creek Indian man in Oklahoma, so he fled the state.

At eight years old, I was the oldest of four children. I didn't gather everyone up in the aftermath or otherwise pick up the pieces—like an obedient and maternal first daughter. Each of the children was stunned, and we all scattered into different survival modes: my little brother was just learning to walk, my sister stalwartly behaved, my brother who was next to me in age started down my father's path, and I decided I would leave Oklahoma as soon as I could to find my own life.

All these questions converged the night Hurricane Carla hit Tulsa. My mother and I had been following the storm on the news, then turned off the television because it was dangerous to watch as Carla's sister storms danced over the city. The other children had been asleep for hours.

My stepfather was out at some event to which he wouldn't take my mother because he was ashamed of her. She wasn't cultured enough, which meant she wasn't white enough.

My mother and I stayed up to watch the storm. The reports said it was losing power, but it still packed danger. It was September of 1961. I was ten years old but felt ancient with questions, most of them unanswerable, or up to this time unaskable. The largest underlying question had to do with the evil field of my stepfather's house and the mess we were in in his house.

As the storm grew closer and the pressure grew, we talked about things that had happened in the neighborhood, and of my mother's hopes and dreams. The woman across the street from us beat her daughter until she was literally cross-eyed, and nobody did anything about it. My best friend next door, a Seminole girl, had her real mother and father. Our family was as different as the two middle-aged men who lived together down the street. I didn't tell my mother about the fights I had with kids at school who gave me a hard time because I was Indian and my mother was divorced.

She wanted the best for us, she said. That's why she was waiting out the emotional storm with our stepfather: we needed a father.

I asked her for my favorite story, the one about being forced to live in a haunted house when she was my age. She told me again of how her father didn't show up when he was supposed to so they had no money at all for food or for a place to live. They got kicked out of their place right before Christmas, all their stuff put out into the snow. The little kids were crying as they walked far out into the country to the boarded-up house that no one would live in because it was haunted. They made a fire. She remembered being miserable as she and her favorite brother hunted in the woods for kindling. Newspaper stuffed in their shoes covered the holes in the soles.

They all stayed on the first floor on pallets made of rags and wouldn't venture upstairs because that's where most of the haunting took place. "Every night" she said, "the party would start. A piano player would start up with that old-time dancehall music and you could hear the clink of drinks and the shouts and talk would grow louder as the evening moved on. Then a fight would erupt. We would actually hear gunshots and then there was the terrible sound of a body being dragged downstairs. We'd hide under the covers. This happened every night."

Our house creaked with the fierce winds beginning their sweep over the city. The electricity flickered with the pressure; the storm had officially arrived. We walked through the house together and checked all the windows and doors. My brothers and sister slept soundly. The more the storm pummelled Tulsa, the more we talked. I valued this time with her. It was rare; since she had married my stepfather, she had taken on yet another job because she had no help with expenses even though my stepfather worked.

My mother told me it had been her dream to have four children: two girls and two boys. We would have what she didn't: a house of our own, plenty of food, good clothes and anything else we needed. She didn't want us to suffer. I looked at the clock, fearful for my stepfather's arrival, to be found talking with my mother.

Suddenly there was the lull of the eye. It was a strange calm, like the bruised sky preceding a tornado. I asked my mother to leave our stepfather. We would be okay. I would donate my babysitting money. We could all help; my brothers and sister and I had already talked about it. We could make it. It was then a ball of fire swooped through the house. She later called it "ball lightning" when she told the story. I saw it as an entity, an eye that could see what I could see, an omen that the storm was not over and it wouldn't be for several more years. We sat through the rest of Hurricane Carla in relative silence. I imagined the storm sweeping lies away. I imagined us safe.

Panhandle Lessons

Nancy Leonard

I grew up in northern Illinois, surrounded by a loving family and supportive friends and having a strong sense of community and my responsibility to it. I was the oldest child and only daughter of parents who instilled in me a wonder of the world and the belief that everyone was created equal. My interests were shaped by my father and grandfather who served in leadership positions in the Illinois State Senate and the judiciary. I have fond memories of traveling to the smaller communities in the district with them to attend county fairs, participate in parades, and learn about the needs of the area. I naturally majored in political science when I attended college at the University of Iowa.

Upon graduation, I went to Washington, D.C., and had the good fortune to work with Senator Everett Dirksen, who was the minority leader of the U.S. Senate. During my time at the Capitol, I met a charming Navy lieutenant from Oklahoma on a blind date arranged by a college friend. Tim Leonard was serving in the Navy JAG (Judge Advocate General's Corps) at the Pentagon and also as a military aide to President Lyndon Johnson at the White House. It was a whirlwind romance; we were engaged in four months and married in eight.

After our marriage, we remained in D.C. for a year and a half before moving to Tim's home state of Oklahoma.

We lived, worked, and gave birth to our daughter, Kirstin, in Oklahoma City. Tim had long wanted to practice law with his father and run for public office, so after two years in Oklahoma City we moved to his hometown of Beaver in the Oklahoma Panhandle, where our two sons, Ryan and Tyler, were born.

Moving to a small, remote community in a new state at the age of twenty-six was quite an adjustment for me. I was far away from my family and a way of living I found meaningful. My lifelong desire to save the world somehow seemed very far away. It was a time of inner reflection and soul-searching, a time that would ultimately make me a stronger person.

In Beaver, I soon became involved in activities relating to my children. I started a preschool and a summer park program for young people. I developed a keen interest in photography and put a darkroom in the basement. I took advantage of opportunities to help in our church and in town. Joining with people of all ages and walks of life to contribute our talents and skills for the betterment of the community was rewarding for me. We shared a sense of pride and belonging that was heartfelt.

As the years passed, I met and became friends with many of the "old-timers." I was fascinated by their ability to relate in great detail the experiences they endured as young men and women in a new land. Their stories were spellbinding. I was saddened to think that, once they were gone, my children and others would miss the gift of knowing them and their wisdom.

What started as a casual interest in photographing these pioneers soon went far beyond a desire to take pictures. Preserving their words became an obsession with me, and I traveled throughout the Panhandle with my tape recorder, seeking to meet as many of the first settlers as possible. I wanted to learn of their families, their thoughts, their feelings, their dreams. There were many with whom I felt a real bond of friendship, a closeness that can only exist when life's intimate experiences are shared.

The history books tell us of the tremendous hardships inflicted on the pioneers by the untamed nature of the new country. Undoubtedly, there were those who suffered greatly. However, most of the men and women with whom I spoke did not dwell on their difficult circumstances; they accepted life's inevitabilities and went on. They lived simply, worked diligently, and helped one another.

As Tom Judy, one old-timer, told me, "It was the rule of the country that, no matter who came along, they were welcome to stay all night and be fed. They'd never charge anything for it. Oh, it was disgraceful to have your house locked. Someone might need to get something to eat or, if it was bad weather, might want to come in to keep from freezing to death. We'd been away at times and come back and find people in the house who we'd never seen before. We never lost anything by anyone taking it."

Few received much formal education. Largely, their knowledge was self-attained. Some were religious; many were not. In most families, the mother's influence was the strongest.

"My father always used to say that early-day women deserve more credit than the men," Tom Judy said. "They had very little to prepare a meal with. They never threw a dress away because it was out of style. They made it over for the children. They used flour sacks to make underwear. They bought a cheap grade of flour made by George Hoover of Dodge City branded Old Gold. Sometimes, they did not get the letters washed out entirely and when a child's dress would blow up, you could see Old Gold stamped on the underwear. They gathered sandhill plums and made plum butter and plum leather out of part of it. They fought fleas night and day. Dad felt the women went through some pretty hard times in those days."

Some of the best parenting advice I ever received came from Nancy Farrell, another pioneer: "I'll tell you what an old travelin' man told me. He said, 'Don't keep these children always tied onto your apron strings. Yes, I know they got to be taught all right and be taught right and wrong. But, you got to let them try their own wings or they can't never get nowhere.'"

It is the people we meet and the experiences we have that shape who we are and impact the decisions we make. My life has been deeply enriched by living in Beaver and by my close relationships with the remarkable men and women of western Oklahoma. Genuine, courageous, rugged individuals, intensely proud of their past, they possess a quiet strength that comes from the knowledge of who they are and where they've been. I learned valuable lessons in leadership from the traits of these Panhandle pioneers: the importance of relying on one's own resources and being creative in solving daily issues, enjoying simple pleasures and giving thanks for each day, helping neighbors in time of need and having a positive outlook, taking pride in heritage, and being loyal to the land.

When I reflect on the meaning of my life in Beaver, I realize that the time spent in this remarkable area, with the men and women who live in what was once called "No Man's Land," has inspired me, guided my decisions, and influenced my family in ways that are deep and profound.

Perhaps the greatest lesson I've learned is that while one person may not be able to save the world by one great act, we can each make a significant difference, one person and one place at a time.

What is truly important in the end is that we give the gifts of love, time, and care to those near us. Then, and only then, can one begin to feel life's purpose is complete.

The Wakita Cemetery

Cindy Ross

Wakita, Oklahoma—my hometown. When I was growing up in the 1950s, Wakita boasted a population of just over five hundred people. The school building housed all grades, one through twelve. There was no kindergarten.

Life was simple and good. My sister and I walked to school each morning, and at noon walked seven blocks to and from Grandma's house for our lunch. Sundays and Wednesday nights found me on the fourth pew in the Baptist church seated next to Grandma. Daddy and Grandpa ran the local service station, and both always had a wonderful smell of gasoline and tobacco.

I raced the streets, rode horses, and alternated between playing football with my sister and the neighborhood boys and playing dress-up in my mother's heels and beads. When it snowed, we squealed with delight as Daddy pulled the town's kids behind his pickup on a homemade sleigh that, to an eight-year-old, seemed fifty feet long.

I loved the quiet of Wakita and still do. The stars light up the sky in a display that city folks don't see. A deep breath fills your lungs with pure air, not the polluted kind.

Come Memorial Day, Grandma loaded me in the car, and we visited the Wakita cemetery to decorate family graves. Grandma introduced me to her mom and dad, a nephew who died in the war—the "big one"—and numerous great-aunts and great-uncles.

I loved going to the cemetery with Grandma. It was a magical place where people I had seen only in pictures came to life through her stories. I still love going to the Wakita cemetery.

In the fifth grade, my family moved fifteen miles to Medford. Medford was more than twice the size of Wakita with a grand total of twelve hundred citizens. I was afraid I'd get lost! The school building was larger, and there were lots of extra rooms for things like band and typing. Still no kindergarten.

Medford also had a nursing home. When I was fifteen, I told Daddy that I wanted a job, wanted to earn my own money. So I went to work as a nurse's aide in the nursing home. There were no other jobs in Medford, Oklahoma, for a girl my age.

Frankly, this was not a job for a girl my age either. My parents were as clueless as I about the duties of a nurse's aide. Otherwise, I never would have applied, and they certainly would not have allowed it.

The work was hard and unpleasant. Feeding, bathing, changing beds, and providing the total physical care for the helpless opened the eyes of this high school sophomore-to-be. The other nurse's aides were much older, all with children of their own.

The morning shift started much too soon at 7:00 A.M. While all of my friends were still peacefully sleeping, Mother woke me up, and Daddy drove me to work on his way to the service station. The money wasn't even good, about a dollar an hour. To a fifteen-year-old, the smells were foul and the residents unattractive. At times, it was more than I thought bearable.

At night, classmates were going to movies and hanging out, but I was always too tired and tomorrow started too early. Being a quick study, I soon concluded this was not the way I wanted to spend my summer, and I announced to Daddy that I was quitting. I learned a lifetime lesson that summer. Daddy told me, "No, you're not quitting. You made a commitment to work at the nursing home this summer, and you'll work every scheduled hour." And, indeed, I did.

And, for some inexplicable reason, I went back every summer for the next four years.

There were other lessons I learned at the nursing home. I learned that most of the residents had few, if any, visitors, even on holidays and birthdays. They were alone and forgotten by relatives and old friends. I learned that keeping someone clean, with hair and teeth brushed, brings that person dignity. I learned to stop and talk, to hear the same story time and again, but to act as if it were fresh. I learned the pure joy of bringing someone so needy a small measure of comfort.

More than thirty years later, nursing homes reappeared in my life. As an adult, I grew to value the routine of life—the every-day days when life is ordinary. But at age forty-seven, my life became most unpredictable, and trips to nursing homes again became the unwelcome routine.

Daddy died unexpectedly and much too soon. He was seventy-one but acted twenty-five years younger. How could a man who rode his motorcycle and could still fly an airplane and play tennis die? It wasn't possible.

Then there was the toughest question of all: how could Daddy leave me with Mother? He had been taking care of her and the chronic health problems that plagued her for years. Mother had always been the difficult family member; and, with my two sisters living five hundred miles away, she was now mine to care for.

Daddy's timing was particularly bad. I had a job that required long hours and high energy, and there were two teenagers in my house. Now the responsibility of my ailing mother was added to the mix.

Mother and Daddy lived in Enid when Daddy died, over an hour's drive from my home and ninety miles from my Oklahoma City office. Yet now in Enid there were vehicles and a house to sell; closets and an attic to clean out; death certificates to file and paperwork to do.

Initially, Mom stayed in Enid. Every weekend I visited, bought groceries, ran errands, and felt guilty when I left. I called every day and felt guilty when we said good-bye. Mom was in pain, alone, and difficult. And, I'm sorry to say that, on many occasions, *I* was difficult too.

Perhaps all mothers and daughters have scars between them—past hurts that have not healed. I married at nineteen. My mother and I had been apart, except for holidays and periodic weekend gatherings, for almost thirty years. We were very different. We never really learned to relate to each other as adult women. But she was mine to care for.

Meanwhile, Grandma had breezed past her ninetieth birthday and still lived alone in Wakita. Even though forgetful, she still baked her delicious cherry pies and Amish cookies.

Mother's health continued to decline, and the physical distance between us did not allow frequent visits. The solution was to move Mom to a nearby assisted-care facility. Once again, I was going to a nursing home every day.

The smells of a nursing home are unmistakable, and they stay with you after a visit. Similarly, the sounds can be haunting. By Medford's standards, Mother's nursing home was a palace. She "enjoyed" more than a bedroom. There was a living room and small kitchen. But the smells and the sounds were the same, as were her needs for physical care.

Mother's joys were few and comforts rare: to have her hair washed, a manicure, and ice cream to soothe a mouth filled with sores. This once-beautiful woman found pleasure in being named the home's "resident of the month," complete with a smiling picture of an obviously sick woman with her now ever-present oxygen tubes.

Then, suddenly, there was another nursing home to visit. A short six months after Daddy's death, Grandma broke her hip and her decline was rapid. My mother's sister, who was already caring for her terminally ill husband, moved Grandma from Wakita to a nursing home close to her and, thankfully, only several miles from my office. Grandma soon lost her words; but when I fed her, she would push her lips together and with a cock of her head and great feeling say, "Ummmm." Grandma also continued to delight in my inept piano playing.

Like Mom, Grandma's physical appearance changed quickly and dramatically. Both ultimately became the patients I had cared for at age fifteen. The comforts were basic: a clean face and hands, easy-to-chew french fries, and warm butterscotch pudding.

Though it was difficult, life-changing and wonderful experiences did come from these trying times. Daddy died eight years ago. Mother followed him a year later; and, in another year, Grandma was gone. My sisters, although a state-and-a-half away, shared in the emotional, if not physical, care of Mom. I am grateful to my aunt for allowing me to contribute to the physical care of Grandma. Long-ago relationships that adulthood and distance had taken are now current and strong with my sisters and aunt.

And I had the great blessing of sharing death . . . first Daddy, then Mother, and finally Grandma. While the anguish of a family member's death is real, the intimacy of sharing that death, of holding a loved one's hand and whispering previously unspoken feelings during those final minutes of life provides ties for an eternity. Perhaps during those summers I worked at the Medford nursing home, death came a bit easier to residents when they held the hand of a young nurse's aide because family members were absent. Perhaps, too, I was learning lessons that I would sorely need later in my own life.

I still go to the Wakita cemetery. It's flat, with few trees and unattractive. The wind always blows. Now I go to visit Grandma and Grandpa and Mom and Daddy. I lay flowers on the graves. I trace the indentation of their names on the markers with my fingers. I talk to them.

I love the Wakita cemetery because it brings me closer to the memories of those I love so deeply, and it brings me closer to me.

Centering the World

Emily Dial-Driver

> Stories have to be told or they die, and when they die, we can't
> remember who we are or why we're here.
> —Sue Monk Kidd, *The Secret Life of Bees*

My mother will die. I find it hard to write that sentence. It's not that I don't know she'll have to die someday. It's not that I don't know that we'll all have to die someday. It's not that death isn't often a "blessed relief." It's not that I don't believe she'll be going to the "better place" we talk about.

It's not any of those things. It's the fact that her loss is too hard to contemplate.

She's the person who holds the communication lines in the family, the one everyone calls to tell the news. She's the one who tells the stories, starting with ones about animals to catch the attention of the young. She's the one who holds the history of the family.

The Christmas my mother, her sister, and her brother received a donkey as a pet, Santa tied the donkey up to the gas meter. The two girls were asleep in their shared room. Their brother, Kay, heard a noise and went to wake them up. When he woke them, saying that he'd heard a noise, they figured he just wanted to start Christmas early. They knew it was almost time for opening Christmas stockings and convinced him that he'd heard Santa's reindeer. He wasn't hard to convince. They all plundered the stockings. Suddenly there was a loud "HaaaaahHeeHaaaahHee."

Their father asked, "I wonder what that is?"

Peggy shrieked, "There's a lion in the backyard!"

That lion was, of course, the donkey they named Tagalong. Generally sweet-natured and patient, Tag occasionally tired of children and contributed to the family collection of bruises. When irked, Tag had the donkey habit of running under clotheslines or turning sharply around fence posts or scooting under low-hanging limbs to scrape the child off.

After the family had moved from town to a section-and-a-half ranch out in the country, my mother claimed she was the only one who worked. By then, Kay had gone to war and, as he put it, "Peggy only waved a little dust rag around." So my mother was primarily responsible for outside chores, telling us, "I was the one had to go down into my grandmother's cellar to get canning jars. There were newts and spiders. I didn't like it, but I went. I was the one who had to pull the dead cat out from under my grandmother's porch. It was nasty, but I did it. I was the one who helped Daddy. We had water on the place. That's the only way you could live out there, of course. But it was gyp water [very hard], and that's why there was a mineral ring around everything that had water. The water came from a well and was raised by a windmill to a water tank high above the ground. High, high, high above the ground. I was the one who had to climb up the tower when there was a problem. Daddy would send me up that tower and I would climb a wooden ladder up up up up. The top of the tank was covered with metal except for one little section covered with screen. I had to pry the screen cover up. Then Daddy would let me down on a rope into the tank. See, that's why I had to do it and not he. I couldn't have handled the rope and hauled him up and down.

"One time when I was down in the tank I had to put a pipe into the drain that let the water down so we could use it. The pipe was to raise the water outflow level so sediment couldn't get into the house water. After that, I had to check that pipe regularly to see if it was secure and functional. I had to be very careful to touch the water as little as possible so as not to contaminate it. I think I even had my feet and legs washed with bleach before I would climb the ladder. When I was finished with the job, I held onto the rope and Daddy pulled me back up. Then I had to scooch over the rim of the tank and climb down down down the wooden ladder to get back to the safe solid ground. I didn't like it, but I did it."

My mother went to college during World War II. No men there, she said. No chances for fun. She was so homesick her tears sprinkled the clothes she was ironing. She was also moneyless. Her mother sent her dollar bills in letters. That extra money made her day, her week, sometimes her month because it meant snacks, books, and maybe a little fun. Once an aunt sent her twenty-five dollars. She thought she was rich and bought a badly needed jacket. That story resonated through our family. It must have meant something to us because I sent money to my sisters when they were in college and I was out. My sister—partly, I hope, as a joke—sent quarters to my husband when he complained he never had any money for the soda machine at his workplace.

Perhaps my grandfather had been frightened by a germ under a microscope at Kansas City Veterinarian College because he was punctilious about hygiene. He shot a pistol for recreation, loaded his own cartridges, and rolled his own cigarettes. He didn't talk much but, when asked, he always had an astute comment: "Oh, you want to know what kind of people we are? We're Scots, Dutch, Irish, French, Welch, and Pekinese," and "You're related to the Prince of Wales, but never forget you had an uncle who was hanged for horse stealing in Texas." But, more importantly, "Whatever you point a gun at, you better want dead," and "There's some language you can't use in the house but you can say anything you want out behind the barn. You have to know the difference between house talk and pasture talk."

We've heard these stories all our lives; but when my mother dies, her stories will be lost. Oh, the facts (or what we think are the facts) might hang on for a while, but her unique voice will disappear.

The stories my mother tells aren't meant to give us a moral or tell us "this is how we live," but they do. They tell us what kind of family we are, what kind of people we come from, and what kind of people we aspire to be. We're a close-knit family of determined individuals, perhaps a bit eccentric, but tied to the land and the natural order. We come from those who have been dogged and maybe a bit perverse, not always following the drummer.

When the stories are gone, the family changes.

My mother is the matriarch. We know that when the matriarch is gone, the family falls to pieces until the next matriarch takes the crown, picks up the family reins, starts the family reunions, tries to hold the family together, tells different stories. It will still be a family, but it won't be the same family.

Going with God

Revelations

Kim Henry

When asked to contribute to this project, I was flattered but leery. I'm not one of those creative types I've always envied, and I certainly don't have a way with a pen. Now, seated in front of my computer, topics whirl around my mind: motherhood, self-esteem, or how one handles all the media attention surrounding me, my husband, and my children. The directions I might take this piece are limitless.

How do I craft a moving and inspirational essay without letting too many of my inner demons show through? After all, I've worked very hard since my husband became governor to show only my confident and self-assured side to everyone. I hide the biggest part of me—that side that is insecure, overwhelmed, and scared to death. I have always been a very guarded person. It's hard for me to let people get too close. I always keep a little of myself locked away, not to be shared.

(*Deep breath.* Here goes. . . .)

Life, in general, seemed to come easy for me. School was simple. Boys liked me. I found the love of my life at the age of sixteen, standing in front of his locker early one fall morning. My life fit "the plan." I married my high school sweetheart right after college graduation and—ironically—got a job as a receptionist in the governor's office. A few months passed, and I found a teaching job in Moore. Three years and one miscarriage later, I became pregnant with twins. But for the miscarriage, life was perfect, and just how I had planned it.

The twins were born in the middle of August, a month early but healthy. Both girls weighed over six pounds and were beautiful. God was surely smiling down on us. For some reason, He had singled us out for the good life.

The good life lasted eight weeks.

By the middle of October, we knew something was not quite right with one of the girls. She was listless and moved very little. We saw several doctors and specialists in the following weeks. A pediatric neurologist finally told us our little girl had a rare form of muscular dystrophy and would not live much longer. There was nothing we could do. Furthermore, our other daughter, we were told, had a 25 percent chance of having the same disorder, but she could not be tested until she became symptomatic.

We took our daughters home. One we knew would not be with us much longer; we had no idea if the other would soon follow her sister. It seemed we were no longer held out for special blessings by God.

I had a hard time with people who, trying to comfort, said, "God will not give you more than you can handle." As if no one had ever had a nervous breakdown or overdosed on drugs or committed suicide. Indeed, many experience situations they cannot handle. Was my strength somehow to blame for my daughter's illness? If I were a weaker person, would my daughter be healthy?

My personal tragedy made me reflect on other traumatic events. Why did God allow the sudden death of a young mother or catastrophic events like hurricanes and tornadoes? If He were such a caring and glorious God, why did He allow such tragedy to occur to His children? Where was God, His healing power, His protection?

I found solace in the words of a very dear friend of mine who happened to be a priest. When asked "Why?" he said, "Kim, it is not her life on earth that was meant to be, but her soul in heaven. God must think you are very special indeed to bestow such a great honor."

At the time I wasn't thrilled to be so "honored." But his words helped because they allowed me to find meaning in our situation.

I began to look for evidence of God and His glory.

I found God in the caring and watchful eye of my neighbor who, unsolicited, brought by groceries when my daughter was too sick for me to go to the market. I found God in the stranger (and friends) who brought over dinner so we would have one less thing to worry about during the day. I found God in people I hadn't even met, including those from other states, who sent cards and messages of love and support.

I found God in the smile and kindness of the store clerk who did not know why I was taking out my bad day on her.

I found God in the strength of another family that had suffered a loss, in watching them muster the resolve it takes to go forward with life, pick up the pieces, and love again.

I found God in the wake of the Oklahoma City bombing, and again in the acts of kindness and love that followed the recent catastrophic hurricane and tsunami. God's love shone in the countless people who were not personally affected by the events but who gave of themselves, their time, and their money, and who grieved along with those directly touched.

God is not in the tragedy, but in the aftermath. God does not cause catastrophic events to occur, but his strength and compassion can be seen and felt in the struggle to mend our broken parts, in the outpouring of love from total strangers and close family and friends alike.

The death of my daughter only strengthened my love and commitment to Jesus Christ. It was his strength that allowed my lungs to breathe, my legs to stabilize, and my feet to walk in the following days, weeks, and months.

Through my grief, I found my self. A self that was more confident and self-assured than the one who had given birth just a few months earlier. As I coped with the death of my daughter, I began to look within for acceptance and guidance. I saw that if I felt good about myself and what I accomplished, then others would as well. I discovered that self-confidence was found not in what others thought, but in the way I walked and held myself, in the way I talked, and in my attitude.

The road to self-esteem, for me, has many forks and diversions. There are moments when I feel I can conquer the world, and in the next moment I feel small and insignificant. I still frequently second-guess my decisions. But I've learned that tragedy can bring to the surface all sorts of emotions and characteristics. For me, Lindsey's death brought self-confidence, strength, resolve, and a renewed understanding of God's glory.

And it revealed that I am, indeed, blessed.

Dreaming

Twila Gibbens-Rickman

I had many dreams when I was younger. I dreamed I would be a mom, a synchronized swimmer, a writer of children's novels.

It was not my dream to be a minister.

It was also not my parents' dream for me to be a minister. My minister father and my teacher mom hoped I'd marry and have a family. Still, they thought I should train for a job "in case something happened."

Truth be known, what I really believed was that, after college, I'd be married and a homemaker. Four years was my limit for schooling. No more. So, after four years, I got my history degree and graduated—with no plan, no boyfriend, and no marriage in sight.

After I graduated from college, I agreed to serve as an assistant to a minister at a church. I led worship, visited hospitals, and preached occasionally.

When I was twenty-five, this same minister encouraged me to go to a theological seminary to "gain a sense of my own authority." The youth group raised money that paid for my first semester. There at the seminary, I learned that there is plenty of scripture and scholarship to support women's leadership, as it is God's nature to "do a new thing." Moreover, Jesus didn't keep religious rules; he changed them.

I still wanted to be a wife and a mother, but I didn't think anyone would want to marry a woman minister. I also didn't believe I could both pastor a church and be a good mother. Fortunately, things happened to open my mind. First, Gloria Steinem came to the university campus to speak, and she aptly stated that some women limit themselves because of what they *think* a man would want or not want. (Hmmm, could that be me?) Then I met other female seminary students who were married, and I began dating men who were interested in co-parenting—and maybe even co-pastoring. So, wow, some men were in fact attracted to women preachers!

I married the best of those men. We created our own dream of ministry, which didn't fit the traditional mold. We co-pastored three churches, taking turns preaching and dividing up other responsibilities depending on our gifts. We resisted assuming hierarchical positions—"senior pastor" and "associate pastor"—and our churches made the transition with us.

Our three sons were of the first generation to admit to classmates and friends that their *mom* was a minister (and their dad was too). We were part of a new contingent which hoped to model to church congregations the equality of power in marriage, shared parenting, and devotion of both mother and father to children. We requested smaller churches (which also meant smaller salaries) and made it clear to personnel committees that family time was a priority.

I have also served some churches separately, and these churches have been gracious, even though the minister's husband wasn't part of the deal. I have been the first woman pastor at five churches. I have been the first pregnant pastor at two other churches. This isn't to say that I haven't been met at times with resistance . . . from women, church secretaries, other ministers. Women in the pulpit aren't everyone's dream. Yet there was also great acceptance . . . from women, church secretaries, other ministers. From the start, I've been welcomed and nourished by comments like "I've been waiting for this for a long time," told to me by an eighty-year-old woman. Or "I think women bring something to ministry that men can't." These statements have never been negative reflections on men; rather they affirm that women bring good differences.

Recently, I turned fifty, and I find myself enjoying the wisdom that comes with having been around that long. Now younger women and men see me as a mentor. And I'm glad to share what I've learned, and what I am continuing to learn.

Currently, of the six hundred-plus United Methodist churches in Oklahoma, roughly one hundred are served by women. We are diverse. There are single women, women with spouses in other fields, divorced women with children, second-career women who are grandmothers, single women with an adopted child, remarried women. All have experience and faith and the great compassion that comes from mother/sister love. We are a solid and maturing body. What was once bursting with wild energy and newness is now comfortable. Our dreams have become stories we didn't know how to dream. We have embodied our ministry. The clothes fit, and we each have our own style. (We like a lot of fabric and color; we like fountains, artwork, and shared leadership. We sing and have liturgical dance.)

We are all individuals. And you should see our clergy robes!

Rebuilding

Althea Constance

I was raised in a loving, and morally upright, family, but my parents were extremely busy and sometimes our relationship was emotionally cold. For much of my life, I had feelings of doubt and inadequacy. Perhaps because of this, I married the first man who I thought truly loved me—for all the wrong reasons. Besides an intense sexual attraction, we had nothing in common. At least, nothing that was substantial enough to build a life together. But I married him anyway, believing that he would be what would make my world work.

How wrong I was.

It was only after I had said, "I do," that I began to realize that this man was even more emotionally deprived and intensely love-starved than I. Within the first year of marriage, I recognized that I had made the worst mistake of my life. The moment came when he threw me against the wall, put his fist through it, and said, "Better the wall than your face."

I didn't anticipate how great these outbursts would be, and how long it would take for all of this to be over.

Once, following the suggestion of a counselor, I quietly stood up to him. Made furious by my new stance, he threw me into a wall, spat "bitch," and put one hand around my throat. In a low voice, he threatened that if I were to move a muscle, it would be my last. When his rage subsided, he sat on the bed, rocking back and forth. He began crying and saying that he couldn't help what he was going to do. He said, "I will kill you, destroy you, and watch you suffer. I will enjoy it." I was terrified. When he finally went outside, my daughter and I locked ourselves in a bedroom, praying for safety until we had a chance to get away.

After he left the next morning, I decided that I had finally had enough and that the insanity had to end, one way or another.* I drove to the courthouse, praying for God to somehow intervene in this nightmare that was my life.

To this day, I believe that God honored that prayer.

After filling out the appropriate paperwork with the court clerk, I waited to be ushered in before a judge who was rumored to dislike giving protective orders. Scared, I prayed, "Lord, if I am to truly leave this man, I need a sympathetic judge."

While I was waiting in the hall, a girl came to inform me that the judge I should have seen had suddenly gotten sick and had to go to home, so another judge would see me. I was elated, especially when I realized that I actually knew the new judge.

As I entered his chambers, he looked up from his desk and kindly asked, "What can I do for you?"

As my story tumbled out, he paused and said, "You know, the next step is that he *will* kill you."

I was amazed. This man believed me, understood, and was in a position to help. I felt that God had indeed intervened on my behalf. He filed the paperwork for the strongest permanent protective order possible, preventing my husband from contact with my daughter and me.

When my husband was served with the protective order, the façade of my marriage disintegrated.

Our eventual divorce was violent.

Repeatedly, my husband broke into my home. After each break-in, strange things appeared in the house: a recording device that monitored my phone calls, a vial of nitroglycerin that had to be detonated by the Tulsa bomb squad, a handgun.

He also engaged in numerous mind games, vowing, "If I don't get the house, no one will get the house because I'll destroy it with you in it."

---

* With the help of my friends, I took the steps that would not allow the abuse to persist. They helped me to find the strength to seek the strongest protective order that could be issued—not allowing for any personal contact, or letters, or phone calls; to obtain a restraining order keeping my ex-husband and his friends off my property; and to purchase a security system. Under the sheriff's direction, I also bought a gun and learned to use it. These things were necessary to keep my daughter and me safe.

His insanity continued. Over time, he damaged the property and stole things from the house, tore the iron bars (meant to keep him out) off the windows, shut off the water supply to the house so that my daughter and I would be without water for days, stalked us, punctured the tires of our car, drained the oil from the car, and telephoned us repeatedly for hours on end.

He also disrupted our lives emotionally by telling friends and neighbors that "She'll be found dead some morning."

My world was upside down for a long time, but, if I had never lived through abuse myself, I do not think I would now know how to recognize when someone else is in such pain that she is thinking about ending her life, or the life of the person she believes is responsible for her pain.

I often wonder whether the divine plan caused these things to happen to me. Maybe God *can* and *has* used my negative experience to bring about good in the lives of others. I like to think so.

The Integrity of Hope

Leslie Penrose

Ministry, for me, has been a dance of integrity and hope.

In 1980, I finally took the leap and left the business world to take a full-time staff position in a United Methodist church—twice the hours, half the salary. The next six years were a roller-coaster journey of an increasing sense of "call to ministry" juxtaposed with growing frustration and disillusionment with the institutional church to which I was feeling called. I began taking religion classes at the University of Tulsa and began exploring my suitability for the ordained ministry in the United Methodist Church—a process I stopped and started, decided and redecided several times before finally entering seminary. Over and over again, I found conflict between what I was learning about Jesus and about the Gospel, and what I was experiencing in and from the church:

"Love your neighbor," Jesus said. *"But not the gay ones,"* the church qualified.

"Feed the hungry and clothe the poor," Jesus commanded. *"But not until you've paid the preacher,"* the church prioritized.

"Visit the sick . . . *unless they have AIDS."*

"Free the prisoners . . . *but don't bring them to church."*

"The world is your parish . . . *but the parish is your world."*

As I stood on the edge of a crisis of faith, struggling with a call that wouldn't go away and a career choice that didn't seem to hold much hope or promise, Jesus invited me to "come and see" (John 1:39) where he dwelt in Central America. I joined a team of people I'd never met on a journey to places I knew very little about; and for three weeks God led me, drove me, dragged me, accompanied me, and carried me through the fire and the waters of suffering and hope and rage and joy and death and faithfulness into new life.

In El Salvador, I was embraced by God in the form of a toothless old woman who had lost three sons to the senseless genocide being committed by her government and paid for by mine. Through tears of hope, she reminded me that at my baptism I had been ordained to be an "ambassador of reconciliation." A five-year-old child whose name was Paz (peace) guided me through her squatters' settlement of cardboard shacks to introduce me to her family, and her mother shared with me that Paz's name was in honor of the dream to which her father had given his life. He had been killed by death squads for organizing a union. A Lutheran bishop invited us to break bread in his home; and while his children danced traditional dances for us, he shared why he continued to stay and work among the poor in spite of numerous threats to his life and his family. "Jesus is here," he said, "living and dying among the poor ones. If I want to be with Jesus, then this is where I must be."

In Nicaragua a young girl gave me the cross she had been given at her confirmation and asked me to "remember her"; an eighteen-year-old man who had lost both legs in the war against the U.S.–backed Contras thanked us for a solidarity of love that was bigger than politics and unconcerned with borders. Everywhere, the Christian faith was giving life and hope and courage in the face of massive suffering and oppression; in community after community, people were gathering to "remember Jesus" by reading the scripture in light of their own experiences and then practicing what they read in their own lives. And in the "re-membering," they were being empowered, liberated—saved.

I had found a God I could believe in and trust. I had met a Jesus I could follow. I had witnessed a faith I could profess in word and deed. And, most life-transforming of all, I had experienced a "church" that bore witness to all of that with integrity, passion, and compassion.

So I entered seminary and celebrated every opportunity it offered to examine, question, doubt, confirm, deconstruct, reconstruct, and, finally, integrate my faith with the new sense of possibility about ministry and being God's church that I had discovered in Central America.

. . .

Late one evening in the mid-1980s I received a phone call from a nurse friend at St. John's Hospital. "We have a young man here who's been here for weeks, waiting to die. He has AIDS and is completely emaciated and covered in sores. There's no reason at all that he is still alive, except that he's terrified to die. He keeps asking me to tell God he's sorry, that he doesn't want to burn in hell. I thought maybe you could help."

I had absolutely no idea what to expect or what to say. With fear and trembling, I went the next day to see the young man. He was gay and Baptist—not a good combination—and the only message he had internalized about God was that "God hates fags." We talked about fifteen minutes before he was totally exhausted. I stayed for a while, holding his hand and rubbing his tender feet. I came back every day and spent an hour or two with him—sometimes talking, sometimes listening, sometimes just touching quietly. I went home at night and cried myself to sleep. Joshua (not his real name) died a week later, and I knew I would never be the same. Like the disciples who had met a stranger and discovered the Christ, I knew that I, too, had been to Emmaus (Luke 24:13–30).

A few days later a friend of his called me . . . and then another and another. Over the next few months, I visited with, counseled with, cried with, and held funerals for a dozen or so young gay men who were afraid to live or die.

A year or so after my holy encounter with Joshua at St. John's, I was invited to spend an evening at a support group for young gay men living with AIDS. "They have some spiritual issues," their therapist told me, "and need someone to help them sort through them." So I went to group that night: they were suspicious and reserved. Finally, just as the group was ending, and there was no chance to really talk, one young man asked me, "What kind of God creates a life and then condemns it to hell?"

There was dead silence in the room. And yet, in the silence, the message those young men had heard from the church for years screamed out: "Homosexuals go to hell." "You are an abomination." "God hates fags!"*

"Only a God that needs to die," I responded.

The next week they asked me to come back . . . and the next and the next and the next. After a few weeks, enough trust grew between us that

---

* Posters bearing these words have been displayed over and over again by Rev. Fred Phelps and his church in anti-gay demonstrations across the country.

the dam opened up. All the pain and rage and anger and hurt of years and years of spiritual abuse and bad theology poured out, and I was baptized* with the depth and breadth of what Christianity had done to the faith of these young men, to their hope, to their relationships, to their lives ... and finally to their ability even to die with any sense of peace.

. . .

I have usually only known I was called in retrospect—as I looked back at an experience and reflected on it, as I realized that gifts I didn't know I possessed had been called forth by a particular person or situation. Like Elijah, who in a time of despair had been given a glimpse of where God had just passed by, I, too, have seen God's back far more often than I have heard God's voice (1 Kings 19: 10–12). And even though I have always had a sense of being drawn to the margins, I have often found—as I did with Central American refugees—that I wasn't even aware there was a particular margin until I was driven/thrown/compelled into it. It had been true again with HIV/AIDS—my "calling" had been more of a "tossing into."

Across the next few years, a number of gay men living with AIDS began attending the congregation for which I served as associate pastor. As their numbers increased, so did the discomfort of the congregation. This was not a ministry they understood or wanted any part of. In the fall of 1992, they petitioned the bishop to have my appointment terminated.

Because of the petition, I was invited by Bishop Dan Solomon to begin a new ministry in Tulsa: a "base community" that would reach out to those who had fallen through the gaps of other United Methodist congregations. That invitation proved to be the beginning of an amazing, "wonder-full," surprising, painful, life-giving, frightening, encouraging journey of hope and faith and struggle. There were no road maps for becoming a base community in North America, no models to follow, no guiding stars. We had no church building, no office, no geographically identified neighborhood to canvass, no expense account, and no official charter—just a common calling, waiting to be embodied. And on June 21, 1993, a small group of

---

* Baptism is a ritual of initiation into the Christian faith. In this case, my "baptism" was an initiation into the terror that one interpretation of Christianity has created in many young gay men's lives.

sojourners gathered in the borrowed basement of a sister congregation, lit a rainbow-colored "Christ" candle, and breathed life into the "Community of Hope."

Several of the gathered sojourners were living with AIDS; some were gay, some straight. Most of us had experienced being rejected by the church and/or marginalized by some other difference or tragedy in our lives. All of us longed for a place to experience authentic community, to celebrate life, to hear ourselves named beloved by God, to wrestle with real issues of faith and life, and to serve our neighbors in the way of Jesus.

Midwifing Community of Hope gave me an opportunity to fully embrace the kind of ministry I felt, and still feel, called to, a place to explore new forms of mission and ministry, a place to reimagine worship and structure, a place to practice the theologies I had discovered in seminary. It also challenged me emotionally as nothing else ever had. I had been significantly involved with a number of persons living with AIDS for years and was already doing several HIV/AIDS–related funerals. But with the beginning of Community of Hope, my involvement in the world of AIDS exploded. The congregation was itself almost 50 percent HIV-infected at first. And during the first year, I did over fifty funerals—fourteen of them for companions of COH members.

Even in the midst of constant dying and grief, my own sense of spiritual connection and wholeness deepened. I found my sense of vocation was reconfirmed every time someone entrusted me with their living, their dying, their spiritual struggle, their questions or doubts or fears. I had come home.

In April of 1996 that sense of belonging and hope changed. A statement was added to the United Methodist *Book of Discipline* declaring that United Methodist ministers were not allowed to celebrate homosexual unions. Many in the Community—gay and straight—felt betrayed by a church that had once again said "welcome" and then slammed the door shut: a church that had once again chosen a "preferential option for the status quo."

For the next several months, we wrestled together toward a response to the ruling. The result was a unanimous decision that celebrating all life commitments, gay and straight, was essential to our integrity; and we affirmed a commitment to continue performing holy unions in spite of the ban. It was an important step, but concern for me kept the Community from experiencing it fully and joyfully. In order to protect my ordination,

they made the decision to do the holy unions without my participation—
as rituals led by lay members. I would still do the preunion counseling and
help the couple plan and prepare the ceremony, but I would not officiate.
That, they thought, would keep me safe from the ecclesiastical charges that
were a constant threat.

My heart broke as I watched the people that *we, the Church*, had invited
to the table of grace offer to sacrifice their own restored sense of self-worth,
their own right to celebrate their relationships as other people celebrated
theirs, in order to protect me. I wondered who was truly *living* the gospel
of Jesus Christ.

The consensus was reached on a Sunday afternoon; and, by Tuesday of
that week, I found myself deep in the belly of a whale—a sense of loss
tearing at the core of my being. I realized I had allowed a decision to be
made for me that, even though made to "save" my life, was already draining
life out of me. What I was grieving was the loss of myself. I know now what
the loss of integrity can do to a person's soul.

The following Sunday, I shared my struggle with the Community—and
my decision to continue officiating at holy unions as I always had:

> Somewhere in the middle of my descent into the belly of that whale,
> I realized that my heart had long ago made the decision about what
> I could and could not compromise in my ministry . . . only I didn't
> *really know where the boundaries were* until I actually tried giving up
> more than my heart was willing or able. I was literally overwhelmed
> with grief and regret.
>
> It's been a difficult three days; but, in that "belly" time, I rediscov-
> ered some very important things. I rediscovered that being "with"
> means for the *whole journey*, not just for the parts that hold less risk.
> And I was reminded that Jesus was pretty clear when he said, "You
> can't serve two masters." I am called to be *with* God's people first—
> even when that means not being *with* the Church.
>
> I relearned how seductive "safety" can be, especially when loss is
> already a big part of our lives and we already feel at risk so often in so
> many ways in our lives and in our ministries; and I relearned that any
> place that *requires* you to hide or deny part of who you are can *never*
> be safe.

I learned *again* that I can't ever do or be or think or plan enough to ensure my safety or yours—all I can do is entrust both of us and the journey to God; and I was reminded that when I have a difficult decision to make I can listen, talk, ponder, pray, and consult before making it, but I can't give the decision to my friends, or my community, or my superiors, or even to God: the decision is finally mine to make.

I rediscovered how essential "integrity"—being true to who you are—is to spiritual well-being, and I was reminded that if I feel like I'm being torn and divided, *I probably am*. I was reminded simply and firmly that *there are no "good reasons" to not do what is right.** "What good is it," Jesus warns, "to gain the whole world, if you have to give away yourself in the process?"

I cannot and will not give up my place as your pastor in the midst of your unions: that is too deeply essential to my understanding of this ministry and to my valuing of your lives and relationships. To abandon that would be to abandon myself. If I can remain United Methodist and honor *who I am, who you are, and the ministry we are both called to do*, that is my first choice. If that is not possible, then perhaps there is another denomination with which we can live and grow and work in creative, joyful, life-giving ways. If not, then I would be honored to serve as your pastor knowing that I have been "ordained" by your lives—by your living and your dying, by your loving and your serving, by your laughter, your tears, your courage, your faith, your indomitable hope, and by the "home-making and the journey-taking" we have done together.

So, my invitation is simply that we continue to do what we have always done—keep putting one foot in front of the other on this journey of faith with as much faithfulness and integrity as we possibly can, trusting the God who goes with us, and refusing to follow our fear.†

· · ·

It took another two years for the charges to finally come. And by the time they did, I was totally exhausted from responding to one judicial demand

---

* Ray Hoover, trans., "Jesus: A Profile in Courage," *The Fourth R*, May/August 1979, 17.
† Excerpt from sermon by Leslie Penrose, February 23, 1997, at Community of Hope.

after another, while trying to pastor an increasingly frustrated community. The "dance" that had started in 1993 between the UMC and the participants of Community of Hope had clearly become a "battle."* An official complaint was filed with the bishop in 1999, media coverage increased the tension, and the bishop gave me an ultimatum to withdraw from the denomination or prepare for an ecclesiastical trial.

That night, my prayer was one Bishop Colin O'Brien-Winters of Namibia had written in a particularly difficult time in his ministry: "Lord, remind me when I need to know; you did not call me to defend your church, but to lay down my life for your people."

The following morning I submitted my resignation to my district superintendent and the bishop:

Date: March 4, 1999
To: Bishop Bruce Blake, Oklahoma Conference, United
       Methodist Church
It is with a deep trust in God's steadfast and unconditional love that I write to inform you that I am initiating the process of withdrawal from the United Methodist Church in order to transfer my ministerial orders to another denomination.

I have chosen to begin this process because I cannot remain faithful to the Gospel and honor the requirement of the United Methodist Church not to celebrate and bless same-sex covenant relationships. As one who has been baptized to "resist injustice and oppression" and ordained to "look after the concerns of Christ above all," I am called and charged to offer the full ministry of the church—including the blessing of covenant relationships—to all God's people, including those who are gay or lesbian. I will do nothing less.

                                              Rev. Leslie Penrose, Elder

A few days later, the Community of Hope also chose to sever their relationship with the United Methodist Church.

---

* George Lakoff and Mark Johnson, *Metaphors We Live By* (Chicago: University of Chicago Press, 1980). The two metaphors "dance" and "battle" were vitally important in helping us to reflect on and evaluate our relationship with the United Methodist Church.

The months following withdrawal were long and hard for all of us. The grief was profound, and we were all weary of struggle. But there is something sacramental about stubbornness at the margins, and something tenacious about hope.* It wouldn't let us go.

We accepted an invitation to join the United Church of Christ and began to take the first tentative steps with our new dance partners. That dance is five years old now. Some of the issues we wrestle with have changed; there are new and different challenges; but ministry for me continues to be a dance of integrity, with hope in the lead—a dance of integrity and hope.

---

* As Vaclav Havel says, "Hope is not the conviction that things will turn out well, but the confidence that what you are doing makes sense regardless of how it turns out." Havel, *Disturbing the Peace* (London: Faber and Faber, 1990).

Choices

Why? Rising to the Challenge

Kalyn Free

Please know that I am quite aware of the hazards. I want to do it because I want to do it. Women must try to do things as men have tried. When they fail, their failure must be but a challenge to others.
—Amelia Earhart, letter to George Putnam, 1937

Life often does not progress as we planned or dreamed. I had a goal, a plan, and the drive to achieve. I have found strength in adversity, determination in opposition, appreciation for others in serving, and success in failing. Life has taught me that the journey is often more instructive than the destination.

During my two political campaigns, I have learned to view others' queries as statements of their circumstances and views on life, not as personal condemnations. I heard many questions and pronouncements on women attorneys: "Why are you running for office? The district attorney is a man's job; yes, being a lawyer is a man's job too."

Some people expressed their views on the races: "You're an Indian and, if you win, you'll let all the Indians off." "You're an Indian; do you drink too much?"

One elderly lady in a wheelchair asserted, "The Bible says that women should be having babies for our Lord Jesus Christ, not running for office." When I thanked her for her time and said that I was just glad she would be exercising her right to vote, she further informed me, "The Bible says that women aren't supposed to vote and you're going to hell for that too." As a former statewide Bible Bowl champion, I was stunned to learn this!

Others felt free to ask about my personal style: "Why do you have long hair?" "Why don't you cut your hair?" "Why don't you color your hair?"

Some felt that only women who had children had proved themselves: "What? You don't have children? Why not? Why aren't you married? Are you a lesbian? What's wrong with you?"

One "informed" law enforcement officer cited "evidence" that I was gay: "I know you're a lesbian because you worked for Janet Reno, and she's a lesbian." After I became DA, I had opportunities to observe his investigations and read his reports; I then had proof in black and white that his logic left much to be desired.

Campaigning for public office in Oklahoma taught me more than I ever could have imagined. I learned that answering some questions on the basis of my initial reaction is not always best—for example, retorting, "My opponent doesn't wear makeup either," when asked, "Why don't you wear makeup?" or "Why don't you wear panty hose?"

I learned that, when I bared my soul, I could be cut to the quick by those who seek to hurt or not to learn or not to understand. Once I revealed my desire to one day marry and have a family, only to have a complete stranger ask, "Then what's wrong with you?" Apparently to some people, I am somehow defective because I do not have a husband.

I am Choctaw; the Choctaws are a matrilineal society with a long history of strong women. In my own family, I have been blessed to be surrounded by strong-willed women who have overcome immense hardship and adversity. My beloved grandmother, Nan, an original enrollee of our tribe, always put her family first. She was a daily inspiration to me, and one of the reasons I fight so hard to improve the lives of Indians. I admire my mother and my three aunts who, out of necessity, worked outside the home to provide for their children. My four beloved sisters, strong and persevering, have demonstrated sacrifice and the true meaning of family.

Life has taught me that I, like countless women before me, can reach to unknown strengths within. I have learned to rely on the indomitable energy shared by women for centuries to keep me going beyond that which seems humanly possible. I have discovered an incredible focus that can be both my strength and my weakness. Most importantly, I have an enduring appreciation for family; family is my foundation, my source of renewal, my refuge, my purpose. And protecting families and their children must be the final and ultimate goal if our nation is to thrive. This has been my dream for decades: to serve the public and help make America a better place for our children and our families. My family has done more than I could have ever asked to help me achieve my dreams.

My life has taught me to cherish the learning as much as the achieving, to love those who teach me hard lessons as well as those who lovingly teach. Oklahoma is a wonderful state, full of caring, intelligent people. Yet a woman running for public office in Oklahoma faces many obstacles. Regretfully, I learned that many, even in my own party, do not embrace gender or racial diversity. Although I was saddened by a lack of action to back the rhetoric of the political arena, I have accepted that I will never be the establishment's candidate and have learned to forgive when some failed to live up to their word.

As district attorney, I learned many hard lessons from those who served with me and from those whom I served. Before I took office, a man killed his wife and her brother. The victims and their family were ordinary people in Haskell County who lacked political clout. The murderer was represented by a powerful state senator, who had successfully delayed the trial for more than two years. Justice demanded that I prosecute. Fortunately, the jury returned guilty verdicts and the defendant is now serving life without parole. This case ensured that I learn quickly about risk assessments, hidden markings, mental abuse, and the effects of violence on children and our communities.

I had to rapidly develop an understanding of things I could never before have fathomed. I learned that women stay with their abuser for a variety of reasons, including fear of the abuser, fear for themselves, and fear for their children. These women are not only victims: they are strong, creative, resilient, and resourceful survivors with many coping skills.

Those who daily live with violence or its threat intuitively learn to survive. When her man says he will kill her and/or their children if she leaves him, a woman may have little choice but to believe him. And I learned that I had no choice but to believe her. Because many live in a world that is dangerous and possibly deadly, a single misstep or misspoken word can result in a succession of beatings or terror-filled nights, even death.

I learned not to say, "If a man beat me, I'd be out of there. . . ." I do not know what it is to fear for my children's lives, to live with the knowledge that my children would be left alone to cope with his violence were I to die or lose a custody battle. I thought I was strong—until I met the truly strong ones, the survivors, the heroines. I learned that, contrary to popular opinion, all are vulnerable and that no person is immune to fear, manipulation, and the desire to survive.

My heart breaks for the millions of women and children who daily live in fear and terror, just trying to survive, not only throughout the world but, yes, in communities in our own nation.

Through my work as DA I came to know, respect, and admire a lady I shall call Sally. Sally was not what many think of as the typical abused woman; she was a lively, intelligent, strikingly beautiful, middle-class woman. Sally and her husband were active and respected in both their church and community. Sally's family, friends, and neighbors had no idea that Sally endured decades of violence, humiliation, and manipulation and was subjected to intense control.

All abuse is about control. Before Sally left her marriage, she was reduced to asking permission to go to the store, visit friends, or choose a different perfume to wear. The permission was withheld as a means of establishing and maintaining tight control. Sally knew that challenging her husband's control could result in violence, loss of the keys to her car, nights without sleep, or, worse, loss of her kids, either in a custody battle or in their abduction.

Sally's world constricted until she thought dying was her only possible means of escape. After decades, she did escape; she worked to become independent and became empowered to make her own choices. She attended college and has touched many lives with her story and her work. In fact, she has had a deep and profound effect on my life. She is chief among the people I most admire; I value her insight, her friendship, her guidance, and her wisdom. I am indebted to her for enlightening me in many ways and inspiring me to continue, in whatever small way I can, to work to eradicate violence in our families.

I learned that children love their parents, even when the parents are neglectful; are physically and/or mentally and/or sexually abusive; or are drug addicts and dealers. I learned that making law and policy concerning the "best interests of the child" is relatively easy but standing by as policy is being implemented, watching law enforcement officers handcuff parents and the Department of Human Services pulling children out of their parent's arms, is heart-wrenching.

I have watched with pain as children were taken from homes where methamphetamine was being "cooked," exposing the children to absorption of the drug or risk of explosion. These children cried in fear, wanting their parents. The children did not want to be separated from the parents upon whom they depended for food, love, and care. Unfortunately, in a meth home all three are in short supply, creating children who will gladly accept the mere crumbs that meth parents cast their way.

I learned that our children truly are the forgotten ones—with too many politicians giving mere lip service to protecting them, providing for them, and ensuring they have a future of safety and opportunity. I learned that problems are plentiful and complex; answers are too often limited and simply inadequate.

I have risked failure and embraced success; I have dreamed large and worked hard. I have always been aware that as a candidate and an elected official, I could serve as a role model for young women and Indians throughout Oklahoma and America. As I ran for Congress, I learned that there are wonderful, progressive women and men in Oklahoma and across our nation who believe in America, in equality, in our families and communities and who are willing to give their precious time and limited financial resources to invest in a campaign that addresses the issues that concern us.

These incredibly dedicated women and men worked for my candidacy, not because I offered them lucrative business deals, personal financial gain, or tax breaks, but because my candidacy offered hope and opportunities for prosperity for *everyone*. I learned that a lot of right-thinking people can and will come together for a common good: Indians and cowboys, organized labor and environmentalists, child and victims' advocates and law enforcement, pro-choice proponents and the religious right, pacifists and hunters, teachers and the uneducated, and lawyers and laborers. We can all work together—sharing a vision for our people.

My life has taught me that "Why?" is an important question, but "What?" is equally important.

Why did I run for public office; why did I sacrifice my personal life and ask sacrifice of my loving and devoted family? What did I learn, what can I give, what can I teach? The larger answer is that rising to the challenge is of utmost importance. Little girls cannot become what they cannot imagine; what they imagine is based upon what they see.

My grandmother Nan was born when women did not have the right to vote. She watched her Choctaw brothers go off to war to fight for a country that denied Indians and women the right to vote.

We must demonstrate, through our actions, values, and choices that women and Indians can serve our communities, our state, and our nation proudly and well. Women and Indians are shamefully underrepresented in state houses, in Congress, and at all levels of elected office. We must work hard to correct this. We must continue to plant the seeds of change in the fertile ground that has been plowed by the brave warriors who came before us if we are to enjoy parity, freedom, representation, and a voice in our own self-determination.

Although I did not win my campaign for Congress, I have not failed. I, and those who labored with me, spread a message of optimism, prosperity, and tolerance across twenty-five counties, from Kansas to Texas. We planted the seeds of change in the hearts and minds of eastern Okla-homans. We fought the good fight. We lost that race, but we proved that tomorrow can be a new day in this state. To paraphrase Amelia Earhart's eloquence: "If I failed . . . I hope my failure is but a challenge to others."

> But now that you're here,
> it all seems perfectly clear,
> UNLESS someone like you cares a whole awful lot,
> nothing is going to get better.
> It's not.
>   —Dr. Seuss, *The Lorax*

I present this challenge to you: Care. Our nation needs you to care "a whole awful lot." We must care enough to run for public office and make the sacrifices to help those who need it most. We, your sisters, will be there for you, standing together, proud, strong, and true. Those who have gone before, who planted the seeds of opportunity, will watch proudly and imbue you with inner strength; those who surround you will support and encourage you. As sisters, we come together from all corners of America to support each other in ways we can only now imagine. In rising to the challenge before us, we can reap the abundance of change, equality, hope, and opportunity, the legacy of those who bravely explored and patiently planted while believing in the promise of a future harvest.

Feminism Is Not a Dirty Word

Cindy Simon Rosenthal

How did a word associated with the noble cause of women's political equality become an epithet? How did a movement dedicated to social justice and basic human fairness become the target of hatred and intolerance? Certainly I have witnessed this transformation in my lifetime; and, among my students at the University of Oklahoma, I see many flinch at the thought of using the "F" word to describe themselves. Thus, for a generation of Oklahoma undergraduate students, it is valuable to recover and revive the meaning of *feminism*.

But I am getting ahead of myself.

I originally learned about feminism from my family. I grew up in a family with four brothers, and all of us were encouraged to think about limitless opportunities and to pursue unbounded dreams. My mother and father partnered in life, parenting, and a small manufacturing business in northwest Ohio. In school, on the playground, at church, and at home, I assumed equality. My brothers always needed another infielder or running back; and, frankly, my basketball skills insulated me from the embarrassment of being the last chosen in a pickup game. My assumptions about equal opportunity seemed to be confirmed by my own experiences.

Growing up in the '50s and '60s, however, I lacked the perspective to see how my own life chances were at odds with the world around me. I ran for high school student council president, failing to recognize that girls had never held the top office. In the era before Title IX, I played Big 10 basketball at Northwestern University but ignored the gross disparity of resources allocated for men's and women's sports. As a student intern for the *Toledo Blade*, I relished a plum investigative reporting assignment on employment agencies, even though the resulting series of stories made little note of the blatant sex discrimination practices of the industry.

Not until 1975, in a year spent in St. Louis with the Coro Foundation, a fellowship program in public affairs, did I begin to experience and understand fully the world of inequality around me. To be sure, my college years coincided with the apex of the antiwar protests, the struggle for civil rights, and the emerging women's movement. I personally joined the marches but never fully confronted my own privileges, which turned mere possibilities into opportunities that others did not enjoy. My best friends in the Coro program—a married African American father living in the projects and a white Catholic social activist surviving on a shoestring—reminded me of the paraphrased admonition of Luke 12:48: "To whom much is given, much is expected." My friends demonstrated daily a sense of social responsibility, which called them to give generously of themselves, even when their own needs were a challenge; and their example inspired me to do likewise.

Fortunately, I married a man whose own family instilled ideals of service, equality, and social justice. We have shared career successes, deferred job ambitions when necessary, raised a family, made sacrifices, and worked out that challenging balance between work and home life. In the navigation of life choices, we wove for ourselves a fabric of everyday feminism, "a system of ideals and practices which assumes that men and women must share equally in the work, in the privileges and in the defining and the dreaming of the world."*

I have tried to convey that definition to students over the past eleven years of teaching political science at the University of Oklahoma. But the classroom has all too often reminded me that feminism has been demonized by those who feel threatened by the promise of "liberty and justice for all." While my students sincerely profess a commitment to equality of rights for all, they shy from the label of "feminist" because they associate negativism and pessimism with it.

To me, feminism is about possibilities and not pessimism. When I ask my students why they are taking a course in state government, I typically get responses from the male students who speak of aspirations to be governor or a state legislator; only one female student in eleven years has volunteered her motivation to run for political office. Even in the twenty-first century,

---

* Gerda Lerner, quoted in Helen Astin and Carole Leland, *Women of Influence, Women of Vision: A Cross-Generational Study of Leaders and Social Change* (San Francisco: Jossey-Bass, 1991), 19.

men and women do not embrace the same prospects. In my courses on gender and politics, I describe the dramatic efforts of the suffragists, explain the research on barriers to women in politics, and report the contributions made by political leaders—men and women—to achieve a truly egalitarian society.

How can the noble goals of feminism be realized in this state in this century? In 2002 with the help of others at the Carl Albert Congressional Research and Studies Center, I started NEW (National Education for Women's) Leadership–Oklahoma. To address the historic underrepresentation of women in political life, NEW Leadership educates, encourages, and inspires women to enter the fields of politics, public policy, and service. Bringing together undergraduate women from all across the state for an annual training institute, NEW Leadership tells a new generation of Oklahoma women that they can, and must, share equally in the work, privileges, and dreams of the world. The program attempts to redress a central reality, documented by empirical research, that women are less likely to think about a career in politics and are less often recruited or encouraged to run for public office. The program allows me to pass on the confidence and encouragement that I always enjoyed.

In 2004, I put my own commitment to a new test. A vacancy on the Norman City Council challenged me to do more than encourage others to run for public office; I decided to see if I could "walk the walk." More than anything else, retail politics at the local level consists of knocking on doors and listening to people. Campaigning made me more aware of the aspirations and trepidations of others in my community. I met the mother of a toddler who expressed concern about the presence of a drug house in her neighborhood. A father shared his fears that his children would not be able find good jobs close to home. I talked with a senior citizen who worried about her health and reports of arsenic in the water supply. A grandmother fretted to me about the reckless and speeding drivers who endangered her grandchildren on her street.

Now on city council, I deal with the seemingly mundane—gravel, septic tanks, and stop signs—and the millions—budgets, bond issues, and major infrastructure needs. At bottom, however, this work of public service holds the essence of what the writer bell hooks describes as feminism: "Visionary feminism offers us hope for the future . . . [b]y emphasizing an ethics of mutuality and interdependency."* Applied to the everyday business of municipal government, visionary feminism celebrates listening to divergent points of view, valuing differences as well as commonalities, solving problems by collective means, and bringing people together.

A significant part of the discipline of political science adopts the view that political actors are driven first and foremost by self-interest. Elected officials, in an effort to secure their reelection, cater to the demands of those interests that will deliver votes in the next election. This calculated view of politics has strong roots in reality and provides a thin form of political representation and democratic accountability. Unfortunately, this view of politics blinds us to the feminist vision of something more.

Elsewhere I have written about a decidedly different form of political leadership behavior, an integrative style of deliberation and decision making where the deft touch of consensus can serve as an alternative to the hard edge of competition.† So far in my brief service in the "real world" of politics, I can now report to my students that this alternative vision of political life can and does exist. It is the essence of Mary Parker Follett's vision of political leadership: "The leader guides the group and is at the same time himself guided by the group, is always a part of the group. No one can truly lead except from within. . . . The power of leadership is the power of integrating which creates community."‡

A feminist believes that as a society we can ill afford not to use all of the talents and energy among us. A feminist believes that we should practice an ethic of care for those whose needs are greater than our own. A feminist believes that our communities grow stronger when we all share in defining, and dreaming of, possibilities for the next generation.

Feminism is not a dirty word.

---

* bell hooks, *Feminism Is for Everybody: Passionate Politics* (Cambridge, Mass.: South End Press, 2000), 117.
† Cindy Simon Rosenthal, *When Women Lead* (New York: Oxford University Press, 1998).
‡ Mary Parker Follett, *The New State* (New York: Longman, Green, 1920), 229–30.

Great Expectations

Anita R. May

My mother expected me to be special. She and my father had wanted to have children for nine years before I was born. And my mother scared everyone by giving birth to me in her seventh month of pregnancy. I was three-and-a-half pounds at birth and one of the first babies to use the new incubators at St. Elizabeth's Hospital in Utica, New York. Well-meaning relatives expressed concern that I would be unhealthy all my life and certainly not very smart. Instead, my mother said that she prayed that I would be healthy and exceptionally brilliant. Perhaps these expectations and her prayers—combined, of course, with the fact that my parents were able to provide for me, their only child, what they never would have been able to provide had they had many children—started me on my path in life.

I grew up in the 1940s in a wonderful Italian American neighborhood. In the mornings when I walked to the Catholic school a block from my home I could smell the bread being baked at four or five Italian bakeries and the coffee beans being roasted for espresso at the neighborhood grocery. In my grandmother's kitchen, where I spent hours, I learned special recipes and watched while she spun a web of food and love over all the members of her family.

But there were drawbacks for a young girl growing up during this time and at this place. Women were expected to learn to cook, sew, get married, and have children . . . in that order. My uncles did not understand why my parents encouraged my love of learning, or why they were so proud of my high grades, or why they would encourage a *girl* to think of going to college. As an avid reader, I spent hours in my books, trying to find female role models who had great careers and families as well. I still remember reading about Elizabeth Blackwell, the first woman doctor in the United States, and Queen Elizabeth I, who refused to marry so that she could give herself to ruling England. But neither of these women accomplished what I hoped for—marriage and motherhood as well as a career.

My aunts and my mother's lady friends told me that if I wanted to be a teacher or a nurse—the only acceptable jobs for educated women at this time—I would have to expect to end my career when I married. In those days, if a teacher became pregnant, she was expected to quit teaching. Given these circumstances, it was certainly compelling to many to argue against sending a girl to college. But not to my father, whom I once overheard saying in response to such an argument: "It's my money, and I guess I can do what I want with it." He wanted to give his daughter an education. He and my mother were more than proud when I graduated with the highest grades from grade school and high school, and they invited our entire family to my college graduation to celebrate the fact that I graduated summa cum laude.

When I think back upon those years, I must give much credit to the Catholic nuns who taught me in grade school and high school. They guided and directed my enthusiasm for learning into channels that later earned me scholarships and prizes to go on to college. They helped me gain the experiences that I needed to achieve my goals—encouraging me to join the debate club, enter speech and essay contests, and become a member of the student council. In my limited experience, those nuns were the only women I knew who had careers. They encouraged me to study and served as my role models, proving that women were capable of running more than their homes and families.

I chose to attend LeMoyne College—a small Catholic liberal arts college run by the Jesuit order in nearby Syracuse, New York. It was the first Jesuit college in the United States to admit women into the four-year liberal arts program. And the Jesuits who taught there believed that women were capable of being educated. This was not especially true of the laypeople who taught there. I still remember overhearing a conversation in which a history professor explained to someone that women were not very capable in the fields of history or political science. Instead, he argued, they were more suited to English studies and languages. But he then went on to say that he had encountered one exception to this philosophy . . . me! I was appalled and determined then that I would prove to any and all doubters like him that the study of history was a place where women *could* excel.

It was the dean of women at LeMoyne who really helped me and other female students to embrace the idea that the world was more open to us than we knew. She called together the women in the sophomore class and encouraged us to begin thinking of graduate education. She mobilized several of the faculty to hold seminars for us on what we needed to do to prepare for graduate school. I was thrilled to learn that I could pursue my love of history by getting a doctorate and, then, by teaching in college. We were warned, however, that women were admitted to graduate schools, medical schools, and law schools under very limited quotas. So we had to get the highest grades and the best recommendations. Loving a challenge, I went right after it. I was offered several graduate assistantships and decided to accept a three-year National Defense Education Act Fellowship. This took me farther away from home than I had ever lived, to the University of Pittsburgh in Pennsylvania.

Graduate school was a frightening affair. Pittsburgh was a very big city, much bigger than either my hometown or my college town, and the demands of graduate school were intimidating. I no longer had kind Jesuit fathers or a terrific dean of women to support me. But I did make friends with students from equally small towns and small colleges, and we stuck together. It wasn't long before I met the person who became my most encouraging supporter and my future husband. We helped each other through graduate school: I helped him with language exams, and he typed my papers. We also encouraged each other through the difficult courses and exams. We married in the middle of our graduate years.

By the time we had finished all but our dissertations we were already proud parents of a two-year-old, and Tom was offered a position at the University of Oklahoma Health Sciences Center. There was actually a position in my field open on the Norman campus as well, but I was ineligible for it because at that time there was a strict nepotism rule. So I took the first year in Oklahoma to stay home with my two-year-old and finish my doctoral dissertation.

We didn't have the money to attend my graduation ceremony in Pittsburgh. When my degree came in the mail, my husband told my daughter that we had to go to the post office to pick up the diploma, and it meant that her mommy was a doctor. She burst into tears and screamed, "She is not! She is not!" When Tom asked her what she was afraid of, it became clear that somehow she thought I would turn into the man with the white coat who gave her the shots she did not like!

I took my brand-new doctorate and went looking for a college teaching position in the Oklahoma City area. I found that the only one I could fit with my parental and research interests was a part-time appointment. There were openings for history teachers that year, and it was not difficult to secure a position. The situation changed dramatically within the next few years, when the bottom fell out of the history market. During the 1970s the elimination of the strict history requirements in lower schools made the demand for history teachers in colleges grind to a halt. Thus, I eventually lost my part-time teaching job.

When my second child was ready for kindergarten, I began to look again for full-time employment at the universities and colleges in the area. A faculty friend was serving on the board of the newly created Oklahoma Humanities Committee, the state program of the National Endowment for the Humanities. He knew I was looking for work, and he encouraged me to apply to be the assistant director. He said they wanted a person with an advanced degree in the humanities, and he explained that it was challenging and interesting work. I applied for the position and was hired. It was the summer of 1975. The very next year, the executive director left and I was offered his position by the chairman of the board and the trustees, who had become very impressed with my work. By this time affirmative action laws prevailed so that promoting a qualified woman within an organization was considered an appropriate action. I have continued to hold that position since.

All these accidents of timing provided an incredible opportunity. Accepting a position as administrator of a small nonprofit organization dedicated to fostering appreciation and learning in the humanities allowed me to share my love of history, literature, and philosophy with so many more people than I could have reached in classrooms. It also challenged me to develop capabilities within myself that I never dreamed I had. I always saw myself as a student, the only child who found the greatest things in life in books. I loved being a scholar, researching in libraries, and teaching. I never saw myself as a person who could put together a budget, manage a professional staff, fund-raise, and continue to develop new and creative ways to present the humanities to many different audiences. But with the help of a wonderful group of board members, a talented staff, and the lively interest of Oklahomans in learning, this has been the greatest position I could have had.

There have been some strange experiences, however, for this displaced "Yankee," as my students used to call me. It took a bit of time, for example, to understand that many people in the state confused the words *humanities* and *humanist* with secular humanism. I had been taught that humanism was a term devised during the Renaissance to refer to a revival of interest in the classics, in literature, and in the history of human accomplishment. The great humanists that I learned about were Erasmus and St. Thomas More. Neither of these men was godless; both were men of great faith. In fact, St. Thomas More died for his faith. I had no idea that, when we used the word *humanist* to describe a professor of one of the disciplines of the humanities, some people might think we were talking about an atheist.

In my first year on the job, I thought it would be a great idea to offer a "Summer Humanist" to the community, a faculty member who would spend the summer in a community developing a humanities program. We received about ten proposals from scholars. When the grants were announced, some people in the state protested, complaining that atheists were coming to libraries or museums in their communities. One woman came to see me, saying she was representing one of the worried groups. While she sat in my office waiting for me to end a telephone conversation, she noticed the large poster of Tutankhamen from an exhibit funded by the National Endowment for the Humanities.

When I finished my phone call, she looked at me and asked, "Is this about culture?"

I said, "Yes, indeed."

She said, "Well, I am in favor of culture."

Then she told me how her grandmother had helped found the library in her town and how, since the days of early settlement, her folks had always supported the growth of libraries and museums and schools in their community.

Then she said, "Well, okay, I'll go back and tell everyone this is all right."

We learned our lesson. From that day forward, we never used the word *humanist* to describe a scholar who does research and teaches any of the disciplines in the humanities.

That woman proved to me that Oklahomans were indeed truly interested in learning. Those who came as pioneers, especially the women, helped assure the cultural life of their communities, setting up schools for the children and starting reading groups that eventually became libraries. It has been rewarding to learn about and travel around the state of Oklahoma and to discover new ways to contribute to the cultural lives of Oklahomans.

Oklahoma is a great place for women. The recent history of pioneer women has fostered a broadly held expectation that women play a significant role in building a good society, one that includes social and political responsibility as well as care for home and family.

Mothering

Lightning Strikes Twice

Carole Burrage

I spent approximately my first decade of sexual activity as most females do, trying desperately to avoid getting pregnant. Nothing, I thought, would ruin my life more swiftly than a baby. I had known girls in high school who had gotten knocked up, kicked off the cheerleading squad, dumped by their boyfriends, and doomed to a life of working menial jobs and living with their parents. Though I love my mother, the thought of living with her for one moment longer than I had to was a most effective form of birth control.

Mom, too, was afraid I might find myself in the "family way." Long before I'd had my first sexual encounter, I caught her reading a thin paperback from the local Christian bookstore. On the cover was a girl with a wedge haircut staring out a rain-spattered window, underneath the title *Christy's Pregnant*. A paragraph on the back of the book described the story of a God-fearing couple who—through no fault of their own—discover that their rebellious sixteen-year-old is with child. When I asked my mother why she was reading this particular book, she said, "One can never be too prepared."

Thanks to maturity and matrimony, I overcame my aversion to procreation. It's ironic, then, that I've discovered that the path to motherhood, which I so vigilantly avoided, is one road I have great difficulty traveling. What is supposed to be the most natural thing in the world doesn't come naturally to me. I'm luckier than many, however: unlike my friends who have had fertility problems, I have been pregnant four times. Conception is not my issue; rather, it's hanging on to the little suckers once they've taken root that I have a hard time with. If this were baseball, I suppose you'd say I'm batting .500, which sounds like a pretty good average. I have two beautiful sons. The older, Truman, is almost eight, and the younger, Carter, is three weeks old today. Like his big brother, he was born two months early and weighed a hair more than 3.5 pounds. Also like his brother, he is spending the first weeks of his life in the neonatal intensive care unit at St. John's Hospital in Tulsa. While I write this in my hospital guest room, he lies in an isolette on the seventh floor, being fed breast milk continuously through a feeding tube that runs up his tiny nose and down into his stomach. He was given a blood transfusion earlier today, and the extra fluid in his body has made him puffy, so he also received a dose of Lasix, the diuretic given to racehorses when they retain water. When the nurse removed the IV from his hand, blood spurted everywhere, causing her to comment, "That was a good line." Right now, he is very probably sleeping. I pray that he is comfortable.

I would give everything I own not to be here again. Though I'm not a weepy person by nature, I burst into tears the moment I found out that I needed an emergency cesarean section because, once again, my booby trap of a body had declared war on the life growing inside me. Not only would my poor baby be shoved out into the world far earlier than he deserved, but my husband and I would have to revisit what was undoubtedly the hardest time of our lives. I've heard of women in rice paddies who pause from work to squat and give birth before getting back to task. Why couldn't I be made of such hardy stock? It's impossible not to feel like a failure when, with the aid of modern medicine, you still can't do what cavewomen accomplished.

This shouldn't have come as a surprise, but somehow it did. Despite a fairly crummy track record of one preemie and two miscarriages, I figured this last go-around would turn out differently. Call me Pollyanna, but I felt better than I had with any of my previous pregnancies, and my chronically high blood pressure had been amazingly normal. Finally, it seemed, my body had decided to behave itself. My hostile womb appeared to have mellowed. This time was going to be different.

But it wasn't, and here we are. As Yogi Berra said, "It's déjà vu all over again." For the second time at roughly thirty-two weeks of pregnancy, my blood pressure rose to levels I'm told would cause most people to suffer fatal strokes. Again, I was sliced open, and we were shown the slimy little baby over the blue curtain and heard him cry. Again, he was whisked away by Dr. Vitanza and the neonatology team. Again, I was stuffed and stapled back together; and, again, I was the last in the family to get to see my baby. Again, my husband pushed my wheelchair through the gray double doors of the NICU; again, I heard the thrum and bang of the scrub station and donned the wash-worn yellow surgical gown before being escorted to the exact same position in the room for the most critical babies where Truman had lain years earlier. Again, my child weighed less than the average Chihuahua; again, he was blindfolded to protect his eyes from the bilirubin light treating his jaundice; again, his mouth was agape from the ventilator tube jammed down his throat to make sure he didn't succumb to the respiratory distress syndrome brought on from being born with underdeveloped lungs. Again, the tubes and wires were attached, the central line was threaded into his navel to check his blood gases, and the antibiotics were administered via an intravenous line inserted in his scalp.

Again, it was days before we were able to hold our baby for the first time; and when we did, it was with eyes anxiously fixed on the monitors overhead that measured his heart rate, breathing, and oxygen saturation to make sure that our touch wasn't causing him harm. Again, we became reacquainted with that swelling of the throat that prohibits speech and eyes that spill over at the slightest provocation. All of this is painfully familiar territory.

The breast pump has become my nemesis. Okay, so perhaps it isn't the pump's fault that I barely secrete enough mother's milk to keep up with my tiny baby's equally tiny appetite. I enviously watch other NICU moms put overflowing bottles—bottles that are labeled last name first, with date, pump time, and mom's medications listed—into the communal fridge. A productive pumping for me leaves a bottle a third of the way full (or two-thirds of the way empty, depending on one's point of view). I anxiously chart my output and calculate at the end of each day whether I have enough milk stored to last through the night so that I can go home; if not, I stay the night in my guest room and get up at 2 or 3 A.M. to deliver breakfast. I don't know what I'm going to do when he starts eating more. Well-meaning friends have told me to let myself off the hook, have one less thing to worry about, and just let him drink formula. I don't think they realize that this is the one of the very few things I am personally able to do for my baby. I predict it won't be too long before I will be forced to throw in this particular towel. One thing I know for sure, however, is that, in addition to "surrogate," I can cross "wet nurse" off my list of potential careers.

I try to stay in the moment, and I find that helps. Not blaming myself or the doctors or fate or God or El Niño or whatever for the past and not anticipating the myriad of potential disasters the future may hold allow me to focus on the staggering beauty and kindness bestowed on us daily. Carter has the most gorgeous, tiny, tapered fingers I have ever seen, and his wee lips are a perfect cupid's bow. The nurses call him "Mr. Cutie Pie" and "Handsome" even when they don't know I'm listening. Every day there are gift bags and boxes and meals waiting on our doorstep, and cards and letters carrying thoughts and prayers arrive in the mail. Friends call and offer to entertain Truman or check on our dog or simply to let us know that they are thinking of us. Some of our dearest friends have just endured a singularly awful miscarriage, yet they have put aside their own grief and been here for us in ways that render me speechless. Times like these make me glad I live in a small town and help me realize that I am blessed with a depth of rich, wonderful relationships.

Trying circumstances also bring clarity of vision, a renewed understanding of what really matters. Merely holding my own baby is a gift; and, though not deeply religious, I never fail to silently say the Lord's Prayer whenever I have him in my arms. Watching Truman—a gangly second-grader with spiky blond hair, big blue eyes, and a snaggle-toothed grin—scrub in to enter the same nursery where he once lay, too sick to cry, is a full-circle moment. I'm awed and appreciative all over again that my older son has grown from a half-hatched baby into a sweet, smart, special little boy. And I am bowled over with gratitude that I managed to marry the kindest, most decent, and most honorable man I have ever known. I ache for the time when the four of us can spend the night together at home as a family, doing nothing more exciting than eating dinner and watching TV.

With experience comes wisdom: the benefit of having been here and done this before is the knowledge that in a few weeks, this "meantime" will be over, and Carter will come home. I look at Truman, and I remind myself that it won't be long before much about these seemingly endless days will fade from memory, and what little is left will become family lore. Diaper changing will become a chore rather than the privilege it is at the moment, and "boys will be boys." I hope, however, that I can retain a bit of perspective from this second time around, take less of everyday life for granted, and recognize the sacred in the seemingly mundane. Sleeping in my own bed, warm with the knowledge that those most dear to me are under the same roof; could anything be sweeter than that?

As I stated earlier, I'd give everything I own not to be here right now. Would I do it again, if I knew this was the price I had to pay to have one of those babies I so fervently didn't want in my youth? In a heartbeat.

Moving Day

A Letter to Emily and Elizabeth

Susan Savage

One morning in 2003 I said a quiet prayer for my daughters, both of whom were on the road, traveling out of state for summer jobs. That same morning, I was moving from their first home, the one in which they had lived most of their lives. My thoughts turned to the transitions that had occurred in our lives over the recent years, watershed events that redefined how our family lived yet also created new possibilities. I contemplated the profound effect physical space has on our approach to the world. I wrote my thoughts in the following letter to Emily and Elizabeth.

July 2, 2003
Dear Emily and Elizabeth,

It is moving day, girls; and, as our beds, rugs, tables, chairs, pictures, lamps, and several hundred boxes are loaded into two vans, I am full of thoughts, memories, emotions, and anticipation. Our time in this grand old house is finished, and it is time for us to create new memories in new places.

Walking through our home this morning among the packed boxes, I marveled at the empty (and clean!) closets; the basement walls devoid of your years of artwork, posters, and camping-trip treasures; the garage inhabited only by the bicycles, a lawn mower, and other sundry items to be moved to Oklahoma City. I was filled with such gratitude and appreciation for this open and airy place where our family lived for so long.

It is important to me that you know my heart and head are filled with happy memories. Sure, there have been sadness and some heartache, but they are part of living and loving. Mostly, I am thankful for the rich life this house enabled all of us to have and for the time—which now seems so very brief to me—that our family was privileged to live here.

The memories fill every corner of my mind as I write: what you wore when you came home for the first time from the hospital, the lunches you carried to Lee Elementary, Halloween costumes, holiday decorations and celebrations, backyard birthday parties, school projects, neighbors, friends, our menagerie of critters, extended family who visited from all over the country. . . . The sounds, smells, and images are so vivid.

Emily, you left for Indianapolis in June, and, Elizabeth, you have been in Wyoming since May. You helped a lot before your respective jobs required you to leave, but I am astonished by the sheer number of things we acquired and collected over nearly twenty-five years in this house. Where did all of this stuff come from? I even hosted a "packing party" after you left, attended by Lucy; Jane and her girls; Scott, Leslie, and Ann; Hilary, Martha, and Anne; and among all of us, we packed the kitchen and the dining and living rooms in one day.

Packing photographs of you at every age became a journey through time—Elizabeth, your birthday when Lucy and I brought Moe, the horse you loved, walked him up the back driveway and watched your expression of disbelief when Dad opened the gate and we all cried, "Happy Birthday!" Emily, your Slip 'n' Slide competitions with Justin and Nick on those hot July birthdays. The cycling competitions, riding horses at the ranch, soccer games, pictures of sweet Molly girl—a dog every child should have—as you dressed her in a horse halter and she pulled you on the skateboard. Photographs of Mikie, Woofer, Chuckie-Cat, Jack, Sam, Raney, Ricky, Tammy, Miss Kitty, the hamsters, snake, lizard—all of the critters who were part of our household. It took me forever to pack those photographs—I laughed and cried; but, most of all, I recalled the noise and energy of your very active and interesting lives.

This grand old home is a special place—a place where your foundation for life has been solid and sturdy and certain—just like this house we love—a place full of good memories, a stable place, and a place where you have been loved and nurtured by your parents and each other and family and friends.

Today's move is a transition to new beginnings for each of us: new places, new people, new houses, new jobs, new experiences. Yet leaving a place you love can be hard—so carry this house with you in your heart throughout your lives. I know I will. Also take with you the knowledge that another family has decided to make this their home. I hope the solid brick walls and the open, airy rooms give this young family the same marvelous opportunities to grow and create memories as we have had.

Picture me sitting in the garage on this hot July day in shorts, a T-shirt, and visor, with the dogs by my side. (I think they're afraid I may not remember they are supposed to travel the one hundred miles to our new home where the cats already await us.) Raney is hunting bumblebees and dipping in and out of the pool. Sam is trying to find a cool spot on which to lie. I am watching the artifacts of our lives—all packed, sorted, and organized—being loaded piece by piece. This evening Scott, Leslie, and Ann will come for a picnic on the floor in the empty kitchen and a final swim.

Emily and Elizabeth, we are so lucky and have so much good fortune. I am looking ahead as you certainly are too. As the dogs and I leave tonight, we will say a last good-bye to this wonderful home. You should know the trees planted on the occasions of your births grow strong. You, as they, are well rooted and ready for all that awaits. It is exciting to think about what comes next.

Take care, my sweet girls. Be safe in your travels. Be strong. Work hard.

Much love,
Mom

And Then There Was Me

Sue Iveson

Mostly I try not to dwell on the past.

My childhood was not what anyone would call conventional. Well, it was conventional at first. The early part of my life was idyllic. From the age of two until I was about seven or eight, we were one big happy family. I was living every little girl's dream, growing up on horseback, as my parents raised Quarter Horses. Then my father's mental illness became the focal point of our lives. He was eventually diagnosed with paranoid schizophrenia, but not until many years later.

Living with him was a nightmare. I have experienced and witnessed things no child should ever have to encounter. My father would become extremely violent with very little, or no, provocation. He believed we were poisoning his meals. He would accuse us of sending messages to each other, or to strangers when we were out, with our eyes. My mother never wanted to rock the boat so she would avoid eye contact with anyone when my father was present. She accepted that he would only eat food from a can (that he opened himself) as normal. I, on the other hand, was not quite so charitable. I would goad him, eating the spaghetti dinner my mother cooked, saying things like, "Look, Dad, I am eating the spaghetti and not dropping dead. Amazing, eh?" Of course, these little torments didn't go over too well. This particular episode happened when I was about eleven years old. It ended with a very hot pot of sauce being thrown at me, landing on my legs and giving me first- and second-degree burns.

I have also dodged knives, hockey sticks, and worse. When I was twelve, my father chased me during another violent rampage. I ran to my bedroom and leaned against the locked door to keep him out. He used a hatchet to try to break the door down, and the blade came through the door very close to my head. Terrified, I ran to the window and jumped from the second story to get away from him. Though I was hurt, I believe it would have been much worse had he caught me.

The event leading to my parents' eventual divorce is a defining moment in my life. After being out one night, I came home to hear my parents fighting again. I heard my father yelling, "God help me! God forgive me!" as he ran up the stairs to our second floor. I assumed he was chasing my mother, intent on beating her again. I started wearily for the stairs after them, bent on protecting my mother, only to find her wrapped in a towel at the bottom of the stairs, screaming at me to stop. By this time I was halfway up the stairs and could see into my parents' bedroom. I watched as, with the handgun he kept in his nightstand, my father shot himself in the head.

My father survived.

I cleaned the bedroom so my mother would not have to see the blood and brains on the carpet and walls when she came home. I never did find out what had set him off this last time. I was thirteen years old when this happened. It was then I realized that the only person I could rely on was myself.

Before and after I left that family, I was essentially a child who lived a wild life with no rules for almost five years. I eventually came to see I was going nowhere. I was afraid for my future and realized I was the only one who could change my life. After giving up my wild friends, I slept on the floor of my new bedroom until I could afford a mattress. But the room was mine. It was peaceful. It was a start. By sheer power of will, I overcame drug addiction cold turkey. Withdrawal was bad, but not as bad as realizing that I had almost become as lost as some of the people in my life.

After my experiences, I met my oldest daughter's birth with anticipation; extreme happiness; and cold, black fear. I had read that children who are abused grow up to be abusers. I never had a real role model for parenting. How could I possibly be a good mother? I was terrified.

Of course, I did have a good idea of what *not* to do as a mother. To this day, I still do not understand why my mother did not put her children first. As soon as I looked into my daughter's eyes, I knew I would die before allowing anyone to harm one hair on her head.

I am who I am because of these people. Remove one and it would change who I am considerably. However, without my *own* strength and determination, I would not be the person I am today.

Cat on the High Dive

Joan Nesbitt

In my dream, my son is far ahead of me, just around the corner, I think. I can't see him, but I hope he is there. I move faster, my eyes scanning the horizon, ravenous for any glimpse of his small silhouette as proof he is not lost. He's been gone for hours, but I control my panic and tell myself if I just keep moving, just keep looking, I will find him. When my fear can no longer be suppressed and I am on the verge of hysteria, I awake abruptly. Sometimes I am nauseous, always near tears. Often I get up and walk down the dark hall to stand over his sleeping form and calm myself. The moonlight barely illuminates the pile of toys beside his bed, much less my psyche, and I am left to wonder, "What am I so afraid of?"

The carefully composed drawing I find in the study—small in size but enormous in import—answers for me. *I am not in the picture.* There is a pickup truck on a winding country road, complete with birds and trees. My husband is driving, and my son is riding in the back. I know the identities of the stick figures included in this illustration of my son's life because, lest there be any question, he has labeled them "Dad" and "Me."

One night I ask my husband if he has noticed my son's drawing. He says, "No," so I describe it. He tells me that on a recent weekday afternoon he took our son on a slow drive down some back roads near our home. A boy of vast persistence, my son was obsessed with the forbidden delight of riding in the back of our pickup. My husband relented, and the resulting adventure was so thrilling as to merit documentation.

I want to be relieved that my son's picture represents an actual rather than an imagined experience, as if that somehow gives less emotional consequence to my absence. Then I am reminded that I am absent because I am . . . well . . . *absent* so much of the time. I am not in the picture because I am unavailable for such spontaneous jaunts in my children's lives.

I am a working mother, with all the same fears and guilt triggers of every other working mother I know. The difference for me is that, as of a year ago, my husband is no longer a working father. He left his job to care for our eight-year-old son, Parker, and our eleven-year-old daughter, Kate. The modern, two-working-parent family has a litany of flaws, according to popular literature, but the arrangement offers a soothing emotional salve we rarely contemplate. When both parents work full-time, both are more or less equally connected to their children's lives. Now that my husband is staying home, he has ascended to the throne of preferred parent and I have been relegated to the second string—a brutal blow to the maternal ego.

My demoted status was hammered home recently when my daughter came down with a sore throat while my husband was away for a few hours playing tennis. While I was scrounging in the medicine cabinet for ibuprofen, my daughter's faithful assistant ambushed me with the question at the top of both their minds: "When is Dad coming home?" Parker blurted out, "Because Kate is shivering!" The clipped words that I think came out of my mouth were something like "I'm fully aware of that, and I'm quite capable of handling a fever." For the record, I usually try to avoid exposing my insecurities so fully to my children, not because I'm a mindful role model, but rather because they are masters at exploiting them. The stark reality I'm facing is that the parent who is home most, rules. It's a comfortable, instinctive role for a mother to fill, but I can't fight the math. I can compile chore lists, establish laundry guidelines, and suggest nightly menus but, frankly, I can't enforce a damn thing. I'm Barney Fife—a deputy with no bullets in a town where the sheriff is both beloved and wise.

For the first twelve years of our marriage, my husband and I both worked, he to build his business and I to pay our bills. My mother provided our child care. As households with two working parents go, ours seemed comparatively calm and functional. Because my mother shouldered a great deal of the domestic burden, my husband and I were reasonably free of the typical worries of working parents. When Mom's age and health forced her retirement, my husband and I were abruptly awakened to the reality most our friends had already confronted: this daycare thing sucks! We stitched together a patchwork solution and spent a year fretting over its deficien- cies. As we faced our first summer—the Grand Canyon of daycare scheduling—my husband made a radical suggestion: he could sell his business and raise our kids rather than turning them over to a surrogate.

On the surface, it was perfectly logical. I made more money than my husband, and my employer provided our health insurance and retirement benefits. My husband, on the other hand, had 100 percent equity in a business with a willing buyer. The new arrangement would require a higher level of budgetary discipline since the sale wouldn't make us instant millionaires, but the idea wasn't financially impossible. Surface assessments aside, however, his suggestion was mired in field of emotional land mines I had no idea how to traverse.

I'm a child of the '70s, which is to say I'm screwed. In fifth grade I watched Billie Jean King beat Bobby Riggs and felt strangely empowered. My favorite television show was *The Brady Bunch*. I wouldn't realize until many years later just how conflicted these two influences made me feel. On the one hand, I identified with Helen Reddy and her feminist roar, yet I still wanted Mike Brady to complete my picture (and to foot the bill for what I expected to be a solidly middle-class life). My career advancement always had more to do with financial imperative than personal desire. I was fresh out of college when I discovered the first law of career physics: once you get on the treadmill, acceleration is tolerated in direct proportion to compensation. As long as my daughter was dressed in Laura Ashley and my son enjoyed the latest PlayStation game, I didn't seem to mind the running so much. With every new promotion, I bought more Martha Stewart books and dreamed of making marzipan fruit at Christmas. Then a friend gave me a box of tiny sugared oranges and attached a note that read, "Real women *buy* marzipan." It was a disingenuous way of saying, "You can have it all." Every working mother I know understands that's a load of crap, but the illusion was secure because there was no alternative on my horizon.

For my husband to suggest that we could and should change our personal paradigm was monumentally unsettling. I had imagined this crossroads all right, but in my version of the dream I was the person "retiring" from the rat race. After all, everyone knew I was the expert cook, chief organizer, and self-appointed arbiter of domestic style. I am the *mother*, for God's sake.

So it was the mother in me that wanted to look him in the eye and ask, "Are you out of your mind?" Did he really think he could master the science of craft making, the intricacies of ironing, the nuances of Crock-Pot cookery, the Zen of bed making? What could he possibly bring to the task?

What I'm realizing is that the task isn't defined by the home, but by the heart. Working mothers—at least *this* working mother—want desperately to check all the boxes on the endless to-do list that is our lives. If we can keep everything tidy, everyone fed, all events on schedule, then maybe our children won't hate us or blame us for our choices. But my husband carries no such burden of false assurances, nor is he shackled by the societal expectations attendant to housewifery. For him, parenting comes first; and parenting is about cultivating a relationship, not keeping a home. He is neither bothered nor distracted by the bread crumbs, junk mail, and dirty socks that litter our lives. *He is in the picture*, delivering homemade cupcakes to classroom parties; attending school assemblies and field trips; coaching soccer, tennis, and basketball; and patiently explaining the mysteries of nightly homework.

While I'm mourning the end of motherhood as I knew it, my husband is staring down his own demons. Since he's no longer employed, he's lost most of his social currency. We live in a state where the citizens have voted to ban gay marriage. Suffice to say, a lot of folks who populate our lives aren't comfortable with domestic arrangements that fall *outside the norm*. That in our lifetime we've known many gay, lesbian, and straight couples, but none like us, adds to our unease. Notice I say "like us" because a marriage like mine doesn't yet have a social label that I'm aware of. Individual role reversals, such as female firefighters and male nurses, are well documented in today's popular culture. But marriages that involve role reversals are still largely unexamined. Our marriage is an oddity to strangers and a curious amusement to acquaintances. Because we so strongly defy easy definition, only those closest to us ask questions beyond the most superficial.

In a recent conversation, a stranger asked my husband, "What do you do?"

"Not much of anything," my husband replied with a smile and a chuckle that led the stranger to believe he was joking.

"No, *really*," came the reply, to which my husband mimicked, "*Really.*"

The conversation ended abruptly then; and when my husband retold it to me later, he seemed disconcerted by the stranger's uneasy reaction and immediate disinterest.

I suggested to him that to make people comfortable, he needed to give them a label they could understand.

"Just say you're a stay-at-home Dad." (Read: "pussy.") "Or say you're retired." (Read: "independently wealthy.") "But when you say 'nothing,' people can't put you in a box and that makes them nervous. For all they know, you're a freak. Or a sociopath."

What I realized then is that my husband is like a cat on the high dive. Everyone looks up, but no one expects to see him there. The first reaction is disbelief—*What's he doing up there?*—followed by morbid curiosity: *What do we do? Should we help him? What if he falls? Good Lord, won't that be something when he hits the water!*

I used to think that everything I knew about marriage could be written on a grain of rice. My family has marched in a parade of spectacularly unsuccessful unions, and I grew up in a sea of marital flotsam. As a young girl, I figured marriage was like a nasty virus, and we weren't a particularly hardy group. I waited far longer than most my peers to give it a try; and, even then, on the cusp of my thirtieth birthday, a nagging inner voice reminded me that it's a bit of a crapshoot. More than a decade later, I realize that the best unions are a grand improvisation. If you're willing to forgo the security of a script, you just might find the marital equivalent of a hundred dollar bill tucked in an old coat pocket. I sure as hell didn't set out to be my family's breadwinner. My husband surely didn't plan to be our family's caretaker. But here we find ourselves, filling roles we didn't imagine, on a journey we didn't plot, in a life we wouldn't trade.

Women and Work

I No Longer Fear Death

Wilma Mankiller

The question I am asked most frequently is why I remain such a positive person after surviving breast cancer, lymphoma, dialysis, two kidney transplants, and systemic myasthenia gravis. The answer is simple: I am Cherokee, and I am a woman. No one knows better than I that every day is indeed a good day. How can I be anything but positive when I come from a tenacious, resilient people who keep moving forward with an eye toward the future even after enduring unspeakable hardship? How can I not be positive when I have lived longer than I ever dreamed possible, and my life plays itself out in a supportive community of extended family and friends?

There is much to be thankful for. Though I am an ordinary woman, I have been blessed with many extraordinary experiences. I learned at a fairly early age that I cannot always control what is sent my way or the actions of other people, but I can most certainly control my thoughts and reactions. I don't spend a lot of time dwelling on the negative. I believe that having a good, peaceful mind is the basic premise for a good life. My sense of faith, hope, and optimism stems in part from being Cherokee and in part from a cool November morning in 1978.

. . .

After a quick glance at the morning news, I poured a cup of coffee and headed out the door. I had no idea my life would soon change forever. About three miles from my home, I started up a slight grade. On the other side of the hill, my friend Sherry Morris pulled out to pass two slow-moving cars. When I came to the top of the hill, her car was in my lane. Our cars hit head on. I have

---

A part of this article appeared in Wilma Mankiller's *Every Day Is a Good Day: Reflections of Contemporary Indigenus Women* (Golden, Colo.: Fulcrum, 2004).

very little recollection of what happened immediately after the accident. I was in shock from my injuries and loss of blood. I vaguely remember there was blood everywhere and people were screaming. By the time an ambulance took Sherry to Tahlequah, her life had already slipped away. I was taken by ambulance to Stillwell, where I was stabilized and then transferred to a regional hospital in Fort Smith, Arkansas. As the ambulance sped toward Fort Smith, death beckoned me with an intense feeling of peacefulness and warmth. I felt a carefree lightness and an overpowering pull toward unconditional, all-encompassing love. Everything in that world was perfect.

I had begun a beautiful and sacred journey toward the land of the Creator when my daughters, Felicia and Gina, came into my mind, and I returned to this world. That near-death experience made a significant difference in the way I have since lived my life. After that, I no longer feared death, and I also no longer feared life. The accident, my near-death experience, and Sherry's death made me much more open to whatever path the Creator might lead me down. These events also helped me learn to appreciate the incredible gift of life and transformed me into a more courageous person with a much greater willingness to take risks.

Now from a distance of almost three decades, I look back on that terrible November day and wonder what Sherry's life would have been like if she had lived beyond her early thirties and been able to watch her sensitive, smart daughter, Meghan, grow into a focused young woman who works on a range of social justice issues. And I wonder what my life would have been like if the Creator not had sent so many challenges my way.

The first challenge after the accident was learning that one leg was so badly crushed that amputation was a possibility, and permanent disability was very probable. The other leg was broken in several places, and my face and chest were crushed. Though no one spoke about it, I knew there had been another car involved in the accident. After three weeks in the hospital, I was coming to grips with my injuries when Mike Morris gave me the devastating news about his wife, Sherry. There are no words to describe the disbelief and pain I experienced during the next days, weeks, and months as I dealt with Sherry's death and my own extensive injuries. By the time I had recovered enough to return to work, I had endured seventeen separate surgeries, mostly on my legs.

I was once told that the most lovely and precious flowers can be seen only in the bottom of a very deep valley. I have been in that valley and seen those incredible flowers. The steep climb out of the valley made me stronger and more mature. After that it was hard to envision what it would take to really rattle me. I am convinced that those experiences prepared me for the position of principal chief of the Cherokee Nation and for the other challenges that awaited me.

When I returned to work eighteen months after the accident, our principal chief, Ross Swimmer, assigned me the task of working with a team to develop self-help housing and water projects in rural historic Cherokee communities. I worked primarily with Charlie Soap, a bilingual Cherokee with a reputation for being able to "get things done," and we developed several successful projects in a number of communities.* All of that work validated my belief that Cherokee people in these communities are mutually supportive and willing to help each other. After these projects were completed, it became difficult for anyone to ever again argue that Cherokees did not have the capacity to solve their own problems, given the resources and right set of circumstances. Based on our community work, the Cherokee Nation Community Development Department was formed, and I became its founding director, a position I held until 1983 when Ross Swimmer bypassed all his male political allies and chose me for his running mate.

Ross Swimmer and I were quite the team. He is a Republican. I am a Democrat. In those days, Cherokee candidates together formed a slate of candidates for all elective offices: principal chief; deputy principal chief; and fifteen legislators, or members of the tribal council. By the time I informed Ross Swimmer I would accept his offer to seek the office of deputy principal chief, all his council slate had been chosen. They all opposed my candidacy—but none more than the Swimmer campaign manager, Councilman Gary Chapman. Chapman had hoped to be chosen to run as deputy chief on the ticket, but Swimmer disqualified him because both he and Chapman were senior officials of the First National Bank, a depository of Cherokee Nation funds.

---

* Wilma Mankiller discusses her work in rural historic communities in more detail in *Mankiller: A Chief and Her People* (New York: St. Martin's Griffin, 1999).

The Swimmer-Mankiller campaign was run out of Chapman's garage. I faced opposition from within the Swimmer campaign as well as from the two other candidates who filed for the office of deputy principal chief. On more than one occasion, Charlie Soap, my future husband, tried to convince me that Swimmer's people were not campaigning for me or even supporting me. Though I knew they did not support me, I refused to accept the notion that some of Swimmer's own people were actively working against me. Once, Ross Swimmer called to ask me if I had been campaigning in bars, something I would not even remotely consider. The source of this rumor was Gary Chapman himself. Toward the end of the campaign, I was asked by Swimmer's campaign workers to take campaign-related information to the Stillwell newspaper. Out of curiosity, I opened the manila envelope and discovered ads for Ross Swimmer for chief and my opponent, J. B. Dreadfulwater, for deputy principal chief. Charlie was right. I finally got it!

Charlie and I developed our own campaign strategy, and we both worked very hard right up until two weeks before the election, when Charlie had to leave for an overseas trip. A small crew of volunteers, along with my mother, my girls, and my brothers and sisters, worked until we were exhausted. My brother Jim had an old van that we loaded up with election signs to erect on country roads. On the day of the election, I decided not to stay at the "watch party" with the Swimmer campaign group. Instead, I went to Tallahassee Muscogee Creek Ceremonial Grounds and danced until the sun came up. In the morning, I called Tahlequah and learned that Ross Swimmer had won the election and that I faced Agnes Cowen in a run-off. After a relatively uneventful campaign, I won the run-off election.

When Ross Swimmer resigned in 1985 to take a position with the Reagan administration in Washington, D.C., I automatically moved into the position of principal chief to fill out his term, as provided by our Cherokee constitution. It was then up to the tribal council to fill the vacant position of deputy chief from their ranks. The names of three candidates emerged: Clarence Sunday, a respected elder and former associate of Chief Bill Keeler at Phillips Petroleum; John Ketcher, a sixty-two-year-old bilingual Cherokee; and Gary Chapman, the Tahlequah banker who had not supported my candidacy. After much debate and several split votes, the council voted unanimously for Ketcher, one of the finest men I know.

John and I served out the rest of that term, and we were elected for two more four-year terms. In 1994 both John Ketcher and I decided against seeking office in the upcoming 1995 elections. After working many years as an employee of the Cherokee Nation and then serving three four-year terms in elective office, I decided it was time for a change for me and for the nation. And I had a nagging feeling that something was physically wrong.

Six months after I left office, while serving as a Montgomery Fellow at Dartmouth College, I was diagnosed with second-stage lymphoma. Since there were no comparable treatment facilities near my home in Oklahoma, I remained in Boston for almost eight months while undergoing chemotherapy. My world suddenly shifted and narrowed considerably. A year earlier, Diné (Navajo) Chairman Peterson Zah and I had led a delegation to meet with President Clinton on behalf of all tribal nations. Now my days were spent poring over results of bone scans, gallium scans, and X-rays; waiting to learn whether my white and red blood-cell counts were up or down; and seeing whether chemotherapy had shrunk the tumor.

During the time I was being treated for lymphoma, I was also being sued by the very controversial Joe Byrd administration, which had succeeded me at the Cherokee Nation in 1995. This suit questioned the legality of granting severance pay to employees who left when my term of office ended. Joe Byrd and the tribal council eventually dropped the civil suit against me when it was discovered they had some incorrect information. By this point, I had already spent thousands of dollars defending myself and months alternating between chemotherapy treatments and responding to dozens of interrogatories and motions.

The time in Boston was very difficult. For the first time in my life, I felt completely alone and vulnerable as I defended myself against my own body and against external threats like the lawsuit. Though many people loved and rallied around me, that period of illness and feeling attacked from every possible front was a solitary journey. Even the most empathetic, healthy person cannot fully understand the tremendous emotional, intellectual, and physical effects of being diagnosed with a serious illness. During this time of trauma and stress, I was two thousand miles from my family and community in a place where nothing was familiar. It was extremely disorienting. I learned a lot from the experience, mostly about myself. Because I had to cancel a lot of activities, I learned that I was not as central to the success of all these events as I thought I was. And I learned that my absence gave an opportunity for younger women, and women who were less known, to step up and lead. Now I am more careful about the projects I am involved in, and I pause to ask myself, "Can someone else besides me do this work?"

I willed myself to remain spiritually strong through prayer, meditation, and relaxation exercises. I sang, played guitar, and tried to do something positive every day. Surprisingly, I never lost my sense of determination or my sense of humor. I still laugh when I remember being startled by unexpectedly catching a glimpse of my bald, pale, thin self in a mirror! Eventually, after chemotherapy, radiation, and stem-cell transplants, the lymphoma became quiet. When I was finally able to return to my home in Mankiller Flats, surrounded by the land that I love, the first thing I did was walk to the freshwater spring of my childhood, sit in my usual spot facing east, and say a heartfelt prayer of thanksgiving that I was able to come full circle to this special place where my life had begun.

Labor Omnia Vincit
Labor Conquers All Things

Pam Henry

When I decided to enter broadcast journalism, there were virtually no women in the field. In fact, in 1968 no women were employed as reporters or news anchors in any TV news department in the state of Oklahoma.

As a high school senior, I won a spot at a three-day broadcast career seminar at the University of Oklahoma, sponsored by WKY Radio and the Oklahoma Association of Broadcasters. Speakers included Ross Porter, the WKY-TV sportscaster who later won a news spot at NBC in Los Angeles, and other local TV newscasters. All of the newspeople at the seminar were men.

Returning home from the seminar, I told my parents the news: I wanted to attend the University of Oklahoma and major in speech and broadcasting. That would prepare me for a career in television news. My parents really weren't that surprised but they warned me that there were no women in TV news and that I likely wouldn't be able to get a job. I made an appointment with an OU speech professor who had assisted at the broadcasting seminar and who had encouraged to me. My parents went with me. Dr. Ansel Resler told my parents that, by the time I graduated from OU, he believed local TV stations would be hiring women. I was beginning to see women reporters on national television, so I believed him. Fortunately, Dr. Resler was right: while I was in college, Oklahoma City TV stations began hiring their first women reporters. While I was still in college, KWTV hired me as an intern, and I met the newswomen on their staff.

I wanted to be a news broadcaster because of my love for current events and public speaking. Women were getting those jobs around the country, and it seemed only right that I should have a chance. I not only didn't mind working with men, I enjoyed it. At OU, as an extra-credit class assignment,

I attended the workshop of the National Press Photographers Association. The impact of television news struck me. It seemed that pictures added tremendously to a broadcast news story.

I began to look at the Oklahoma City TV stations as places where I would love to work. But my first professional job was in the KTOK Radio newsroom. I was in heaven as the first woman hired by the news department! There was a little resistance from the staff, but there was much more help and encouragement. My first duties led to reporting, anchoring, and handling the City Hall beat. One Tuesday, in the press loft at an Oklahoma City City Council meeting, I asked the reporter from WKY-TV (now KFOR) his opinion of my applying for a job at Channel 4. Although I was working in radio, my dream was to segue into TV news. I will never forget his answer: Channel 4 "would never hire a woman."

Fortunately, I thrive on challenges like that.

I had learned in my college newsroom internships that newsanchor jobs were coveted and held by senior members of the staff. I would need to apply for a reporter's job if I wanted to get into broadcasting. So, at KTOK Radio, I focused on demonstrating that I could go to news conferences or fires to cover a story, even though I was on crutches.* And that was noticed.

Ultimately, I applied for a reporter's job at Channel 4 because I had heard rumors that they might be looking for a woman to hire. *NBC Today* correspondent Bob Dotson told the newsroom leaders that he had seen me at fires jumping over fire hoses, and he thought I could do the job. Another reporter said he wouldn't work with a woman; but, since I was one of the few women in the state with broadcast news experience, I had a head start and was hired as the first woman reporter at WKY-TV in 1972. The reporter who had said he wouldn't work with a woman left the station shortly after I was hired.

---

* When I was fourteen months old, I contracted polio in one of the summer epidemics that preceded the polio vaccine. As a result, I walked with crutches and braces. Surgery eventually allowed me to discard my leg braces, but the crutches were a fact of life. When I was eight, I was chosen as the National Poster Child for the March of Dimes. For a wonderful year I was exposed to the world of news. My mother and I spent one full month on the road meeting First Lady Mamie Eisenhower, Senator John Kennedy, newscasters Walter Cronkite and Edward R. Murrow, and scores of other celebrities. I posed for pictures with Eleanor Roosevelt, widow of polio victim President Franklin Roosevelt, who founded the March of Dimes. The exposure planted in my soul a fascination with newsworthy people and newsworthy events.

The staff was very supportive. The only drawback to being the sole woman in the newsroom was the lack of conversation on topics of interest to females! Of course, we talked a great deal about news, but we also had many, many conversations about sports. Several members of the staff worked on the Sooner football coach's TV program and covered all of the games. They were experts in the field and would tell me the inside stories of what the various Big Eight (the sports conference of the 1970s) teams were like up close. I loved hearing their stories, but I was really pleased when a woman photographer was hired. It was nice to have a friend with whom I could talk about clothes and nail polish!

The next major challenge was to be assigned stories of importance. The biggest honor in a newsroom is to have the lead story. I had a lifelong interest in politics, and I gravitated toward campaign and State Capitol news. Over the next few years, I was gradually given more responsibility. The corrections beat opened up, and I volunteered for that. It was shortly after the July 1973 prison riot at the Oklahoma State Penitentiary in McAlester, and the Oklahoma Corrections Department was big news. There was some hesitation about giving me a beat that could be dangerous, but I convinced News Director Jack Ogle and Director of Information Ernie Schultz that the vast majority of prison reporting was at meetings of the Board of Corrections, not at prison riots. At the same time, my bosses allowed me to anchor the midnight newscast. That led to the local 7:25 A.M. and 8:25 A.M. cut-ins on the *Today* show, and eventually to being the weekend news anchor.

As a woman on the corrections beat, I decided I should tour a Texas prison to see how Texas handled penal problems, but the Texas Corrections public information officer denied my request, saying that women reporters were not allowed inside prisons. I was shocked. I had been inside the Oklahoma State Penitentiary many times, as well as in other facilities in Oklahoma. I reacted as a cool, hardened reporter: I went to the women's room and cried. I continued to cover Oklahoma Corrections and was eventually allowed to cover a riot at the Oklahoma State Reformatory in Granite. It was hardly dangerous. Reporters were escorted to the warden's home to wait in the living room for news. But I got our story.

Television reporters and photographers carry a lot of equipment with them to various locations. When I covered the Corrections Department, the photographer carried all of the heavy gear, but I always picked up the lightweight lighting box we took with us. Some news sources gave us funny looks when they saw a girl on crutches carrying a piece of equipment, but I was always proud to contribute what I could to the effort.

More women were being hired in TV newsrooms by the late 1970s, and it became obvious that hard work was overcoming the earlier roadblocks to women. That is the lesson that helped me throughout my entire career. The men in newsrooms were willing to work with a woman if she did her part and more. Able-bodied co-workers were also willing to accommodate a person with disabilities if she did her part and more.

During the 1974 U.S. Senate campaign, I covered a plane accident involving Democratic candidate Charles Nesbitt. Photographer Oliver Murray and I raced to Will Rogers World Airport when we heard on the police scanner that Nesbitt's plane was coming in for an emergency landing because the landing gear would not go down. We stationed ourselves with other reporters and photographers along the foam-covered runway, waiting for the emergency landing. The plane came down, touched down on the foam, and slid safely down the runway at high speed.

Suddenly, the reporters and photographers were running after the sliding aircraft. I realized that it would take me ages to make the trek on my crutches, and I was looking around in despair when a baggage cart appeared. I asked the driver if he could give me a ride to the spot where the plane had stopped. He agreed and we were off. I reached the airplane along with all of the other media and got one of the first interviews with the candidate. Nesbitt eventually lost that election, but I gained a faith that somehow I would be able to complete my news assignments.

When speaking to groups of persons with disabilities, I often joke that, in 1971, being a woman was more of a handicap to me than walking on crutches.

Times have changed in TV newsrooms since the early 1970s. Virtually all of the TV stations in Oklahoma have had, or do now have, women as news directors. In my last position before retiring for health reasons, I spent twelve years as manager of News and Public Affairs for the Oklahoma Educational Television Authority. My previous jobs all prepared me for that wonderful and important position.

The motto of my beloved state of Oklahoma is *Labor Omnia Vincit*. That is the lesson I learned working as a woman in a man's field and working with a disability. When I think back that women weren't supposed to major in broadcast journalism and that polio could have made it hard for me to be hired, I can only surmise that labor does, indeed, conquer all. And that it helps if you love that labor.

Women's Work

Otie Ann Fried

I've been a lobbyist for a little over twenty years, walking the marble floors of the Oklahoma Capitol, working the house, senate, and governor's office. On occasion I've tried the Washington scene but it's just never felt right. I find D.C. to be too impersonal, too self-absorbed, and lobbyists too removed from the elected representatives. Congressional staffers now rule the District, and while most of them are talented and hardworking, I find more enjoyment in dealing directly with the people who cast the votes and write the laws.

The fifty state legislatures—the so-called laboratories of democracy—still afford that opportunity, and it is there that I find the personal contact that is so rewarding.

As with most people, the beginning of my career led me down another path. After graduating from college, I entered the field of education, starting out as an English, speech, and drama teacher in a Lawton, Oklahoma, junior high school. Teaching was a profession that was considered "fit" for a woman. I loved it, though I must say it was one of the toughest jobs I've ever had. Maybe *the* toughest.

I consider teaching to be the most important job in the world. But something else was in my blood, and I grew restless. So I had a decision to make. Should I stay in teaching or roll the dice and move on to new challenges?

· · ·

One night after the inauguration of President Jimmy Carter, I found myself sitting in the White House movie theatre between the President on my left and a sleeping First Lady on my right. Rosalyn Carter was worn out from a speech she had given that day at the National Press Club. My being there was pretty heady stuff, but President Carter and his family made it all seem normal and comfortable. That evening marked the culmination of another road I had chosen to travel.

When I left teaching, I had decided to participate in the 1976 presidential race. It was a fascinating time. Watergate was behind us, and the sky was the limit. The little-known peanut farmer from Georgia energized the volunteers in our campaign, young people whom President John F. Kennedy had first inspired. I immersed myself in the Carter campaign in Oklahoma, feeling as excited as a child, willing to do any job that was thrown at me.

I learned politics for what it really is, which is far from a glamorous game. It's hard work. But the more I was asked to do, the more I *wanted* to do. There was no job too small. I walked neighborhoods in ninety-degree heat, knocking on door after door, telling the Carter story. I helped make hundreds of yard signs, then struggled to get those signs into rock-hard red earth during the heat of the summer. I handed out brochures, made hundreds of phone calls, addressed thousands of envelopes, and engaged in countless debates. I found that my energy and enthusiasm were boundless. The experience was intoxicating. This was democracy at work, and I reveled in it.

Jimmy Carter won the election, and those of us who had worked so hard were proud of our success. But success was accompanied by the realization that the world hadn't stopped. The election was over, and I had no prospects of a job. I didn't know how I was going to pay my bills, where I was going to live, or what I was going to do with the rest of my life.

So, as I sat in the White House that night, I was faced with another defining moment.

When I looked around the room at the "first family," watching the President, the First Lady and their son Chip, who had become a friend, I realized they were just "regular people." There was nothing special about them other than their love for what they were doing. And something more: they had a purpose. They were engaged in work that affected people's lives all over the country.

I wanted some of that.

Inspired by my experiences, I applied for and was accepted as a research analyst with the Oklahoma State Senate. In effect, I was going back to school, this time at the State Capitol. It was quite a learning experience.

During the next few years, I was fortunate enough to staff the Education and Appropriations Committees, working closely with the committee chairs. My assignments at first were menial. But I didn't mind. I was learning government from the ground up; and by the time I started getting more important tasks, I felt that I had earned them, that I had paid my dues.

I began observing the few women who had been elected to the house and senate, marveling at the hurdles that were placed in their way, pulling for them as they battled in an environment that had been controlled for decades by men. Most of the women legislators took time to help the young women at the Capitol while they fought their own battles, but a few seemed to place their own roadblocks in front of other women. It made no sense to me, and I vowed never to become that way. Women competing in a man's world have enough obstacles to overcome without having to fight against the jealousies of other women.

My four years of experience as a legislative staff member, just like my experiences as a teacher and campaign worker, were highly rewarding. I had learned the legislative process and developed relationships with most of the legislators and staff members at the Capitol. But now it was time to move on, to do more than merely carry out someone else's strategies and simply follow orders.

. . .

In the spring of 1981, I attended an event in Kansas City for my father, Otis Delaporte, who was being inducted into the National Association of Intercollegiate Athletics Hall of Fame in honor of his career as a college coach. My father had coached high school and college athletes for forty years in Oklahoma in all areas of athletics. Other halls of fame had honored him, but that night represented the culmination of his professional career. When his name was called, I proudly watched him approach the podium, then listened as he spoke of hard work, dedication, and teamwork. More importantly, he talked about having the courage to take chances in the pursuit of a dream.

He was the most important role model in my life. It was from him that I developed my focus and drive. He had a simple work ethic: work hard; *earn* your rewards.

During my high school days, he took me inside the male world of sports, and it was immensely educational. I became totally engrossed in his teams. I knew about the coaches, knew which opposing athletes were the best, knew what our game-day strategy was. From these experiences I learned how to organize, how to set goals, and how to develop the means to accomplish those goals. During games I would sit in the stands or walk the sidelines in total silence, so engrossed in the competition that I could not yell, too tense to even fully enjoy our victories. Unlike my peers, these games weren't about sports. They were business. There was work to be done. And when the game ended, there was a scoreboard to display to the world our success or failure.

My father would invite me to sit with the coaches after each game. It was intriguing to listen to them talk about what had transpired on the field, what worked, what didn't. So much of the psychology of the game was played out in those discussions that it became a part of my psyche. At some level I began to understand. Even though I was a woman, I was a part of something few *men* got to experience.

Though I didn't realize it at the time, these experiences prepared me for the future. Because I interacted with hard-charging, aggressive men, I wasn't intimidated when the time came for me to compete in a male-dominated world.

Sitting at the Hall of Fame induction and recalling those early days with my dad was a special experience, one that I have treasured even more because it was the last time I saw him; he died just three weeks after his induction. That night I realized what I needed to do. I wanted to use the experiences of my life the time with my father's teams, my teaching career, the Carter campaign, and my years working at the Capitol in a way that would put me in charge of my own fate. The thought both frightened and excited me.

I decided to become a lobbyist.

Few people know what a lobbyist really does. The perception, I'm afraid, is that the job consists of simply talking to a few legislators each day, then taking them to dinner every night. There may have been a time when that would suffice, but those days are long gone. Lobbying has become highly specialized. Today, a lobbyist must know how the legislative process works, how to move bills through the legislature, and how to get them signed by the governor. But she must also be part public relations expert and part grass-roots organizer. Lobbying no longer is confined to the halls of the Capitol. It is a year-round experience, and much of the effective lobbying takes place in the cities and towns throughout the state. It is a high-tech business. Computers, cell phones, and personal-assistant computers are standard tools of the trade. Communication with in-state and out-of-state clients requires instant access. It's a far cry from my early days in the business.

I am a self-employed "contract lobbyist." That means that I don't work for a single company or association. Like a lawyer who works in the judicial branch of government, I represent many clients before the legislative and executive branches. While my main area of concentration has been health care, I have also represented retail, energy, telecommunications, and financial services interests. In addition, I have represented numerous education clients, aviation interests, insurance companies, and various other interest groups.

This variety is highly stimulating. I look forward each day going to the Capitol and working with legislators, legislative staff members, the governor's office, and various state agencies as we engage in the democratic process and help write the laws under which our citizens must operate. It's a challenging job and is both rewarding and frustrating.

I have learned that to be successful I must be part salesperson and part educator. I've had to learn to control my emotions, never letting myself get too high from successes nor too low after defeats. In many ways, lobbyists are similar to professional athletes. We have our *season* (the legislative session) and our *off-season* (the interim between sessions). As with athletes, a lobbyist must work in the off-season to prepare for the competition that inevitably comes when the house and senate convene each winter.

A good lobbyist does the little things well. *Everyone* takes care of the big things.

Like I said, lobbying has changed drastically since that day twenty years ago when I stepped into the Capitol representing my first client. In those days there were far fewer lobbyists than operate today. And there were virtually no women. I was one of the first female contract lobbyists in Oklahoma. To say that lobbying was a male-dominated business would be a gross understatement. As with female legislators, women weren't expected to participate.

There were those who thought I had no business doing what I was doing. Some saw my entry into the lobbying field as an affront to the established order. There were roadblocks to overcome, battles to fight. But my experiences had prepared me, and I set myself to the task of proving that I belonged.

I don't want to leave the impression that I had to fight every man at the Capitol in my early days. That simply wasn't the case. I was fortunate to have a number of important male mentors, legislators, and staff directors who gave unselfishly of their time to teach me the business. Women getting into their field didn't threaten those men. For them, my entry represented the natural progression of life in our state. I owe them a great deal.

I have had a successful lobbying career for longer than I ever thought possible. And the beauty is that I love the job today as much as I did when I started. My experience lets me do things a little differently, and I believe that I do a better job representing my clients than I did in the beginning. But the main thing is that I was willing to pay my dues and learn how the process works. I can honestly say that I've never backed down from a challenge.

I realize there are many other women who have fought far tougher battles. My journey has been an easy one in comparison with some of those women. Still, I take a measure of pride in knowing that perhaps I have helped open doors for other women who have entered the field after me. At least I hope I have.

The current lobbying landscape can best be summarized by an experience I had a couple of years ago. An important corporation decided to create an expanded government-relations arm in the state, and they interviewed a large number of lobbyists for the job of "chief lobbyist." I was one of about ten lobbyists who interviewed for the position and was fortunate to be selected for the job.

When the interview process was over and I had been tendered the offer, I sat down with the corporation's selection committee to discuss their issues and what their goals were. At the end of the meeting I asked why, out of all the lobbyists they had interviewed, I was the one they had chosen.

Their answer was a compliment to all female lobbyists, not just to me. Women, I was told, had the reputation of being the hardest-working, most-dedicated professionals at the Capitol.

"We want the best," I was told. "And we believe that women tend to make the best lobbyists. They are tireless workers, take the issues to heart, and put everything they have into the job. And they work like they have something to prove, which makes them even *better* lobbyists."

Work like we have something to prove. I don't think I would argue with that assessment at all. Women, like many minorities, have always had to prove themselves. We have come a long way, and we've done it in large part by out-working our competition. Today, Oklahoma has many talented, qualified women lobbyists. A trip to the Capitol will find them strolling the halls, working with other lobbyists and legislators male and female representing numerous clients. They are an instrumental part of our state's governmental process. Oklahoma is a better place because of it. And I consider myself fortunate to have played a small part in this change.

No One Can Fire Me

Sandy Ingraham

Oklahoma and I had a rocky beginning. The first time I questioned a government policy—the Vietnam War—the administration at the Oklahoma college I attended suggested to my conservative, military parents that I sit out a year. The first time I tried to get on a career track, I bumped my head on a very low glass ceiling: at the Oklahoma company where I worked, women were not eligible for the flexible work schedule necessary to participate in a company-sponsored education program required for promotion. The first time I tried to get a government loan to attend school on my own, my Oklahoma bank told me I made too much money at my waitressing job to qualify.

Did my career path result from my experiences as a young woman in Oklahoma? Maybe. Maybe not. I am the sum of my experiences. As a product of the sixties, a woman, a social worker, and now a lawyer, I was expected to care, to be a "bleeding heart." But it was more than that. I grew up wanting a lot. I still want a lot. I want all children to be loved and nurtured. I want babies to be born healthier and grow up happier. I wish fewer women were battered, fewer killed. I want everyone to be better fed and to have a bed to sleep in at night. I want every person to have a good doctor, a good education, a good job. I had to do something because I could.

So I put myself through college and spent the next thirty years focused on policy change in Oklahoma. I have tried to wage a war against the brutality of poverty which discriminates against the most vulnerable and the most helpless. Oklahoma poverty is sexist, ageist, and racist. It mostly hurts women, little kids, older adults, people with disabilities, and people who are not white.

In the early 1970s, when I first started lobbying on social issues at the Oklahoma State Capitol, I thought that bad policy might be a result of

uncaring people. Not that easy. From my perspective in Oklahoma's political system, I have seen the best and the worst of people. I can report that
there is more good than bad and more reason to be optimistic than
pessimistic. I have seen politicians, closeted but determined in their support
and desire to help poor people; wealthy people privately putting their
money and time where their hearts are; social workers staying in jobs that
break their own hearts; poor people giving everything they have to
someone who needs it more. My dream is for Oklahoma public policy to
be as compassionate as most of its citizens are.

I have tried to help people who have little or nothing. Weaving hundreds
of projects together into full-time work, I have walked legislative halls,
consulted with agencies and communities, trained advocates, taught
college students, researched and written about issues, packaged data, and
filed lawsuits. I have tried to provide policymakers with a real view of Oklahoma and have suggested creative responses to anyone listening.

In a nutshell, here are some things I have learned along the way:

First, *policymakers act differently when they are watched*. During a state
budget crisis, a program helping people with disabilities was pulled from
the chopping block after concerned Oklahomans flooded the state capital.
While admonishing his committee to fund the program he initially tried
to eliminate, a powerful but shaken legislator said he never wanted there
to be "more wheelchairs and seeing-eye dogs than senators in the State
Capitol again." Even when a policymaker is racist, he or she will act differently when the committee room is full of nonwhite people. Even when a
policymaker is sexist, best behavior will be the rule when women come to
visit a legislative office. Even when a policymaker is ageist, a vote will be
made for older people when they pack the gallery to watch the process.
Without saying a thing, people's presence makes a difference.

Second, *policymakers are doubters and usually say no first*. The complex-
ities of product-liability law created doubts that nearly killed Oklahoma's
"Good Faith Donor" bill. Oklahomans running food banks, desperate for
donations needed to serve poor and hungry families and children, found
their efforts stifled by distributors, grocers, and restauranteurs whose legal
liability was more costly to them than their products. Corporations threw
away good food rather than chance that a food bank's subsequent mishan-

dling would become a lawsuit against them. As I advocated for a solution, I discovered legislators confused and hesitant to remove unnecessary liability for these "good" corporate donors. During the same legislative session, less-than-stellar corporations confused the issue by attempting to shed liability necessary to protect Oklahoma's citizens from some dangerous products. Doubt spread like an infection among legislators. Success required tenacious explanation, information, and assurances. If you want to be successful in politics, don't let people get used to saying no to you. Give people information that helps them understand your position and gives them a basis upon which to agree with you. Ask until the answer is yes. Giving up is the only thing that makes an answer final. "Good Faith Donor" protection became law, putting more food on the tables of Oklahoma's poor families and children.

Third, *power is perception*. I remember once, a few years ago, at the state house, a senator came running up to me and said, "Sandy, you have to get your people to call and respond to Crisis X." I remember looking behind me and beside me. Who was it that he thought I was leading? Never claim to be powerful; but, if you hang around long enough, someone will assume you are. Another time, when I was the only nonlegislator sitting in one of the never-ending appropriation subcommittee meetings, a senator turned to me and asked, "What do you think, Sandy? Should we fund this mental health program expansion in Anytown, Oklahoma?" I said, "I would." And they did. I was not at that meeting to advocate for that particular program, but I knew it was needed. Whatever you care about will benefit from the support many people reserve for those they perceive as powerful.

Fourth, *you will fail if you worry about who will pay you*. All along, I have made a good living. If you want to do something, do it. If no one can pay you, do it anyway. Some of my advocacy efforts have been funded by both small and large Oklahoma poverty programs. During one dramatic state budget downturn, national funding from "Hands across America" supported my work with the Oklahoma Conference of Churches during an entire legislative session as I successfully opposed brutal cuts to Oklahoma's poverty programs. Much of the time, no one paid for the advocacy. The work I did for no specific financial compensation paid in successful advocacy for the poor—and in bolstering my reputation. Neither compassion nor success goes unnoticed by legislators. If you really care about what you are doing instead of what you are getting, someone else will gladly and purposefully overpay you later . . . with money or influence. Believe me, it all comes out in the wash.

Fifth, *you will fail unless you know more and work harder and longer than everyone else.* Hopes and dreams are not enough. At some point, you have to do something more, even if you think you cannot. Understand the change you want to make. I find it essential to spend an enormous amount of time and energy collecting data and then compiling it into studies and reports that show the hard facts that make the need for change undeniable. The most successful programs and funding with which I have been involved are the result of tedious, time-consuming research and writing: Oklahoma's outstanding early intervention program for children from birth to thirty-six months, SoonerStart; the 1984 Perinatal Plan, which created a comprehensive system of care for pregnant women and their infants; and ongoing focus on chronic problems like poverty and the escalating cost of prescription medications, to name a few. You must take it one step at a time; keep at it; be tenacious; and be creative. If you fail, embrace a different strategy and go on. You will get there. The impossible requires flexibility and just takes a little longer.

Sometimes when I look back, I feel like I have accomplished much. Sometimes it feels like nothing. One thing I know for sure is that no one can fire me. But don't tell my mother; she thinks I have a real job.

Don't Call Me Baby

Kathy Taylor

In the 1970s, I worked my heart out in Republican campaigns for Senator Dewey Bartlett and Governor Henry Bellmon. I represented Richard Nixon's platform in a high school presidential debate. When the Republican Party withdrew their support for the Equal Rights Amendment, I questioned how a group that I worked so hard to support could believe that I did not deserve to be treated equal to the men I was helping elect.

In law school, I studied constantly, acutely aware that, in many ways, securing a "good job" would be more difficult for me than my male colleagues. I finished law school in the top 5 percent of my class but felt deflated when I went to job interviews and heard comments like "You can't eat in the board room; you don't belong here," or "Didn't I interview you yesterday? Oh, I guess it was the other blonde," or "What does your husband think about your practicing law?"

I began my law practice as a securities lawyer. I once represented a client who had a particularly difficult problem with short swing profits which, if not properly handled, could have cost him millions of dollars. The firm's senior partner called me into his office and gave me the facts. I researched tirelessly until I devised a solution. In the middle of my report to the client, the partner interrupted, saying, "Honey, could you get me a cigarette?" It was obvious that my work was viewed as valueless, and I never returned to the partner's office that day. That was the 1980s.

The year 2003 marked my thirtieth year of life in the business world. I sincerely believed progress was steadily moving toward equality for all. I was filled with hope and triumph as I walked with a group of bright, passionate young college women into our state legislative chambers. A moment later, however, I was stunned to witness state legislators greeting the young women with demeaning catcalls. These students, meeting at the

135

Capitol to discuss opportunities for public service careers, did not fail to miss the irony of the situation. Many of the legislators giving this inappropriate welcome have daughters, wives, and sisters; and all of them have mothers. I wondered if they viewed their female relatives differently, or if this was how they treated all women?

Shockingly, these discriminatory put-downs do not diminish as one ages. During my first month serving as Oklahoma's secretary of commerce, one state senator asked if I intended to visit Oklahoma's commerce office in Europe. He continued by implying that my primary purpose for this trip would most likely be shopping in Paris, not the betterment of the state. Initially, I thought he was joking. He was not.

In 2004, the Governor's Commission on the Status of Women issued a report from the Institute for Women's Policy Research decrying the state of women in Oklahoma. According to the report, Oklahoma has the highest rate of women living in poverty, the fourth-highest rate of women dying from heart disease, and the highest rate of incarceration of women. Progress moves at a snail's pace, yet problems swoop in with deft speed. Sometimes it can seem like a waste of effort to continue the fight for equality.

But then I look at the intelligent young women—my daughter among them—who dream of making an equal contribution to the world and who see in their lifetime the possibility of electing a female president or female governor of Oklahoma. These women want to deal with the issues that treat women most severely, particularly in Oklahoma: poverty, lack of access to health care, drug use, and incarceration.

Women finally gained the right to vote in 1920, though the dialogue to give women a voice in the United States began much earlier. Women like Susan B. Anthony and Elizabeth Cady Stanton fought against all odds to keep the dialogue truly moving so that women would have the opportunity to voice their opinion in choosing their representatives. Without their efforts, the risks they took, the passion they exhibited, the perseverance they displayed in the face of defeat, I would have neither the voice nor the responsibility to work for those who do not have a voice. Though I, too, am often guilty of taking my right to vote for granted, I honor these women; and I am grateful for the strength handed down to me by my mother and grandmother. The work we do today to further equal rights is the essential sequel to the work of the suffragists.

I do not claim to have the exact remedy to break the glass ceiling and dissolve the gender gap, but I know that one way to chip away at the problem involves developing positive female role models for both young women and young men from every background. It takes the initiative of those of us positioned to have our voices heard to keep the dialogue going and to keep women's issues a priority. We must convince others that it is important to take action to counter the ills and the negative attitudes. If we fail to fulfill our responsibility, the cure will never be discovered, and change will never be implemented.

From my little corner of the world, I try to take small steps that make a difference:

- Mentor other women at every opportunity. I hire women, support their political campaigns, and write recommendations; and I include women in circles in which I am involved that support and give women exposure.
- Support organizations that help women rise above the circumstances often dictated by their gender. One particularly compelling program assists female offenders in learning parenting skills and work skills and provides them clothes to begin the difficult interview process as a person with a felony conviction.
- Support policymakers who believe women's issues are important to the overall quality of life for all. This is a litmus test for any political contribution—it is not a partisan issue but a humanitarian issue.
- Effect policy when possible by accepting positions of policy responsibility and comment—despite the personal risk.
- Be a positive role model to my daughter, my granddaughters, my nieces, and also my nephews because the next generation of men can make a difference in this dialogue.
- Do not stand aside or be quiet when funding is cut for needed women's programs, but take action. When funding for the program to help female offenders was terminated suddenly by city political

action, I worked with a group of women to identify the funds privately.

- Most of all, continue to believe that change is possible.

And so, for my daughter, for my stepdaughter, for the young women I work with, and for my grandchildren, my passion is to contribute, to fully develop a world that respects the worth, needs, and work of all will continue to burn brightly—despite the pace, despite the odds.

As Margaret Mead said, "Never doubt that a small group of thoughtful, committed citizens can change the world; indeed, it is the only thing that ever does."

My current translation of this profound statement is "We haven't come that far; don't call me 'baby'; and let's get to work!"

Misfit

Anne Roberts

I've always been a misfit—in so many ways it's hard to count.

I would probably have been diagnosed with ADHD if that had been a popular diagnosis in the '60s. I was so hyper that I resembled the character of Samantha on *Bewitched* when she sped herself up to get all the housework done before Darrin got home—kind of creepy. I realize now that I should have patented "multitasking" years ago.

When my mother needed a respite from my frenetic activity, she would say, "Let's see how long you can stand on your head!" I got so good at it that I am now the envy of my yoga class.

My clever parents created many distractions along the way to help me become socially acceptable, keeping me busy with music lessons and summer camps and trips to the library. So I became a musician, a hiker, and an avid reader.

Because I was a reader, my mom made a special pact with each new teacher to allow me to have a library book at my desk to read so I wouldn't bounce off the walls after I finished assignments. To this day, I can read anywhere, even standing on my head.

Athletic girls were called scrappy tomboys in those days. Girls weren't allowed to play team sports, so I honed my skills at tree climbing and tetherball. I learned archery at day camp, and later "bought" my own bow-and-arrow set with three books of Green Stamps. I could ride my bike faster than any boy on the block, so my mom's admonition of "Honey, you need to let the boys win" planted the seed that grew into the understanding that being "me" was risky.

Even my music was affected by my being a misfit. I don't remember a time when I wasn't singing. My church had a wonderful music program, and the choir director encouraged me by giving me little solos to sing. Every summer, he took his singers to music camp where we learned a short musical. I was nine or ten when I experienced my first stage kiss. The show was *Johnny Appleseed*, and I played Johnny's girlfriend, Apple Brown Betty. It was a foretaste of things to come: being 5'2" with big blue eyes has sealed my destiny to play "sweet young things" until I'm eighty. I recently returned to the University of Oklahoma for a master of arts degree in music (at age forty-six), where I was cast as the love interest to another grad student in an opera called *Gianni Schicchi* (pronounced Johnny Skeeky) and we had to kiss three times. The other student was twenty-eight, and he thought I was about thirty-five. Imagine how grossed out he would have been to learn I was old enough to be his mother!

I suppose you could say that those summer shows at music camp were the start of my career in music. But, even there, I was a misfit. I had a foot in two very different camps: sacred and secular music. By the time I was in high school, it was obvious I had fallen out of favor with both. Each camp insisted I had to choose—as if my very soul were at stake. "No servant can serve two masters," they said. It seemed I was no longer sweet and submissive enough for my church friends. And I never quite learned how to be wild enough for my theater crowd. While they were out carousing after a gig, I would be at home quietly mending our costumes for the next show. At heart, I was a good little Baptist girl, but one who could "shake my booty" in a rock band.

Bridging these two worlds—and finding a place—has been a lifelong struggle. Looking back, I can see that this very struggle helped me develop skills in diplomacy that would serve me well in my future work in politics.

Throughout high school, I sang my fool head off. By the time I got to college, I was truly exhausted, and ready to try something new. But when I told the enrollment counselor that I would like to major in French (which I had also been studying since elementary school) and maybe take a few music classes, he looked over his glasses at me and said, "My dear, there's no such thing as dabbling in the fine arts." So—poof—I became a music major. Turns out that the counselor was the dean of the music school; and, lucky for me, I had been randomly assigned to him.

In college, I experienced all the typical things girls experience. I fell in love with the first guy I met, also a Baptist musician, with struggles of his own. After a long courtship and engagement, he broke it off a few months before the wedding. He said I was too "loud and boisterous" to be a good Baptist wife. He was right, of course. I went on to marry a man who delighted in my quirkiness and shared my struggle to fit in to two very different worlds. He had only recently become a Christian, and he tried really hard to please our church friends. In the end, the lure of the sex, drugs, and rock and roll of his former life proved too much for him; and we divorced after only a couple of years.

After the trauma of divorce had dissipated, I set about figuring out how to harness a boisterous, scrappy, and passionate musician and create a life where there was room for all of me.

The first challenge was to convince myself that it's really okay for a girl to be the way I am: smart, talented, and driven. For modern girls, it must be inconceivable to imagine the mindset of my generation of women, and particularly Southern women who grew up in a fundamentalist community. To put it simply, there were no expectations for girls. Our lives were to be lived in the shadow of men. Yet I was a straight-A student and driven to succeed. I was a textbook example of the old adage "A girl must work twice as hard to be considered half as good as a man." So work I did. In the process, I discovered an interesting phenomenon. Developing a proficiency in one area of life, especially overcoming obstacles to do it, can give you confidence to tackle other areas. To this day, in my lowest moments, I sing. I work a difficult crossword puzzle. I do something that reminds me that I am competent.

My co-conspirator in accomplishment was my mother, who must have said to me a million times, "You can do anything you set your mind to." Over the years, that phrase, and the love behind it, engendered in me a rock-solid belief in myself and gave me the confidence to take risks, try new things, and perfect old ones. Fifteen years ago, finding myself in a less-than-optimum work situation, I began quietly seeking another job. I was intrigued by a position announcement for the executive director of a nonprofit children's advocate organization. I had been working in the nonprofit field for a few years, writing grants and conducting trainings. But I certainly had no experience in running an organization, and I had not been to the State Capitol since my fifth-grade field trip. But I had a passion for children; and, with my mother's words ringing in my ears, I applied and got the job.

I took over the helm of the Oklahoma Institute for Child Advocacy in 1989. I was the only employee, and my first paycheck bounced! My parents became my staff, and my board provided hands-on support. I worked night and day to get the organization up and running. Then my mom called one day to tell me about some upcoming auditions for an opera at a local university. I told her she was nuts, that I was drowning in work and didn't have time to sing. Yet in her motherly wisdom, she said, "Honey, you don't have time *not* to." She seemed to have the inside scoop on this strategy of doing something you love to regain your confidence and feed your spirit. Turns out, I starred in the opera, which reminded me that I was competent and that I could do anything I set my mind to. I had set my mind to making this organization succeed. So I kept on working and singing and working and singing. And it's paid off. Today, OICA has sixteen employees and a million-dollar budget.

Now you're probably asking, "How in the world did you end up running an organization after getting a degree in music?" This is where the misfit part comes in. First of all, you can't make a living singing in Oklahoma. It's interesting that Oklahoma has produced so many incredible singers, from Reba McIntyre to Leona Mitchell to Kristin Chenoweth. But they had to leave the state to make it. Let's face it. If your goal is to become rich and famous, New York or Los Angeles gives you a better chance. If, on the other hand, your goal is just to sing, you can make quite a wonderful life right here. Most of my peers who left for the Big City back in the '70s spent lots of time waiting tables or driving cabs and very little time on stage. All the while, I was back in Oklahoma doing five or six shows a year, singing with the symphony, and, at the same time, building business skills that people would actually pay for.

I have truly had the best of both worlds—a job I love and a passion I live. In my job as a child advocate and director of a nonprofit organization, being a misfit is actually an asset. Being hyperactive allows me to "multitask" with ease and keep lots of balls in the air at once. My compulsion to read helps me to devour reams of legislation the likes of which would make some people cry. My lifetime on stage has given me the confidence to speak in front of large audiences and conduct interviews in front of TV cameras.

I have finally come to understand that weird can be wonderful, and the very traits that make a misfit can also make a success. People who love you and believe in you are the key, yet these assets are not always available to us. This is probably why I became a child advocate, because I believe that every child deserves the kind of parents that I had—or at least one caring adult who can help her believe in herself and find her place in the world.

Transitions

Prison Saved My Life

Claudia Lovelace

Things were tough growing up. My parents divorced when I was three. My real dad gave up his rights to me when he was given the choice between paying child support and terminating his parental rights. I remember saying good-bye to him. My mom's new husband adopted my brother and me, and then he and my mom had two more children.

I was nine when I told my mother that my adoptive father was molesting me. She didn't believe me, so the molestation continued until he finally admitted it when I was twelve. My mother stayed with this man for many more years. My mother was a good mother. Some people say, "How could this be, when she couldn't see what was going on?" Yes, I was angry at her for not protecting me or standing up for herself when she and my father disagreed, but I forgave her.

I started running away from home and was finally placed with the juvenile authorities at age fourteen. I went to a foster care facility, then to a school for girls, and eventually to a group home. Right before my seventeenth birthday, I ran away, and I have been on my own ever since. I left the group home to go live with a boyfriend in his apartment in Hollywood. We were there for a couple of weeks, and one day he said he was going out for a while. He never came back.

After about a week, I was going to walk down the hill to the store to purchase what I could with the pennies I had found around the apartment. When I stepped out, a wind caught the door and slammed it shut. It was locked, and I had no key. I began walking the streets, contemplating what I was going to do. I knew there was a warrant for my arrest and that if I were caught, I would probably be locked up until my twenty-first birthday.

I chose what I considered my only option: to live on the streets. I became a prostitute and remained one for eight years. There were many arrests. I had pimps, and my money was not my own.

147

During the first six months, there were quite a few pimps. If one would mistreat me or become violent, I would run away. I met a man who had just come from Vietnam. We became close, and he wanted to take me away from that life. I convinced him we could accomplish more, faster, if I continued to work as a prostitute; he became my husband and my pimp. We tried to have children but couldn't.

In that life, pimps have more than one woman. My husband probably wouldn't have had, but during one of my "runaways," his friends convinced him to find another, and he did. Shortly thereafter, she became pregnant, and that was the beginning of the end of our marriage. I could not compete, I felt, with the love a man has for his children.

I got out of that life when I was twenty-four, after many years of beatings, partying, unhappiness, and disappointment. I received help through a government program that gave me the opportunity to get on-the-job training. I attended a year of college and carried a 4.0 grade-point average.

I would like to say my life straightened up then, but it didn't. Although I was working every day, my lifestyle did not change. I partied, went from relationship to relationship, and had no clue how to live life on "normal" terms. My drinking progressed, and it did not look as if there was any hope that life would get better.

I moved to Oklahoma in 1979, when I was twenty-eight. I thought if I moved away from Los Angeles, I would be all right. Eventually, I found a job in an insurance company, and I began to be promoted.

My job was always my saving grace. Even though my personal life was in constant turmoil, I rationalized, "I can't be such a bad person: look how well I do my job." I merely existed; I was not living.

There was another failed marriage and more failed relationships. The insurance company I worked for closed; I was asked to leave the army with a general discharge because of my drinking; and I had three DUIs in four years. My addiction was out of control.

The first time I got sober was in 1993. I was in treatment for a year and then became a counselor at the same treatment center. In 1995, I was accepted to nursing school. While I was in nursing school, the man I was involved with got another girl pregnant, which devastated me. This was the second time this had happened to me. I thought I would not recover from the pain that I felt. My boyfriend's attention was focused on the mother of his future baby.

Whatever self-esteem I had regained during my two-and-a-half years of sobriety could not stand up to the feelings of inadequacy I let take over my every thought. I relapsed on cocaine and alcohol. One day when I was drinking, I called my mom in California. I told her how depressed I was and gave her the devastating news that I was no longer sober. She said, "I will be on the next plane." I was grateful she was coming. My heart ached because I knew I was breaking her heart. I took my boyfriend to work (yes, I stayed with him even after what happened. Somewhere in my fairy-tale mind, I thought maybe he would get custody and we could be a family), and on the way home I backed into the car behind me. The lady in the other car insisted the police be called, even after I told her they would take me to jail. This "driving under the influence" was my fourth offense. When my mom landed in Oklahoma, I was in jail with no way to contact her, and she was there with no one to pick her up. This incident was one that made me realize my addiction was not hurting just me.

When I went to court, the judge gave me three years in prison. As they led me away, my world became unimaginable. I was not frightened: I knew what was coming because I had done time in juvenile hall. But I was now forty-six years old and I was going to prison. I felt so alone. Once again I had built my bridges just to tear them down; it seemed that had been my life story. I would climb out of the messes I had made of my life so many times, just to return.

In going to prison, there is a threshold. It is a crossing from "out there" to another world "inside." There is a process of forgetting that "out there" exists. You begin "living" in prison. I guess the technical word is "assimi-lating" into your surroundings. Imagine going from everything that is familiar, everything you have in the world, to a foreign land.

I left everything I owned in the care of another human being. I cannot say I left everything with a "friend" because, when I was loading my stuff into the truck, there was a feeling that told me I wouldn't see any of it again. That really made me sad. Your belongings are part of your personal iden-tity; they hold your memories, everything that connects you with the world.

When I got to the facility where I would do my time, I didn't say too much. Just as anyone would do when going to a place that is totally unfamiliar, I went in looking, taking inventory. You see who the "heavies" are, who has power, what is acceptable, what the rules are, which guards have compassion and which guards to avoid. I do not think that "fear" is the correct word to describe going into prison; it is more the loss of freedom that is so strange to a person. You often do not understand your own feelings. No one can really put into words those feelings. Three years seemed a lifetime.

After about three months, you begin to loosen up. You have had time to meet people, maybe run into some that you know; or, after sharing stories, you meet people that know some of the same people you know. Prison gives a person time to reflect. As you look around, you begin to see where you are and know exactly why you are there. At least that is how it was for me. I made friends; but as I did, I realized I did not want to "like" this place. I needed to learn what kept me destroying my life.

You make friends. There were five other women in my room. You get close to some, cry with them when their visitors don't show up, watch TV and cry over sappy movies, laugh at silly jokes. This may sound like it's not so bad. To some extent, it isn't; but the sense of loss of freedom never leaves. The feeling that the world is going on without you is ever present, every day.

It is a little world. You have your room that you share with others. It is a tight squeeze, but your space becomes your home. Many times, when some of the other women would hear me call it home, they would spout off, "This is not *my* home." I would reply, "It is until you leave."

Everyone has a job; some jobs are better than others. I had office skills, so I always got good jobs. But because I often got into trouble, by the time I left, my job was picking up trash along the highway. Sometimes when I was in an area where, if I looked a certain way, I couldn't see the highway, I used to pretend I was strolling in a meadow and life was good. Then the guard would holler my name and bring me back to reality. After work, you come back to the "center" (that's what they called the prison), and you would either go to classes, watch TV, go to the dayroom and play cards, or just read on your bunk. I don't know how else to explain it, except that it is a world within this world, and you can get lost in that world.

I was not a model prisoner. One time I was trying to help a friend get a birthday present she wanted to give to a loved one. Because I was working at community level outside the prison, I went across the street from where I worked and purchased a cross. When I got back, I gave the cross to her. I also gave her the receipt with my name signed on it to show her I did not cheat her. I told her to be sure to throw the receipt away, and she assured me she would. About two months later, she got in trouble. The guards searched her room and found the receipt. That evening when I returned from work, one guard called me in and asked me about it. He was one of the guards that everyone got along with, and he looked at me like he was sorry I had done such a stupid thing. I was charged with "being in an unauthorized area," and that charge cost me 180 good days from my sentence.

As they led me to lockup, I again felt so crazy. I asked myself, "What is wrong with you? Here you are—going to jail, in jail! Something is definitely wrong with this picture."

I searched my soul for answers, and God helped me to see my darkest places. It was then that it dawned on me that, even though I rationalized I was doing a good thing, I was still using the same behavior. I prayed for God to reveal the things I needed to learn. God answered my prayers.

God revealed to me that all the things that had happened in my life were gifts that could be used to help others who are lost and feel that there is no way back to the light. God gave me a life-sustaining message: God did not put me on this earth to be miserable. God was "keeping me just for a time as this" (Esther 4:14) to help others overcome adversity and troubled times.

Prison saved my life. In prison I took an inner-child workshop designed by John Bradshaw. At a local church, I took classes called Choice Theory and Life Plan Seminar. By attending these classes and going to twelve-step meetings, I began to empty my soul of all pain, anger, resentments, old coping skills, and disappointments. I started filling this void with God's word through Bible studies and the disciple class and by rededicating my life to Christ. I received encouragement from my pastors, and I relished the responsibilities they entrusted to me.

When I got out of prison in January 1998, I completed the treatment program I was in before my incarceration.

I took the exam to become a nurse and passed with flying colors.

I worked at Drug Recovery, Inc., Community House, in Oklahoma City. I started out as the nurse/administrative assistant and was promoted to nurse/primary counselor. I became very active in the prison ministry at my church. I've learned that Oklahoma is number one in the nation in the number of incarcerated women, and it has been my experience, with those I know personally and those I work with through prison ministry, that women often take the rap for the men they are with. They let the men convince them that, as women, they will get less time (and they usually do). The men promise to "take care of them" while they are in prison, and then the men abandon them.

I received my BA in religion in May of 2002 from Oklahoma City University. I am now attending Perkins School of Theology at Southern Methodist University in Dallas, Texas. I am a United Methodist licensed local pastor, serving two churches in the Oklahoma Conference. I hope to get married again, but I am not actively seeking a husband. Because of my studies, I have not really had time for another person in my life. I believe it will come, but on God's time.

The moral of this story is not to give up on yourself or anyone else because of feelings of hopelessness. We must reach our troubled youth and let them know that they are worthy of a good life. We must help their self-esteem. We have to realize that we are all God's children, and God does not make junk. We have to "be there" for all, not just for those who we feel deserve God. This is hard, I know, because we all fall short of Christ's perfection, but we must try. No one is better than anyone else, we are only different, and that is what God intends. We have to find a way to love one another. God has a plan if we just open our hearts to see that plan.

God bless to all!

From Volunteer to Career

Jean Gumerson

"Jean can do it," my parents used to say. Early on, that became a conviction in my mind and heart: I can do it. Each time a barrier has arisen within a particular project or life event, I have known that somehow, in some way, I would find a way to "do it." That determination has served me well. The fact that that particular phrase has stayed with me for all these years gives testimony to the power that words and phrases have when parents repeat them to their children. We can forge an image or an idea for that child through the power—or the abuse of the power—of our words.

I relied on the image my parents fostered during one of the biggest challenges of my life, when my husband, Dow, died at a relatively young age. Dow had always felt that he was going to die before I did: he worried about that, about what would happen to me. In those days, people looked down upon a husband who allowed his wife to work. I really did want to work, so when he was so sick, I said, "Don't worry about it; I will go to work." I had always wanted a career, but he really didn't want me to have one.

Almost immediately upon his death, I needed a job—a real job—to support myself. People didn't understand that. We had a beautiful home and lived an enjoyable life with many opportunities, some of them glamorous and exciting. It might have appeared to the world that I was set for life and only wanted to work to keep myself busy or to help me with my grief over losing Dow.

Those would have been good reasons, but it went beyond that.

I didn't know what I'd do. The hardest job I had was convincing people I was serious, that I really wanted a career and would work at it.

For any career person who's single or widowed and has chosen to stay that way, there are times when it's lonely. Why didn't I remarry? I've never met anyone else that I've even been tempted to consider marrying. Who in the world could replace Dow Gumerson?

Though I didn't realize it at the time, Dow's death marked the ending of one very important stage of my life and the beginning of another I could never have imagined in my wildest dreams: a twenty-five-year career, begun in my mid-50s.

A friend once said, "All the easy jobs are taken." The tough ones are left, and we must determine how we are going to tackle them, because tackle them we must.

So my first job was to prove to people that I wasn't empty-headed nor did I expect to be treated any differently from any other newly hired employee. I knew I had skills to use if I just had a chance. I had done a lot of volunteer work and had been involved in politics; still, the hardest thing when I was looking for a job was to convince people that I was willing to work and that I genuinely needed a job.

Much of my success is the result of people who believed in me and my abilities at a time when few people believed I truly wanted a career, much less could succeed at one. Two people get that credit: Guy and Chris Anthony. Being able to work for the C. R. Anthony Company (1979–1987) gave me the opportunity to prove my business capabilities. I wanted a stimulating job, but I also wanted a decent salary. C. R. Anthony Company gave me both, and I think I gained the respect of the Oklahoma City business community.

Chris and Guy Anthony came up to me at a cocktail party and the topic came up about my coming to work for them. I said, "I have nothing to offer. I don't know a thing about the retail business."

Chris said, "Well, you know how to dress, don't you?"

I said, "Yes."

That settled it.

In some ways, that statement was not as flippant as one might assume, because knowing how to dress is one of those skills that can make or break a career or derail a personal or business negotiation. I can look at someone I've never met before and instantly "know" a great deal about that person just from their clothing selection and coordination.

However, Chris knew much more about me than just that I dressed well. I had been president of the Women's Committee of the Symphony

Orchestra, and Chris had worked closely with me. She knew I could organize projects efficiently and effectively for fund-raising. It takes a certain business sense to accomplish fund-raising projects and that's what she saw in me. She knew if I said I'd do something, I'd do it.

After C. R. Anthony came a brief but rewarding time at the Oklahoma City Art Museum, where I further honed skills I would use in later positions with the Children's Medical Research Institute and the Presbyterian Health Foundation. Starting the Children's Medical Research Institute and getting to work for the Presbyterian Health Foundation are two of the most important and wonderful experiences I've ever had.

How I became involved with the Children's Medical Research Institute can be summed up easily: Ignorance is bliss!

Creating this type of private foundation to support state-run children's medical research had never been done anywhere in the country prior to that time. It was the first of its kind. I have always said that it's easier to be the first person to do something than to be the person in charge later on, after several people have worked on it. When you're first to do it, no one has anything to compare it with, so how can anyone criticize you? When you are the first to do a project, you have no one around saying, "We've never done it that way," or "You can't do that because we tried it and it didn't work." You're free to do anything you want to do.

Initially, I was an unpaid volunteer working to create the foundation. Later, I was the second president of the board and eventually was hired as the second executive director of the Children's Medical Research Institute. The early years of creating the foundation, just after the Oklahoma oil boom went bust, were not easy. Everyone who lived in this community at the time remembers how devastating that was to any fund-raising venture. So it was a slow start. But over the years, the foundation has raised millions of dollars. Millions more will be raised in the future because the goals are so worthwhile, so unselfish.

Creating the Children's Medical Research Institute was the highlight of my life, at that point. Anyone who has ever had to create a dream from scratch knows that the early years are unglamorous, full of difficult turns and problems to solve. Many people won't get on board until the hardest years are over, and we had some very tough years early on. But the foundation was finally established and has accomplished wonderful things over many years. I am very proud of all the people who made this happen and am grateful I got to play a part in it.

Then there was the Presbyterian Health Foundation.

Though Dr. Mike Anderson and Stanton Young had been courting me to put my name in for consideration as president of the Presbyterian Health Foundation, I was terribly reluctant to do so. I didn't feel my resume was sufficient for such a job, but as Mike continued not to take no for an answer, I realized I had over thirty years of volunteer experience in the mental health field, considerable experience on local and national boards, and love for and intellectual interest in all topics relating to health. Though there were many doctors coming to the table with extensive medical knowledge, I knew I could bring one of my strongest traits: common sense. Still, it was a monumental decision to make. I pondered it for a long time before saying yes. People may assume it was a quick and easy decision, but it certainly was not.

News articles have mentioned that many people were very skeptical about my taking that position. Many weren't thrilled about my coming, and I knew that.

They thought, "What does *she* know about it?"

I really didn't know anything about it.

I was fully aware of those attitudes and could sense the reservations some people had about whether or not I was the right person for the job. That gave me great pause. I was concerned that my decision be the right one, both for myself and for the foundation. That's why it took me so long to make the decision. I've learned that you can't be afraid to make decisions and you can't be afraid of criticism because, if you are, you'll be paralyzed. You must focus, focus, focus. Keep in front of you what you must do, and then do it.

I began working at the Presbyterian Health Foundation on November 1, 1989. At the time I was hired, the foundation had assets of approximately $90 million. Over the years, it grew to a high of $225 million before the economy dropped it back, as it did for every foundation and everyone's personal accounts.

Never in my wildest dreams did I envision growth of that nature, much less that we would end up giving nearly a thousand grants totaling $100 million over all those years. Funds for research and education in the medical arena are the primary focus of the Presbyterian Health Foundation. I firmly believe we have made a lasting impact via our grants, certainly in the state of Oklahoma; but with many of our medical research grants, we have also made an impact on the health of nations across the world. Major break-throughs have come from the research we've supported. I feel honored to have been a part of all of these changes that the Presbyterian Health Foundation has precipitated and supported.

All of the volunteer experiences over my entire life came together to a pinpoint focus for doing the best job I could for both the Children's Medical Research Institute and the Presbyterian Health Foundation. I've been priv-ileged to have been on the other side of things—having to raise funds. I knew what that was like. I also knew how important it was for groups to collaborate toward a goal. It's been a good match, for me and for them.

Of all the people who initially opposed my going into positions with both the Children's Medical Research Institute and the Presbyterian Health Foundation, an amazing number of those very same people have come to me over time to ask my advice. To this day, I get calls from people who say to me, "Jean, we don't know what to do; you need to tell us." But I don't. I just listen to them and they find their own answers. Perhaps it's a matter of all of us needing a sounding board at times, during which process our own wisdom comes forward.

There have been times people will ask me to do something because they need somebody who is respected and not a threat to anyone. I usually respond, "You mean, you need someone so old that they can't be rude to her; they have to be nice!"

In truth, what it means is that I'm old enough to be mature and not easily shaken up or deterred from a project's goal. When I observe younger people not focusing on the project but instead strategizing about personal glory or gain, I think that's very sad because the outcome could be emptiness for that person and in most cases it's not good for the project.

I think many would say that I've reached the glass ceiling and broken it. I always have an impulse to respond, "Yes, but you won't let me get out of there!" Here's where I am. I'm not going to go any farther. But eventually, someone will, perhaps within the next ten years. My granddaughters Katie and Lissa would be good candidates to go farther. As I've said to them, "Don't close any doors behind you. And don't ever put a man in a corner where he can't get out. You've just got to play the game, even now."

As my career years come to a close and my free time opens up, I look forward to continuing in volunteer roles that I'll choose, but more and more I plan to focus on enjoying personal time with friends and my family. You'll see me flying by in my new car, still busy, but with things I carefully choose for the enjoyment and satisfaction they'll provide in my life.

I think I'll always be busy because there will always be a project that I think is so important that I just can't say no.

$\mathscr{E}\sim\sim\sim\mathscr{E}$

Beyond Statistics

Becki Hawkins

I wasn't sure when I was in high school exactly what I wanted to do with my future. My home economics teacher told me once that she sure hoped I could type.

I ended up working as a nurse's aide in a nursing home not long after high school. Talk about hard work! But, oh, the worth of a day with the elderly: priceless! I fell in love with these dear people, often castaways, very often thrilled to see a skinny young aide show up for duty. It was from this exposure to caregiving that I decided to go to nursing school.

I graduated in 1980 and immediately went to work on an oncology (cancer) floor in Tulsa. I was in my element. For weeks I could not believe they were paying me to be there; but, of course, that soon wore off. Still, I loved the challenges, the experiences, the opportunities for mental and emotional growth, and the satisfaction at the end of each shift of having helped these precious patients. There were always lessons to learn. Over the next twenty years, whether caring for an in-patient or out-patient, hospice or home-health patient, all of them contributed to my continuing education, teaching me as much about living as they did about dying.

Very early in my career, I'd been working one evening nonstop, attending to the needs of a young female patient. She was in her twenties and beautiful, even with a balding head and pale, chalklike cheeks. Her disease was aggressive, and the doctors had done all that was medically possible. Just before I'd arrived for work that evening, they'd told her and her sweet, devoted husband that they'd run out of options. No more chemotherapy would be given, only comfort measures.

Mustering as much courage as I could, I knocked on her door. The couple seemed pleased to see me and welcomed me into the room. I listened to their anguish, sorrow, grief for a denied future, and fear of how to face this news they had refused to believe would ever come.

After they calmed down some, I retreated to our nurses' station work-room to gather my supplies for the evening and felt as if I would choke as I tried to stifle tears of disbelief, anger, and heartbreak.

One of the seasoned nurses observed my visible pain and pulled me aside. "Hey, kiddo. You can't be that sensitive up here on this floor. You got to have thicker skin to work this unit."

Another co-worker overheard her and spoke up, "Hey, Ms. Nightingale, leave her alone! She's new. Didn't you ever tear up when you first started?"

I exited with as much dignity and professionalism as I could and got busy. At one point that evening, during break, I sat in a darkened family waiting area in our unit. Another patient's wife saw me enter and came to sit with me.

"Becki, I know about the bad news that young couple received today. News like that doesn't keep still. I've been watching you tonight, and I wanted to share some thoughts with you while my husband is resting."

Gently she put her arm around my shoulders and began softly speaking. "You've been taught how to give these patients their medications, their chemotherapy, their nutrition, blood products, oxygen, how to monitor their pain and whether the pill or injection or patch is working, and the list goes on and on. You've even learned how to take time to listen to hard questions, hear the fear in our voices, respect our need for privacy, send for clergy, or to put up a NO VISITORS sign.

"But, my dear, listen to me. You're not here to save us. Yes, you're here to do all one can medically do, but, Sweetheart, it is what it is. There aren't any guarantees. It's called Life. And it's going on every day, not only on the cancer floor, but everywhere." She paused. "Come over here and look out this window. See all those little people down there, each one living and learning life lessons? All kinds of folk in all kinds of situations all over the earth. What we're supposed to do is help one another the best we can along the way. We have to trust God with what's out of our control.

"Does that mean we're not to question God or feel anger or disappoint-ment or confusion? No. Listen, Sugar, and don't let anyone be telling you any different. God's shoulders are big enough to take anything we bring to Him. God doesn't cause cancer. Someone needs to print that up to hand out with the admission paperwork up here." She patted my hand and smiled. "But let's save that talk for your next break."

I've never forgotten that chat, nor her kindness in taking time to help me that night. I can't remember her name anymore, but I still very often hear her words.

Did I quit being so sensitive? Nope. But I did learn how to balance what I could do and what I could not.

At one point in my career, I was giving chemotherapy two days a week in an out-patient setting in one hospital while making hospice visits another two days a week for another hospital. Our out-patient chemo room in those days didn't accommodate many patients at once. There were two recliners, two beds, a couple of chairs, and two rolling stools.

Henry had been coming for his chemotherapy injections once a week for quite some time. He had only little tufts of cotton-white hair left on his leathery, round head. But his sea-green eyes were bright, and he could see more than most.

"Martha," he gruffed to his wife, "you go ahead and do that shoppin' and come back in time to get me back to my bed by naptime. There ain't room for you in here and you make me nervous anyways."

Martha sighed and nodded; and then, when she thought he wasn't looking, she winked at me. Of course, he caught her and muttered something under his breath.

"Okay, Henry, which vein do you want me to use today?" I quizzed as I rolled up next to him on my stool, eyeballing his hands and forearms.

"How come you asked me? The other nurse always picks the one she wants. She never listens to me. These here veins roll. You hafta listen to your patients when they tell ya about their vein personalities. Ever been stuck five or six times? Oh, use this one and hold off on so much of that antinausea medicine till we talk a little."

"Okay, I've got everything ready. You talk, I'll listen, and we'll get started," I agreed while slipping on the bright-yellow chemo gloves and gown.

"Nurse, do you think we get to come back? I mean, after we die?"

"Why, Henry, do you ask?" I glanced up from my syringes.

"Well, I sure hope so. I been thinking. I haven't done everything the way I should have. My son died with a heart attack when he was forty. I never told that boy I loved him. I think he knew, but I wish I'd said so. I'd treat Martha better. She ain't perfect either, but she's put up with a lot outta me.

I'd let her go with me to more places, instead of always leaving her behind. Shoot, she even gets a kick outta hangin' out with me even if we aren't talking. And reckon I'd go to church with her some. I was always gonna go someday, just never got around to it. Nothing against God, you see. I like Him all right, but some of those church folk talk outta both sides of their mouths. Well, anyway, wouldn't hurt me any to go with her. It'd have made Martha happier than it would have God. And I guess, Nurse, I might try if I come back to be neighborly. You know, care about someone else's needs besides my own. Well, who knows, our timing is in God's hands anyways. Hell, I might live to be a hundred years old. I might wake up tomorrow and just start over. Might do'er and fool everybody, well, 'cept God."

I pulled off the chemo gloves and trashed all the supplies appropriately, washed with soap and water, removed my gown, and rolled up next to Henry and hugged him up close with salty tears stinging my eyes.

"Nope, Henry, I don't reckon you'd be foolin' God and seriously doubt you'd surprise Martha much either."

One of the reasons I really enjoyed being a hospice/home-health nurse was the element of adventure with each visit. I never knew what I might encounter, especially on the first visit. Once I was sent back into the deep woods of Bogacheeta. As I drove up to the remote address, I wondered, "How in the Sam Hill did anyone decide this was a place to build a house?"

Then I noticed how nice and quiet it was. I could actually hear birds singing and squirrels chattering while chasing each other around very old oak trees. The front yard fowl honked and hollered when I got out of the car.

The house was sixty or more years old and probably had not been painted or remodeled since its construction. Inside, the wood floor in the living room had a few holes, large enough for critters to use as entrances. Tacked up on the walls were calendars from the '30s and '40s, very dated Christmas cards, and Sunday school pictures curled at the corners. An antique potbellied stove warmed the early spring morning. And right in the middle of this cozy living room stood a modern electric hospital bed.

My patient had yellow-white thinning hair hanging in a loose braid. Her cataract-covered eyes still revealed a steel-blue hue. Her voice was steady but weary. "Come on in, my dear. I can't see well anymore. Come, let me touch your face and feel your hands. Then you may tend to my leg like the doctor said you would."

People have a way of setting up a trust in you when you're bathing them, washing their wounds, administering their medications, and teaching them about their disease. Sometimes they even open up and begin to share their story. And, when I was smart enough to be still and really listen, I could learn who this soul was, where that soul was really wounded, and what that person had to offer anyone willing to hear them. She was no different.

"You know, I taught little kids about Jesus a long, long time ago," she proudly told me as I wrapped the gauze gently around the ugly, oozing wound. "I don't get to church anymore. Shoot, I don't get out of bed that much. But, God knows where I am. And by the way, don't forget to save that bathwater in the pan there for the chickens out back. Life is much simpler than what folks make it out to be. Why kill yourself trying to accumulate a bunch of stuff that you ain't gonna take with you anyway?"

More than once she'd try to get me to wrap a piece of bacon or salt pork around her wound to make it heal quicker. "Antibiotics are good I guess, but sometimes you just gotta get back to basics. Just because we have modern medicine doesn't mean we need to throw away what's tried and true, right, Nurse?"

"Yes, ma'am, something to be said for tried and true," I replied in earnest. But I encouraged her to keep the salt pork for the brown beans.

Silly me, thinking there couldn't be much way out in the middle of nowhere.

I've spent over twenty years working with patients. I've also worked as a hospice chaplain. And I've never forgotten the lesson I learned so early in my career: everyone has a story. We've just got to be smart enough to listen.

Infidelity 101

It's Okay to Want to Put Arsenic
in Your Cheating Husband's Tea

Elizabeth Woods Pennington

"I had an affair."

The four little words that a spouse dreads hearing. A subject and a verb. It's the simplest of sentences yet carries a ferocious wallop. It has been over a year since my husband confessed to having an affair with one of his colleagues. If truth be told, I wasn't surprised. I had suspected that very thing for quite some time, even throughout my pregnancy. But suspicion and reality are two very different things, and I was unprepared for the emotional aftermath that this simple sentence, this one little independent clause, would bring in my life. Sure, I had the basic knowledge about affairs gleaned from daytime TV and bad Lifetime movies, and what person, married or otherwise, wasn't aware of Glenn Close's knife-wielding, mistress-gone-psycho performance in *Fatal Attraction*? No matter how well armed I was with sound bites from Oprah and Dr. Laura, I found myself wholly and completely unprepared for the events that would follow and for the emotional roller-coaster ride that I would be on.

To friends, I describe my life of the past year as a soap opera, but this isn't really true. If this were a soap opera, I could drug the Devil (one of my nicer nicknames for *her*), kidnap her, mutilate her body in any number of depraved and delicious ways, and dispose of the remains—all while wearing Vera Wang separates (unwrinkled, of course)—with no fear of being discovered, and all before noon. Ahh, but this isn't really a soap opera. In my world, I still have a small child who depends on receiving love and stability from me, a high-profile job that doesn't allow for *Days of Our Lives* antics at the workplace, family and friends, a house to take care of, and a husband (yes, there is still *him*).

The bomb dropped two days before Thanksgiving, a cruel irony. It should come as no surprise to you that it's next to impossible to feel thankful about anything when you discover your husband is an adulterer, and you're facing the prospect of spending four days with a family—his— under orders of "don't tell anyone." Add to this, the guilt that I felt as a new mom—this should be the Thanksgiving for which I had so much to be thankful, yet I found myself seeping pain. Needless to say, that was a memorable Thanksgiving, one which I wish I could forget. And, no (because I know that you must be wondering), I didn't say anything to his family, though this required frequent trips to other rooms so that I could hide my tears and mourn in peace.

Discovering that you are the victim of a cheating spouse is tantamount to experiencing a death. This is why I purposely use the word "mourn." The discovery of an affair marks the end of a relationship, at least as it once was, and that innocence, once gone, can never be recovered. In fact, I rather suspect affairs may be even more difficult to endure than a death because there is no closure, as there is with a death. Instead, there is grief, endless at times, and the ever-mounting iteration of *what-ifs*. I'm sure that you're familiar with that condition because we all do it—*what if* I had done this, said that, reacted in such-and-such a way? It's even worse in the case of infidelity because the what-ifs ultimately lead to one of the worst of all questions: what if I had been a better wife?

I was totally unprepared for the range of emotions that I experienced in the weeks and months after my husband's confession. I wondered, and doubted, that I would ever climb my way through that grief and find life again. Even now, so many months later, the pain is there, sometimes as fresh as it was that night that he told me the truth. But what I couldn't see at the time, even though I longed for it and even though I felt my life was in shambles (and in many ways, it was), was that things would gradually improve. The situation doesn't go away—so many times I've wished for a magic wand so that with one wave, *poof*, order could be restored. While I can't erase the reality of my life, I have learned that I really do have the strength to move forward and to deal with a pain that for many months seemed to me absolutely unbearable.

In my case, my husband's confession to an affair snowballed into other problems. Unlike some spouses who will do anything to make amends after an affair is confessed (or so I believed), my situation was different. I longed for a man who would tell me every day how sorry he was for what he had done and the pain that he had caused me, someone who would bring me flowers, jewelry, and cards—how silly of me!—as tokens of his sincere apology. That is not my experience.

On "good" days I took care of our son, did my job, and made sure that the laundry was done at home and the fridge stocked. From the outside, I'm sure that we looked like the perfect family: an infant son, a nice house, successful careers, and two people who seemed like a "cute young couple."

Reality was far different. There was very little contact between my husband and me during the early days, and let's not even talk about sex, a four-letter word for me at the time. I was adamant that I wanted us to stay together, but I hated him for what he had done, and I did everything I could to avoid seeing him, let alone have a conversation.

On most nights I would retreat upstairs once my son was asleep so that I could be alone. During this time I shut myself off from everyone. I didn't want to share what was really going on in my life, so I stopped contacting friends and ignored e-mails and phone calls. Because I had a new baby, people assumed that I was the typical harried and exhausted new mom and respected my absence; it wasn't until much later that people started to suspect something was wrong.

This self-imposed disconnect was one of the first mistakes (of many) that I made during this period. I needed my friends more than ever, but I pushed them away on purpose.

Somehow, I made it through the holidays. I put on a good show for everyone: I decorated for Christmas, bought gifts, sent out Christmas cards, attended Christmas parties where I dutifully smiled and laughed. I pretended that my life was the fairy tale, even though a little of me was dying with each passing day.

At the time, I thought that things would surely get better, and the pain that I was feeling would lessen, if I could only make it through a few months. I was wrong.

Soon, I was so depressed that I worried whether I would be able to take care of my son, let alone myself. My mother—one of only a handful of people who knew the truth—worried that I was going to have a nervous breakdown. I assured her that I wouldn't (I thought of a nervous break-down as a luxury that I couldn't allow with a baby in the house), but inwardly I doubted myself.

Inside I was eaten up with hatred: hated him, hated her, and hated myself (if I weren't so fat/too old/not pretty enough/not funny enough, this probably wouldn't have happened). I am a strong woman, but there were many days that I truly wished I were dead; I thought death represented solace, a freedom from a pain that I was beginning to doubt that I could endure.

On one particularly bad day I even carried a jar of prescription-strength sleeping pills in my pocket, wishing that I could take the next step and swallow them all. If not for my son, I might have done it. Before this, I thought of people who admitted to contemplating suicide as being weak; this experience taught me that, given the right circumstances, anyone can be depressed enough to think of suicide as the answer.

So how did I cope? To be honest, at times I didn't think that I would survive, but somehow I kept going from day to day. I had days when I didn't feel as if I could keep going; but, short of suicide, I really didn't have a choice. I might not want to get out of bed each morning, but I couldn't—wouldn't—neglect my son; and, since I didn't know what was going to happen with my marriage, I had to keep my career as stable as possible. These responsibilities helped to keep me focused and, yes, did help me to cope.

Ironically, my husband's confession of his affair wasn't the proverbial rock-bottom of this experience, as some might think. My therapist (one of the good choices I made during this period) warned that worse days would follow. At the time she said this to me, I couldn't imagine things being any worse than they already were—I certainly didn't think I could be *any more* depressed than I was—but I didn't foresee the surreal consequences of his confession.

In the days, weeks, months to follow, my life suddenly seemed it should be the feature story in the *National Enquirer*. As soon as my husband's mistress discovered that I knew about her, she retaliated by threatening to kill me and my son. I didn't call the police because I didn't actually hear the threat—she told my husband, who would later deny that she ever said this to him. (I'm glad to say that, today, I *would* call the police.) She later proclaimed that if she couldn't have him, then maybe she could work out

an arrangement of "sharing" him with me. I know what you're thinking—
crazy bitch—and I agree. To think that I would actually consider happily
engaging in a threesome with my husband's mistress? Crazy talk!

Soon the phone calls started—at home, at work, on my cell phone. On
only one occasion did she actually say anything, and that time only because
she had my husband on the other line, trying to trick him into saying something incriminating. "But you made the decision to be with *me*," she whined.

I will never forget those words. As if this weren't bad enough, her soon-
to-be-ex-husband was also calling me at home and at work. A dutiful wife,
I ignored his calls. Things were already bad; I didn't need him to make things
worse by supplying me with details of an affair that I didn't want to know
about. At home, my husband was acting irrationally, telling me how sorry
he was for everything and how much he loved me, yet he also called me
terrible names—a "fucking whore," a "dumb-ass," a "bitch." He threatened
to kill himself so many times that I eventually felt like yelling at him to
"please just do it already!" He punched walls, loaded and unloaded his rifle,
even asked me to pull the trigger. On my birthday I suffered the indignity
of being tested for AIDS and other sexually transmitted diseases, yet I still
didn't run for the divorce lawyer (though I did consult with one . . . another
good decision).

Did I behave like a rational, independent, and educated woman? Looking
back, it's amazing to me that I tolerated some of the things that occurred
and that were said. I never thought I'd stay with someone who cheated on
me, let alone with someone who emotionally badgered me day after day.

But I also know that making life decisions is difficult to do when you're
at an emotional low, as I was; and, though it's not an excuse for his behavior,
I also realized that my husband was grappling with his own demons. And
I certainly wasn't an angel as all of this was occurring. Once the shock lessened, I fought back with words and actions of my own. This was the man
I loved so very much, my first love, and I had been betrayed by him. I wanted
him to hurt the way that I was hurting.

· · ·

Hard to believe, but as time passes, I more and more distance myself from
these events. Not so long ago, I longed for this type of distancing, yet

doubted I would ever find it. I hated—*hated!*—people who advised, "This too shall pass," thinking that the wisdom of such a trite saying would somehow soothe my bitter wounds and help me to endure. I wanted to yell back, "How the *fuck* do you know what *this* is like?" I forgive them today because they were well-meaning, but I also pledge to never tell someone that "time heals all wounds" when they're going through a struggle of their own. Take my word for it: it's not helpful.

So how did I get through it? This, for me, is the million-dollar question. How can I possibly articulate what pulled me through the most challenging experience I have yet had to endure in my life? To a certain extent, I really had *no* choice but to make it through. No matter how much I longed to kill myself at times, suicide really wasn't an option because I felt such a responsibility to everyone I would leave behind. Seeing a therapist once, twice, sometimes three times a week, certainly helped. At times it seemed like I was telling her the same thing week after week—I probably was—but having someone who understood the psychology of infidelity, and who was also truly objective, was extremely helpful . . . though she didn't always tell me what I wanted to hear.*

Temporarily separating from my husband was also a good decision, despite family members who warned that separating was just a small step from divorce. What they could not see is how miserable both of us were, living in the same house with tension omnipresent. I was a constant reminder to him of his guilt, and he was a constant reminder to me of things I wanted to push from my mind. Separating allowed me moments of peace, if nothing else. After months of punishing myself (thinking that I was somehow responsible for the affair), I rediscovered little enjoyments: a candle-lit bubble bath, a glass of wine, a new color of eye shadow, buttery popcorn.

---

* I learned that over 50 percent of spouses cheat on their partner; that some spouses have the ability to get over an affair quickly, but that because I have an obsessive-compulsive-perfectionist personality it was difficult for me to come to terms with the affair and make a decision about my future; that just because my husband chose to have sex with another woman didn't mean that his feelings for me had changed; that I needed to stop dwelling on painful thoughts because they were self-destructive; that I should stop trying to identify *when* my husband had last screwed his mistress because a specific date didn't matter. (One of my frequent mind games was to say to myself, "If I find out that he fucked her when I was [blank] months pregnant, I'll leave him for sure.")

Separating didn't mean that we had no contact with each other. Occasionally, we went out to dinner together, and we chatted on the phone every evening, the irony of which was not lost on me because this was so oddly reminiscent of our courtship. On most weekends we arranged to do something together as a family. These little things helped to keep us connected.

Having a sense of humor has also really helped. I never thought I'd be able to laugh about any of this, but there are times when I'm actually able to joke about this life of mine. One day the Bitch-Whore-from-Hell's (another nickname) phone number appeared on my caller ID at work, and I answered by saying, "Barnes and Noble, this is Elizabeth." For a brief moment, I felt oddly exhilarated—this from the woman who only a few months before was so broken that she could barely function. During another call I launched into a monologue about how I was praying for her (not entirely true) and her children (this part was true). Imagining the shock on her face was a nice reward.

This experience has taught me many things. For one, it has taught me who my true friends really are. For such a long time I shut myself off from people. Part of this is because I was so emotionally overwhelmed that I could barely function, but part of it was also because of embarrassment.

Infidelity has a stigma associated with it, for the adulterer *and* the spouse. I worried whether people would think that I had done something wrong, whether I had driven my husband to another woman. More, I worried whether people would pity me if they knew the truth. *"Poor thing. Her husband cheated on her. How does she go on? How can she ever trust him? How can she stay?"* This is the question that tormented me the most. To outsiders the decision to stay or leave must seem so black and white. This is how I used to think before I became entangled in this mess. I used to tell my husband that the one unforgivable sin to me was adultery; ironic, then, that forgiving this transgression has been my greatest challenge.

It wasn't easy for me to confide in anyone, but I now know whom I can really depend on when things get bad. True friends will come to your house at any time of the day when you need them. True friends will offer you the sanctity of their house even if they're out of town and their kitchen is dirty. True friends will remind you to eat lunch even though all food is now unappetizing. True friends do not judge, only listen, and offer a shoulder and a hug when they're needed. I want to be the kind of friend that others have been to me.

I have also learned tremendous empathy for others. I've always considered myself to be a compassionate person; but, if truth be told, human beings are very judgmental of each other, and I think women are even guiltier of this than men are. We dissect each other's clothing, hair, and makeup, so why not our choices too?

It's so easy to slip into the *"if it were me, I'd   "* syndrome. *If that were me, I'd kick him out. If that were me, I'd leave him. If that were me, I'd cut his fucking balls off and send them to her on a fucking silver platter.* But until you're placed in this situation—in *any* situation—you don't *really* know what you'd do. We need to remind ourselves of this more often.

More than a year has passed and I remember everything that happened, though the sting is not as great as it once was, and I find myself enjoying things again. There are still bad times, and I still have moments when I'm uncertain about whether I even want to stay in this marriage, but I am a different person today. I can survive anything. Of that I am certain. A good friend recently confided that he thinks I am one of the strongest women he has met.

Some days I do feel strong, like I'm Buffy, the Vampire Slayer, and I can kick demon—er, ex-mistress—butt. On most days, however, I probably wouldn't tell you that I feel strong. On some, I might even tell you that I feel broken, that I'm the shell of the person that I used to be. I have sobbed uncontrollably at home, at work, in my car, on the phone, and with friends.

On the other hand, I always get out of bed the next morning and make myself put one foot in front of the other. What I have discovered over the past year is that we don't really know what our capacity is until we are stretched.

Forgiveness is slow. I am a Christian woman, and part of me wanted to think that forgiveness, bingo, could happen overnight, partially because that is the message I hear in church.

Forgiveness is an ongoing process. It is a decision that I make every day.

To forgive means that I don't hold my husband's infidelity against him and that I don't remind him of it. I know that he remembers it every day when he thinks of his own father and the pain his father caused his mother because of his own adultery. I also know that he thinks of it when he looks at our precious son and thinks about the time that was robbed from us, his family, because of his betrayal. I know that he fears our son might one day discover the truth and worries about what I will say if our son should ever ask me whether Daddy ever cheated on me.

While I will never forget the pain that my husband has caused me, I *choose* not to dwell on it. What happened, happened. It's unfair, it pisses me off, and on more than one occasion it has made me want to hire a hit man (whom, a friend tells me, I could hire for fifty dollars and a case of beer). But nothing can change the past. Even if I were to opt for divorce—for me, I think, an easier route—the pain and memories would not be erased.

I now understand that we as human beings have an ability to forgive and endure—to forgive and endure what, at previous times, we might have conceived of as unforgivable and unendurable. This is a lesson I wish I had not had to learn and especially not in this way.

One year ago today I was most likely dreaming about putting arsenic in my husband's tea. Today, I might (do!) at times still wish to poison him, but what wife doesn't feel this way at some point in her marriage? At least I might now add a little chocolate syrup to it, which, for anyone who knows me, is a *huge* statement because I love chocolate with unbridled abandon. That is what time has given me. And it's enough . . . for now.

One Moment Changes Everything

Choices

Billie Letts

Forty years ago I told a lie. And not just once. I told it over and over. I told it to my parents, to my husband's parents, to my extended family, to my friends.

No, it wasn't one of those little lies like "I know I gave the keys to you," or "Those cigarettes in my purse do *not* belong to me," or "If you'll just do this for me, I promise never to ask you again."

And it wasn't one of those bad little lies like "I've never been drunk in my life," or "If she said I dated her boyfriend, she's a liar," or "I really intended to pay you back on time."

In addition, I didn't think that once I'd told the lie the first time, I'd have to live with it the rest of my life, that I'd have to tell it again and again. And even worse, I'd have to tell people I love.

The year was 1958; I was nineteen years old, unmarried... and pregnant.

For those of you who are younger than thirty, you might not understand the stigma attached to a pregnant, unmarried teenager then. The guilt the girl had to live with, the shame her family felt. The whispers, the jokes, the out-and-out ridicule.

Choices had to be made. Should the girl have an abortion (illegal, dangerous, and expensive at that time)? Should she leave home, leave the state, have the child, then give it up for adoption? Or should she give birth to the baby she had neither the resources nor the stamina to raise alone, leaving the child to face its own kind of shame by being branded as a "mistake"?

Fortunately, the boy/man who was the father of the baby I was carrying cared about me and I cared about him. We had talked of marriage many times, but we hadn't finished college. We had no money or insurance; we couldn't afford an apartment, and I had no idea how to be a mother, much

175

less a wife. But more than all those disadvantages was this: my parents objected to my boyfriend, an "older man" of twenty-three who had been briefly married and was already the father of a young boy.

But despite all our reasons not to marry, despite our fears, despite our lack of resources and the absolute refusal of my parents to accept Dennis into our family, we married anyway.

I was almost three months pregnant when we drove to Stigler where we were married by a justice of the peace while our witness, the wife of the justice, was taking a bath. We spent the rest of the weekend in Oklahoma City where we went to a movie and ate at Beverly's, an "upscale" place known for its fried chicken.

Then it was time to face my parents. So, armed with a marriage license on which I'd attempted to change the date from November 30 to September 1, we went to my home to announce that we had been married secretly weeks earlier. My father demanded to see the wedding certificate, which I had tampered with in much the way a child might try to change a grade on a report card . . . not well.

My parents, not fooled, were furious; they told me to get out of the house. Next stop? My new in-laws.

Though they clearly saw through the lie, they were gracious about our situation and invited us to stay with them as long as we needed.

Days later, my mother called to say I could stop by to pick up some clothes and my check, which had been delivered from Arthur Murray's Dance Studio, where Dennis and I were working. Soon word of the "secret" wedding spread to other family and friends who were obviously suspicious, but quietly accepting. Six months later, I gave birth to a baby boy, a child who stole my heart. With his delivery, all was forgiven by my folks, who were also smitten with this beautiful new being.

Sounds like a pretty nice ending to what had started as a desperate situation, doesn't it? But here's what I hadn't counted on when I told the original lie: every year on the date of our make-believe anniversary, I would have to tell the lie again. And every time I told it, I felt guilt and shame. Not that I'd accidentally gotten pregnant, but that I was lying to my son.

Six years later, we had a second son. . . . No falsehood required. Yet every "anniversary" the old deceit surfaced.

Finally, on November 30, when my older son was eighteen and the younger twelve, I decided I'd lived with the lie too long; it was time to tell the truth and live with the consequences.

I told my husband what I was going to do; then the two of us sat down with our sons, and I admitted the truth of our marriage, the whole truth, and nothing but the truth.

And you know what they did? They laughed, hugged, and kissed me and their dad.

Pregnant, unmarried teenagers face a difficult time; they must make a decision they will live with forever. Do I have any answers? No. But I have two lovely sons who have brought me great joy and a husband I've adored for forty-five years. Do I have any advice? No. But I'm so glad I finally made the truth work for me instead of a lie work against me.

In *Where The Heart Is*, one of my characters says, "Maybe you never told a lie so big it can eat away a part of you. But if you ever do . . . and if you get lucky . . . you might get a chance to set it right."

I know I'm one of the lucky ones because I got a chance to set it right.

Fragile Madness

Paige Douglas

Thinking back on the ordeal, it frightens me to realize how thin the line between sanity and insanity actually is.

I was twenty-four years old, the mother of three children, married to a man who, after the first few years of marriage, became emotionally, verbally, and physically abusive.

Only a year and a half before I broke, I experienced the first attack of physical violence at the hands of the man I loved.

He asked, "What's for dinner?"

"It's in the oven," I said as he opened the oven door. He was instantly pissed off.

"What the fuck is this slop? You put fucking sour cream in the oven!"

I explained that the only reason I had done so was to keep everything warm. That was not good enough. He wanted to fight about it. Okay, so I could handle getting yelled at, called a few names, and that would be the end of it.

But that is not the way things went that night.

To my surprise, he took the hot plate of nachos and threw it across the room. The plate shattered, and beans, cheese, and meat splattered all over the floor.

He turned toward me and said, "Clean it up, bitch."

"No! What the hell is wrong with you? People don't throw food across the room and then tell the person who made it to clean it up! You clean it up!"

"Fuck you!" he said as he grabbed me by my hair and pulled me toward the nachos on the floor. "Clean it up! Now!" he said, as he shoved my face down into the broken plate and food.

The kids and I curled up on the couch in the living room. Clinging to each other, none of us said a word. We fell asleep like that. In the morning, I awoke as my husband was walking out the back door for work.

"What do you want me to do?" I asked. "Do you want me to leave? Do you want a divorce?"

He just looked at me and calmly said, "No, I can't do that to the kids."

Then he left, no apology, nothing.

The kids, I thought, *what the hell? I have to go. I have to get all of us out of here now. He's gone insane.*

However, after only two months, I went back to him, believing his promises that he would never hurt me again. That was a very big mistake, as I have since learned. *Once a snake, always a snake.* Shortly after my return, I found out I was going to have another child.

When he found out about the pregnancy, he was elated.

Then he quit his job.

I had a small support system from the church I attended. I can tell you that I thought my prayers were answered on more than one occasion when one of those wonderful women would show up unexpectedly. Usually they brought groceries or, on the rare occasion that I did have money, offered to take me to the grocery store. Of course, there was no logical reason to remain in these circumstances. I could have admitted to myself that I was married to an abusive male and that I was a victim of the classic social isolation that is often part of controlling relationships.

But I did not know this at the time.

I wanted to be a good wife and a good mother. I kept thinking that if I tried harder, prayed more often, became more submissive, somehow things would improve.

They never did.

At one point, I sat on the edge of the bed, cold, my mind reeling with a thousand thoughts at once. I thought about how I wished to die. I thought about the many times I had contemplated driving off the road or a bridge. It would be so easy.

Suddenly, it occurred to me, *Why should I be the one to die? He should die!*

I put my robe on and went to the closet where I knew he kept a gun. I picked it up, looked at it, found a bullet, and put it in the gun.

I stepped out into the hallway where I could see him. He was sitting in the middle of the children watching cartoons.

I aimed the gun directly at him. I wanted to blow a hole right through his head.

I hesitated. The kids were there, right in the same room with the monster I wanted dead.

Even though this was definitely insane thinking and behavior, my mind never felt clearer.

But I could not pull the trigger.

I could not kill my children's father right in front of them.

I could not reconcile the thought of spending my life in prison for killing a jerk.

I could not abandon them.

. . .

It took me several years to get strong enough to break free of my marriage. For a long time, I deluded myself into believing that there could be a happy ending for us. I gave him more chances than he ever deserved.

I listened to the counsel of church leaders and other women who attended the same church that I did. I finally realized that my religion, in essence, was asking me to live a miserable existence, to be unhappy and unfulfilled, and still to feel blessed.

Finally, I faced the truth. It was painful; it was scary; and it took more courage than I thought I had in me. This was not an easy process. I walked away from everything I had ever believed to be true. In doing so, I was able to leave behind an incredibly sad and sick marriage.

I have never regretted that choice.

When I think about how much I experienced and how close I came to danger, I am amazed that I survived. I have come a long way from the young girl of twenty years ago. I am not perfect, but I have learned so very much. I have grown spiritually, emotionally, and intellectually and hopefully will continue to do so.

My life has been like a carnival ride, full of highs and lows. There are times, as I am sure there will be in the future, when I get down. But at least now I can say I understand depression. I have parted that thin veil that separates rational thought from irrational. I know how fragile our minds and our hearts truly are. I do not regret my past experiences. After all, they are part of me and have helped shape the woman that I have become.

And that is a very good and powerful thing to be able to say.

$$\gtrdot \sim \sim \sim \lessdot$$

Grace, Grit, and Gratitude

Jane Jayroe

It was a moment like no other. I was nineteen years old, a girl from a small rural town in Oklahoma, standing on the end of a runway in Atlantic City, New Jersey. There was a crown on my head, and memories of all the Miss America pageants I had watched on television were rushing through my mind.

"Don't cry," I told myself. Crying for some people means a few dainty tears cascading down their faces, adding a little shine and an image of sincerity. For me, crying meant red-rimmed eyes, mascara tracks down my face, and a drippy nose. It was not a picture I wanted to present to the millions of people watching the Miss America pageant in the fall of 1966.

It was an incredible experience to go from being a girl from Laverne, Oklahoma, who played basketball and had never flown in an airplane, to someone of such celebrity status that she needed security guards to get through a room. And this transition came in one moment in time, the moment when Bert Parks announced that I was Miss America.

How grateful I am for this unexpected blessing in my life. It was indeed life-changing.

But then my life has been like that since 1966—unexpected. My beginnings were very predictable and incredibly good. My parents taught school, and my older sister, Judy, was the best sibling imaginable. Life was all about school, church, and community. It was filled to the brim with loving family members, fun friends, and hopeful days. Adult life would surely be more of the same: college, a teaching position, marriage to a good man, and several children.

Yet I always had a secret dream. It was the dream of performing, and that dream led me to Oklahoma City University and the Miss America program.

Instead of having a life that went on a lovely line from here to there, I've had a roller-coaster life. I'm grateful for every high and low and pray that I've gained some insight to share concerning the journey. The wisdom I can share is best summed up in the form of three Gs: grace, grit, and gratitude.

Grace

My mother's middle name is Grace. It's perfect for her because the word means "unmerited favor." Helene Grace (my momma) is the greatest grace that God could have given to me. She is an extraordinary woman—loving, selfless, generous, fun. She deserves most of the credit for any success I've had. She never pushed me to achieve greatness; I was just encouraged to do my best. She has said to me in recent years that she and my dad would have been voted "least likely to succeed" in school. I don't believe that; she is an uncomplicated person in many ways but amazingly wise in important life lessons. She is a person with a joyful heart.

Mother had very clear goals for my sister and me. We were expected to be nice to others, attend church, use our gifts (music) for God, do our best in school (no pressure for specific grades), and find joy in the simple moments of life (not that she would have used that phrase). She loved her family beyond measure.

She intuitively knew the inner desires of my heart and simply helped me to achieve them. Whether it was driving me to voice lessons after she had spent the day teaching school or convincing my daddy that, even though I had a full scholarship elsewhere, they needed to send me to Oklahoma City University, regardless of the financial sacrifices. She was my support system (along with my sister, Judy). Mother was my encourager. She would have loved me just as much in last place as first, on the bench as on the basketball court, looking plain as being pretty.

What a model for God's grace Mother has been. I certainly didn't deserve or earn her love in the abundance it was given. So it is with God's love. He has showered me with grace. I haven't always known how to receive it. Sometimes I was afraid that His grace would take me to a place that was uncomfortable. And indeed it has.

It was not comfortable for me to enter pageants, and I would never have had the courage to enter the Miss Oklahoma City pageant without the encouragement of my Alpha Chi Omega sisters at OCU. Even though I had planned for some time to enter a Miss America preliminary pageant, I was going to wait until I was older, had more performance experience, and hopefully had gained a little sophistication. I was such a shy, small-town girl.

Winning Miss Oklahoma City and then Miss Oklahoma were experiences that top the chart of exuberance and joy. Representing Oklahoma on the runway in Atlantic City was the highlight of my nineteen years. And then Miss America . . . wow! It was a year of traveling, with experiences that few people have. I visited almost every state in the nation, plus Canada, Europe, and Southeast Asia. I threw out a baseball to start the season for the Kansas City A's, conducted symphony orchestras, attended pageants throughout the country, and met people from all walks of life.

The most important weeks for me were those spent in Vietnam entertaining American military troops. I was the first Miss America to visit a combat zone, and it was indeed my greatest privilege to bring a piece of home to the men and women who were serving our country. After Vietnam, I was summoned to the White House, where I met with President Johnson. I stood with Vice President Hubert Humphrey for the signing of a GI Bill. My mind is full of incredible memories. I still don't know why I was chosen Miss America, but I'm grateful.

I have experienced God's grace and love in the very highest of experiences and in the lowest as well.

Through many dangers, toils, and snares,
I have already come;
'Tis grace hath brought me safe thus far,
And grace will lead me home.
     —"Amazing Grace," words by John Newton

Grit

Another important insight that I have gained through years of a rewarding professional life is the importance of "grit." That's an old-fashioned word that means perseverance or determination. That is the stuff of which real life is made. It's the difference between the runner who crosses the finish line and the one who doesn't.

Whether it's working out of the emotional hole of despair or patiently working to achieve goals, that dogged walk of the determined person is necessary for success. Following my divorce in 1976, I had no job, no money, no self-confidence, and no home. I had a tiny baby to support, and I had never been lower in my life. It was especially tough because of the incredible high of being Miss America just a few years earlier.

God's grace found me in the bottom of a hole and restored me, but it was not a speedy turnaround. It was a plodding kind of recovery, one foot in front of the other. Grit is what matters when things go south in life—and sooner or later they will.

Grit is the character trait that gave me a career in television news. I had no prior experience as a journalist when KOCO-TV in Oklahoma City offered me the opportunity to be the first female news anchor on their prime-time newscast. There were few women in the newsroom and none on the air as anchor. Because of my high name recognition, General Manager Al Parsons offered me the chance to audition for a spot as co-anchor with a longtime television journalist. I didn't have the journalism credentials they would have preferred, but Barbara Walters, Jane Pauley, and Diane Sawyer didn't when they began either. I did have a lot of experience communicating under stress. That was one of the gifts of being Miss America. I had to speak in front of people, and often I did not do a good job. But it was in the "doing" that I learned. In television, too, I learned on the job. My liberal arts education helped as well . . . especially the writing in both undergraduate and graduate courses. (I received a bachelor of music from Oklahoma City University and a master of arts from Tulsa University.)

When I was offered the job as the six and ten o'clock news anchor, it was double the money that I was making at the Oklahoma State Department of Education. As a single mom, I didn't feel that I had a choice, even though the prospect of working nights did not thrill me.

While the hours were never ideal for a personal life and raising my son, the career was a perfect fit for me. I loved the fast pace of the job. I loved the on-camera work, but I also loved the writing, producing, and editing. I loved being on a team with photographers and assignment editors and producers and reporters. I loved doing something that mattered. I loved being a part of the lives of people in Oklahoma. I loved the process of communication that traveled from a cold studio with three cameras, a flimsy news desk, and lots of lights through the camera lens into homes in Oklahoma.

I did not like my first co-anchor. He was totally rude to me and seemed to be completely offended that they had hired a "beauty queen." Reportedly, he was indignant and feared he would have to write all my copy. I don't know if he was fired or quit, but he left. My second co-anchor was recruited from out of state and became known as "that blond guy." He did not do well in Oklahoma, but he was helpful to me in learning how to write. So, too, was Jack Bowen, who was the third co-anchor that I worked with in a two-year period. Our team was awesome and led by the greatest news director Oklahoma City had seen at the time, Tom Kerby. He took our station from the bottom of the barrel to number one in a very short time. Part of the team was producer Barbara Geddie and her husband and photographer Bill Geddie, who is now the producer for *The View* and Barbara Walters's specials.

After one year on the air in Oklahoma City, I had lots of job offers throughout the nation. I was interested in only one—the Dallas/Fort Worth television market. I didn't apply for a job there, but when KSAS called to ask me to audition, I leapt at the chance. It would be tough to leave Oklahoma with all my family and friends, but Dallas was a "top 10" television market, and the salary offer was double what KOCO paid. It was definitely the big time, and I felt proud that they wanted to hire me—and not because of the Miss America background at all. In fact, the hire was in spite of the title. The station never used the Miss America title in any of their publicity efforts. They liked my work as a television journalist and wanted to hire me to co-anchor with Chip Moody, Harold Taft, and a new sports person. It was an awesome opportunity. How could I say no?

I took the job. Early in the summer of 1980, we moved to Fort Worth, where the main studio was located, and I went to work for News Director Bill Vance and with some of the finest journalists in America. Interning from Southern Methodist University in the newsroom and then hired as a reporter was Karen Parfitt, better known as Karen Hughes, who is today a close advisor to President Bush. Working as a reporter, and later as our late-news producer, was a young man named Scott Pelley, who married a reporter from Moreland, Oklahoma—Jane Boone. Scott is now at CBS. When Chip Moody left KXAS, I worked with Dave Layman and Brad Wright. I loved the work.

Before I went on the air in Texas, a television critic wrote an article in the *Dallas Morning News* with the headline: "KXAS Hires Barbie Doll." It was a very negative article. In time, I proved the critic wrong.

It was grit that made the positive difference in that job and many other situations in my life. I was determined to be taken seriously as a television journalist. I worked hard day after day in the heat of that first Texas summer. I was the news anchor who went live from the Republican National Convention in Detroit. I did special news reports on the hardest topics I could think of, just to prove myself. Whether it was working with the sex crimes unit; attending a union meeting when Braniff Airlines was going under; covering politics, weather disasters or the Dallas County jail, I worked hard, risked failure, and did my best every day. There was no magic formula—just determination . . . grit.

That same reporter who wrote the negative article chose me as the first journalist to be on the cover of a special feature in his newspaper a few years later.

Those early years in television news were groundbreaking. It had always been a male-dominated field, almost exclusively. Barbara Walters had been on the NBC's *Today* show doing feature stories, but other than that there were few women in television newsroom. Then it all changed in a hurry. In many ways the news directors didn't always know what to do with women. There was no dressing room or decent lighting for a female on-air person. Men slapped powder on as they walked into the studio. In Dallas, when the male anchor was off, the producers put someone else in his place to co-anchor with me. When I was gone, the male anchor did the news by himself. I pointed this out, and they agreed to let me anchor alone as well. It wasn't my abilities they were concerned about as much as audience reaction. The final results were not yet conclusive on public acceptance of hearing the hard news of the day from a woman.

The most difficult part of the job was trying to balance it with my family. It was a constant challenge. In Oklahoma, when I first started the night schedule, I did what the other journalists did and ran out for dinner, something like a lunch break. In time, I went home to see Tyler. Other people followed my lead: the men I worked with were just as dedicated to their families, but usually they just didn't have the full parenting responsibility I did.

When I moved to Texas, I bought a house less than five minutes from the station. I went to work at 2:00 P.M. but left and picked up Tyler from school at 3 and got that precious time when he was young. Following school he would jump in the car with enthusiasm and tell me everything that went on at school. (Later, if I asked him over dinner about his schoolday, the response was often, "Fine.") I was back at the station by 3:30.

I was almost always able to go home between newscasts in Texas because I was close. What I missed out on was the going-to-bed routine. Like picking up kids from school, the rituals of getting up and going to bed are special in a family. Tyler always had great caretakers (the Terpening family in Oklahoma City and Maria Sanchez later in Texas). He didn't miss out so much as I did.

Being on television makes you a local celebrity and people are incredibly kind, but there are also awful sides to the business. People criticize you for all sorts of things (such as the way your hair looks), and you are often plagued with stalkers. But, in balance, it was worth it a million times over. I got to see the very best side of human beings, too, in their generosity, in their achievements, and in their compassion for others.

When Governor Frank Keating asked me to serve as his cabinet secretary of tourism, I knew it was God's call in my life, and I didn't hesitate to accept this piece of grace. It was tough duty from the beginning. But it was an awesome experience to spend time promoting a place I have grown to love so deeply. Oklahoma.

The job as a cabinet secretary especially put me in a position to be brought down. The culture of politics and government can encourage very mean behavior. Yet I also worked with some of the greatest people in my life: Doug Enevoldsen and Leann Overstake top the list.

Sometimes I've wondered why I haven't been like many movie stars and just ridden off into the sunset and let people remember me as a nineteen-year-old Miss America. I can't do that. God has always called me into positions of influence, and it is in response to His incredible love that I step forth. In tough times, my faith has sustained me. Having good friends, a wonderful family, and a somewhat balanced life have sheltered me from a lot of the more difficult moments. God was faithful during those days as He has always been.

Gratitude

My final observation is the importance of adopting an attitude of gratitude toward life. We experience joy when we look at life with a grateful heart. The apostle Paul writes a lot about the importance of joy and how we find it even in the dark times of life. In fact, he says to count it all joy, and I'm beginning to understand what he means. God can bring something good out of every situation.

If I had never divorced, I wouldn't be married to Jerry Gamble today. If I had not been broke and desperate for money, I would never have found a career that was so incredibly satisfying. If I had not faced a demotion in television following my return to Oklahoma, I would never have worked with the Presbyterian Health Foundation and the Oklahoma Health Center. All of these "failures" led to wonderful opportunities, including serving on Governor Frank Keating's cabinet (and getting to know Cathy Keating). Even today, the joy of working with President Tom McDaniel and Oklahoma City University is the result of all my experiences, both wins and losses.

I feel such appreciation for all of life. As I look over my shoulder and back at my life, I thank God that I was born in this country; that I live in Oklahoma; that I'm married to Jerry Gamble and have Tyler, Elaine, and Luke in my life; that I have the greatest and goofiest girlfriends in the world; that I enjoy good health; and that I can attend a church led by Dr. Norman Neaves and filled with God's presence. I am so grateful that I was born to Pete, Helene, and Judy.

. . .

Living an unexpected life by accepting grace, meeting life with grit, and loving with a grateful heart is a blessing beyond description. May my dear friends, the women of Oklahoma, be blessed in every way.

My Double Life

Sally Emmons-Featherston

I lead a secret life. Not in the Sydney Bristow, dodging bullets and round house kicking way (though I do have a good roundhouse kick, and I do know a spy . . . well, she works for the CIA and she *might* be a spy, though she can't really tell us). By day, I am a university English professor who valiantly fights the good fight against comma splices, split infinitives, and plagiarism. My weapons are my ballpoint pen and Google. By night, my "You must have a thesis statement" mantra ends, and I transform into my alter ego: a Lycra-wearing and booty-hustlin' gal whose weapons of choice are a killer stereo system, a really good electric fan, and a resistance tube.

Nobody expects this from me. Heck, I don't even expect it from me. Sometimes I'm still shocked that at the end of many days I shuck my stereo-typical English teacher guise to become my other self as a J.T. (Justin Timberlake, for the uninitiated)-playing, weight-pumping, cardiovascular queen. "Sadistic Sally" and the "workout Nazi" many in my classes call me (fondly, I like to think). I'm talking about my aerobics classes, though I'm sure that some of the students in my university classes might agree. For many years, my secret life has been just that: my little secret, privy only to a few. Only my best girlfriends knew that at the end of the day, my day was not yet over. While most faculty return home to grade papers, research, cook dinners for their families, or just relax, I instead rush home, change identities by donning my other work outfit, grab my iPod and a quick snack, and am out the door.

The women who come to my Jazzercise classes laugh about my double life. In fact, they often joke that if I were only to break out some of my dance moves in my composition classes my students might be more interested in my lectures (they're probably right). I haven't shared my private life—until now—for a variety of reasons. For one, nobody expects a well-educated and ambitious university professor to teach aerobic classes. *Aerobics!* To donate

189

time at a local library, *yes*; to speak at community events, *yes*; even to work for a political campaign, *yes*. But to willingly don spandex and lead a fitness class, *no*. Although we live in a health-conscious society, we seem to think that fitness instructors must be young, tanned, beautiful, and not particularly well educated. Tell the truth. You've probably thought these very things. To say that I don't fit the mold for the supposed "typical" fitness instructor is a gross understatement of facts. Secondly, I didn't really want my students to learn about my other occupation. It's not that I really minded them knowing; it's just that I didn't want them to come to one of my classes out of curiosity. Call me strange, but the thought of sweating profusely—in spandex!—while working my tail off (and trying to motivate other women to do the same), all while trying to be witty . . . well, it sounds like a recipe for disaster.

The road that led me down this fitness path is long and full of bumps. To explain how I came to be an aerobics teacher, I must first make another confession: I am also the survivor of an eating disorder. However, unlike the average victim of eating disorders, my bout with anorexia didn't occur until graduate school, when I was in my midtwenties. It was at the height of stress for me: my general exams were looming, and thoughts of *What if I don't make it?* were intermixed with *What if I do make it; then what? Will I even be able to find a job?* Add to that mix an up-and-down relationship, family hundreds of miles away, and professors who expected nothing but excellence from me (my expectation for myself too). I was more than stressed.

As anyone who is familiar with eating disorders knows, it's a disease about control, not food. Food—lack of it—is merely the means by which the sufferer feels some semblance of control over things occurring in his or her life. (Yes, there *are* men who suffer from eating disorders too.) At my worst, I weighed myself dozens of times per day. I knew how many calories were in my coffee each morning and how many calories were in each piece of fruit that I might allow myself to eat. Strangely, I would eat three meals a day. I guess I rationalized that I was "okay" by doing this. But what I ate on an average day would barely amount to a thousand calories: a cup of dry cereal in the morning, no sugar, skim milk; reduced fat popcorn for lunch; a salad for dinner, nonfat dressing, or maybe some baked fish if I was feeling particularly thin that day. On most days it was even fewer calories than that. And there were never any snacks. Ever. I hated people who indulged in what I wouldn't: chocolate cake with icing, french fries, steak, homemade bread. I remember once even disliking my boyfriend (now husband) because he was eating a PB&J.

Of course, it took a long time before I realized I even had a problem. I dropped from wearing a size 14 (and sometimes a 16) to a size 4 within a matter of mere months. At first, people commented upon how good I looked; I was overweight and did need to lose a few pounds. But then people started to whisper comments. "My god, look how thin she is," I remember one classmate saying in an art history class. I didn't know her and assumed that she must be jealous, not understanding that, to onlookers, I looked skeletal. But I couldn't ignore it when my parents were visiting one time, and my dad, who rarely expressed his feelings, gave me a big hug and said, "I love you. *Please eat something.*"

I laughingly joked that I would, even though I knew that I wouldn't. And I was shocked that my parents knew that something was wrong, as if my *"I'm just trying to eat better"* lie had actually convinced them that everything was okay. Slowly, I noticed that I felt winded just climbing the stairs to my second-story apartment, and I began to wonder what was wrong with me. And I was unhappy. There was no joy in anything. I felt as if I was just going through the motions of life.

It was during an epiphany—triggered by what, I don't remember—that I finally accepted the truth that so many people had tried unsuccessfully to tell me. I fell to the floor in my apartment and cried. No, I didn't just cry; I sobbed. For who I used to be and for the person that I had become. After a while, I walked into the bathroom and looked at myself in the mirror, and I distinctly remember thinking that a stranger was looking back at me. The face that I had looked at every day of my life was sunken, and my eyes lifeless. I didn't recognize myself. I stared, transfixed, unable to stop. It was that day that I realized what I had been doing to myself. It was that day that I picked up that bathroom scale and threw it in the Dumpster.

Recovery was slow. I began by making myself eat three small meals per day, real meals representing the basic food groups. I felt guilty for every bite that I consumed, but I forced myself to swallow the food. How I managed to overcome an eating disorder by my own sheer willpower, I still wonder about. So many others aren't as fortunate as I. Agonizingly, I waited for my clothes to grow tighter. It took a while, but it eventually happened, and the size 4 went back up to a size 6, and then higher. But then I noticed something else: the apartment stairs that had once been so hard to climb were suddenly easy for me. And I wanted to do things again: go to festivals, go shopping, go on bike rides, and even go to restaurants, though I still couldn't bring myself to eat some of my favorite foods. In fact, I often wondered if I'd ever be able to eat without guilt again.

Going to an aerobics class was a suggestion made by my boyfriend. He knew that I had crazily jumbled, mixed-up messages about my body and thought that working out would be good for me. When I balked at the idea, he picked up the phone book, selected a gym, and called the owner to find out about the schedule. I had never worked out before, but the idea intrigued me. And (another confession) I worried about the weight that I was gaining and when, if ever, it would stop.

So I went to class. All by myself. I understand now what a big step that was because most women who are new to exercise partner with a buddy (it's always easier to go to a class if you have a friend with you). And I was amazed at the diversity of the class: there were young women, middle-aged women, and women in their fifties . . . whom I marveled at. I stood in the back row and was out of breath after just a few songs. I felt clumsy and uncoordinated and probably looked clumsy and uncoordinated. Even so, I liked the music, and I felt that I was actually doing something good for myself. For so long, I had focused on depriving myself. And I was jealous, actually jealous, of the women who were older than I, but whose energy and fitness levels far surpassed my own. I couldn't keep up with them, and I knew that, even though I probably looked the epitome of health to outsiders, I wasn't.

The woman who taught that class later became my friend. Now she's in graduate school; having raised her family, she's doing something for herself. She once told me that she started off in the back row of aerobics, too, fully clothed and embarrassed; but over the years she started to move forward in class, shedding clothes on the way. And then, one day, she was on stage. She warned that this would one day happen to me. Of course, I didn't believe her, but it turns out that her words were prophetic.

It took time—a lot of it—and hard work, but I eventually overcame my eating disorder. It wasn't easy, and even today I still feel guilt when I indulge in what my brain whispers I shouldn't. I'm jealous of others who can treat themselves to pasta, and muffins, and bacon, and a Hershey's bar, without guilt. I may never fully rid myself of that whisper inside of me that held me hostage for so long—*don't eat it*—but over time I have managed to harness it.

Working out saved my life. Truly. I quickly became addicted to the rush that I felt when I conquered a really tough class, and it was good to have an obsession other than food. Coming from a family that never went to the gym, I didn't know how much fun working out could be, or how much a person's mentality could shift simply by doing something physical. Even on especially hectic days at work or at home, I find that, if I can work out, I eventually feel better and have a more positive attitude.

Gradually, my stamina grew, as did my strength. I started to feel better about myself and started to feel a little less guilty when I ate. Mental-health professionals now know that people with eating disorders suffer from a mental illness. They are also known to be perfectionists. When perfection isn't attained, and the circumstances are just right, something clicks in the brain, and slowly, insidiously, an eating disorder develops. That's what happened with me; and, of course, I never imagined that I'd be in this situation. Anorexia was an illness for young girls, models, and actresses, right? Or so I thought.

Becoming a Jazzercise instructor was a natural step for me, though it too was unexpected. I attended class for a few years, started to learn the routines even better than some of the instructors, felt more comfortable in class and more confident in myself, and slowly started moving forward in class—until I was soon in the front row! Even then I wasn't thinking about becoming an instructor. But as things happen, one day the owner of the facility shocked me by telling me that I moved well and that I should consider becoming an instructor.

A seed was planted. What seemed like an alien idea suddenly took hold and I began to seriously think, *this is something that I can really do.* And I started to get excited at the thought of selecting my own music and of catering my workouts to me—all while being paid to do something that I enjoyed! So I trained, passed a movement screening, then passed a written fitness exam, and then tried out in front of dance trainers, also certified Jazzercise instructors, so they could assess my physical ability, safety, and technique. And I was certified! It was my last year of graduate school. The extra money was nice ... *and I was being paid to do something that I enjoyed!*

Upon graduation, I had to decide whether to continue teaching fitness classes. After all, I was launching my academic career; did I have time for this? What if one of my students came to one of my classes? *What if one of my colleagues came to one of my classes?* Ultimately, I decided to continue to teach because this is the one special thing that I do for me. Work can be consuming; and now, as a new mom, I usually feel rushed. I have very little "me" time now. Working out is my time, the one luxury I allow myself. Escaping from the daily stresses, even if just for an hour, a few days a week, helps recharge me. There will come a time when I'm ready to relinquish the stage to another instructor; I'm just not there yet.

Because I like to think that something good can come from even the bad, I talk freely about my eating disorder to people in my fitness classes. What I've discovered is that there are an awful lot of people out there who have suffered from eating disorders, yet remain "hush-hush" about them because they're taboo subjects in American society. Even more people— especially women—have conflicted ideas about their bodies and wish they could change something about themselves. The people who come to my classes have a variety of backgrounds. None of us likely fit the image that most people think of when they think of people who work out. I've had stay-at-home moms, lawyers, doctors, hairstylists, and CEOs of companies attend my classes. I've had both men and women in class. Once, two members of the Oklahoma State University football team came to my class . . . and swore that they'd never come back because we all outdid them. And I've even faced one of my biggest fears when one of my university students showed up for class . . . and then kept returning! (Imagine the shock *she* must have felt upon seeing that *I* was the instructor on stage.)

So I teach. I am a successful woman by society's standards. I am well educated and am blessed to have a career that I enjoy. During the day, I (hopefully) broaden the minds of college students and help them to become better writers and readers. On most nights, I do what other people do: I play with my son, watch TV, drive my husband crazy, iron, cook, shop, search the Internet, read. . . . But a few nights a week, my alter ego emerges, one that likes loud music, being a little wild, and working out hard. And I'm a better person because of it.

Politics

May 1 . . .

Carolyn Anne Taylor

May I be free from danger
May I have mental happiness
May I have physical happiness
May I have ease of well-being*

May I be free from danger

Politics is tough, hard, and fast; it is an intellectually and physically challenging world, where you are only as good as your last vote, speech, or deed. And I loved every minute that I was in it.

Most women who hold elected political office run later in life, after they have raised their children. For them, politics is a second career.

Not me.

I began, like most, by working for others as a campaign volunteer, learning the nuts and bolts of campaigning. When I was a young teacher, summers provided an opportunity to work to help elect pro-education candidates.

In the summer of 1984, however, I applied for a Fulbright Scholarship to study politics and history in the Middle East and was accepted.

As I told my family and friends of this magnificent opportunity and prepared to travel, many said, "Why do you want to go there? Don't you know it's a region filled with danger, where war has been waged for centuries? And you know how they treat women!"

---

* Andrew Harvey, *The Direct Path* (New York: Broadway Books, 2000). This prayer is from the Buddhist practice of "loving kindness" (*metta*).

A week before I was to depart for Tel Aviv, the popular incumbent state representative announced she would not run for reelection. It was only days before the deadline for filing. A handful of friends encouraged me to consider running, but it meant turning down the scholarship. This was a hard call, yet running would be an opportunity to fulfill a dream at the young age of twenty-seven.

I announced I would run for the office and stayed in Norman to quickly put together a campaign. Immediately I had to tell friends and family that instead of going to the Middle East, I now wanted to go to the Oklahoma House of Representatives in Oklahoma City.

Some said, "Why do you want to go there? Don't you know it's filled with danger, where war has been waged for decades? And you know how they treat women!"

During that first campaign, it was interesting to me the number of people who commented, "You are too 'nice' for politics." I wonder what that means. Do you have to be "mean" to serve in elected office? Perhaps those issuing such warnings saw danger because I was not perceived as "tough" enough. I was young, female, and relatively soft-spoken; the common view is that opposite characteristics are required to succeed in public life.

It's funny. After I served my first term in office, not once when I ran for reelection did someone say I was too "nice." The truth is, some of the nicest, kindest, smartest, and most caring people I have ever known were other elected officials. What is truly dangerous, I think, is that the public's perception of their elected government is vastly different from reality. Does this largely inaccurate view reduce voter confidence and participation? Does it discourage good people from serving in government and running for office? If so, that is the greatest danger to our democracy.

May I have mental happiness

Recently, my husband and I were having a talk about the future. He said that he will never fully retire from his law office because "men always need somewhere to go." He teasingly added, "to get away from their wives." But I know what he means. His father, as long as he was physically able, went every day to the local coffee shop to solve the world's problems with the other men in town. I remember my dad spending many happy hours cleaning, arranging, and rearranging his tools in our garage.

Women also need somewhere to go. Someone once asked me, "Where is your healing place?" At the time, I thought they were nuts. Believe me, the State Capitol is *not* a healing place. Now I understand. For some women a healing place involves exercise, prayer, or gardening. For me years ago, it was aerobics. Today it's hiking and yoga. For some it's drugs or alcohol or both. For my mother it's her weekly bridge club. My grandmother never let a day pass without devoting at least an hour to embroidery. I guess my other healing place has been inside a book.

How we choose our place I do not know. It is an active decision, and one each of us desperately needs to make, especially in today's world, in order to have any sense of mental happiness.

May I have physical happiness

In the movie *The Breakfast Club*, high school students from every stereotypical group—jocks, nerds, geeks, druggies or stoners, and the popular and beautiful—for various reasons have to spend a Saturday together serving detention in their big school library. These are students who have never spoken to each other, much less spent time together. They are strangers to each other because they belong to different groups.

By the end of the movie, the students have become friends and have developed an appreciation for each other as individuals. This scenario has always reminded me of the Oklahoma House of Representatives. In high school it is not always popular to be identified as "smart." In the Oklahoma state legislature, it was also not advantageous to be labeled "smart," although that accusation wasn't made very often. We were elected from every region and part of the state—jocks, brains, geeks, nerds, the cool and beautiful—and would likely never have associated with each other, yet we also had to stay in a big room together and not leave until we learned to get along and be somewhat productive. This application has profoundly affected my belief that anything in this world is possible, including but not limited to, "brains" being athletic and "jocks" being smart.

May I have ease of well-being

Every morning, on the way to the Capitol, I drove through McDonald's and told the huge, colorfully lit, talking menu that I wanted a "bacon-egg-cheese biscuit, bacon burnt please, and a large coffee with one cream."

"Pull around, please," was always the response from the sign.

Often the same woman worked the breakfast shift. She always smiled, handed the bag through the small window, then the cup of coffee with one cream carefully balanced on the center of the lid. She would then cheerfully say, "Have a nice day."

During the spring of 1990, the Oklahoma legislature was working hard to pass a landmark education reform and funding bill that became known by its number, HB 1017. As chair of both the Education Committee and Education Appropriations Subcommittee, I had been heavily involved, first drafting and then defending the legislation. It was controversial and received a great deal of media attention. Teachers from across the state came to the Capitol to urge passage of the bill. For three days, hundreds of educators marched around the Capitol, often in the rain, carrying signs, chanting, "Never Last Again," and lobbying their individual representatives and senators to vote yes. It was high drama.

The news coverage on the day of the vote was extensive because of the anticipated closeness of the vote and the heavy pressure both for and against the measure. Most Oklahomans had an opinion on the matter. That morning, with butterflies the size of pterodactyls in my stomach, I really needed that "bacon-egg-cheese biscuit, bacon burnt please, and a large coffee with one cream."

"Pull around, please."

She was on duty. I smiled; she didn't. She pushed the small window open and pointed to the decal on my windshield, a parking sticker with the seal of the Oklahoma House of Representatives. She held tight to the bag in one hand and the cup of coffee in the other and said, "How are you going to vote?"

I was stunned, but I managed to reply, "I'm voting yes."

She smiled, handed me the bag and cup, and said, "Have a nice day."

The week after HB 1017 passed, a letter to the editor appeared in the University of Oklahoma student newspaper, the *Oklahoma Daily*. It was from a student. He wrote that, although he agreed with the cause, he had gotten a big kick out of watching the teachers protesting at the Capitol on the news. He had seen the teachers shouting, "S.O.S.! Save Our Schools!" One night, he turned on the evening news and couldn't help but smirk at how silly the teachers looked, freezing their butts off while protesting and holding posters smeared by the rain. All of a sudden, he said out loud, "Holy Spicoli! There's my mom!"

Yes, his mother. He called home to Tulsa to check with his dad, and, sure enough, it was she. In fact, she had just been on CNN. The next morning her face was plastered on the cover of the *Tulsa World*. He found all of the coverage of his mother amazing. As he thought about it, he realized that she had not tried to get on TV. Her goal had not been to call attention to herself, but to support her fellow teachers in a crusade she believed in.

He closed his letter by writing, "I felt proud of my mom. She went to the capitol, not for glory or to showboat, but to stand up for House Bill 1017. . . . As a son, I haven't looked at mother in the hero sense. . . . But when I saw her on the steps at the capitol, not making herself the center of attention, . . . I became proud. . . . I saw an aspect of what makes this country great—those who will stand up for what they believe in. I always thought that you had to make a lot of noise to be heard. This is not true, I saw my mom not open her mouth and make more noise than she ever has. I'm proud of you mom."*

You want a better world? Then start building it. Who is stopping you? Build it with those who want it. Build it small and it will grow. Words, dreams, and ideals without actions are nothing. Both of these women— the one at the McDonald's window and the one protesting at the Capitol— strangers to me, are my heroines. They acted on their beliefs, in their own way, to make this state and world a better place and gave themselves, in return, ease of well-being.

---

* Jason Clark, Guest Editorial, *Oklahoma Daily*, April 24, 1990.

All Used Up

Sally Freeman Frasier

"You can be who you are, and what you are, wherever you are," my mother once said to me. This advice followed me into adulthood and has become part of the mind-set that now guides my actions. To know me, you must know that I married into a very political family. Even so, in the early years of my marriage, I didn't soak up much of these politics—even when my husband ran for the state legislature, and I helped him by walking precincts, knocking on doors, and introducing myself. My mind was elsewhere: teaching and raising our children.

As our children grew, I began to realize just how much the political issues meshed with the subjects I had grown to care about, what some people call the "kitchen-table issues": good public schools; help for the less fortunate; fair labor standards, practices, and pay; and environmental concerns. About the same time, I found myself becoming increasingly frustrated with the general public. I watched as citizens would spend thousands of their personal dollars on the arts, and yet would then help to elect a representative who made it clear that he or she intended to vote against arts funding. I watched as citizens would repeatedly fall victim to extremist rhetoric and fail to vote in their own best interests. I was especially frustrated with citizens who just didn't vote at all.

I discovered that *I* needed a government that was tuned into the issues that *I* cared about and that *I* needed to support the politicians who cared about these things as much as I did. Government wasn't as far removed from my life as I once thought it was. In fact, strangely enough, I realized that every item on my kitchen table actually had a government tie, and that I needed government to handle the issues I could not—clean water, clean air, and food for my family, for example.

It was at this point that I jumped in with both feet and became deeply involved with first one, and then several, presidential campaigns.

"You don't have to win to be right," I told my children when they saw my first candidate lose to his competition. "You have to continue to fight for what you believe in."

No matter the odds, I continued to help the candidates who shared my passions and that I believed would serve my family's best interests.

Life is overwhelming in our society today. We are full of worry about jobs, about health care for ourselves and our families, and about the well-being of our schools and teachers. It's good for us to think about these pressing issues, but we must also be careful to pay attention to our government and to those who aspire to act as our representatives. I once read that "Freedom exists only when the people take care of their government." Public policy affects each of us, each day. Each of us has the duty to speak up about the direction those policies take.

There is a well-known political motto: "Each one, teach one." I plan to continue to live up to this motto. And when my time comes, I hope to go out all used up!

The Lessons of Humility

Mary Fallin

humility: *n.* the state or quality of being humble; absence of pride or self-assertion*

I grew up in Tecumseh, Oklahoma, where both of my parents served terms as the city's mayor. Later, I attended Oklahoma State University, started a rewarding career, and married. Soon our daughter, Christina, arrived. It seemed to be a perfect picture: good childhood, carefree adolescence, happy entry into adulthood.

As a businesswoman and young mother, I became aware of a number of issues that had a direct impact on my life. Legislatures set tax rates; they pass laws; they even have a say in what the school curriculum will be. Their actions have a clear and immediate influence on families, business, and the quality of life. At times, I felt there were decisions being made at the State Capitol that were having a detrimental effect on the business I was managing.

So, in 1990, I ran for the Oklahoma State House of Representatives. And that's when I got a megadose of humility. I was in my midthirties when I first sought elective office. As anyone who has run a campaign will tell you, it's a humbling experience. Every candidate for office starts out expecting to be welcomed and acclaimed. After all, here we are, stepping up to serve our neighbors at the Capitol! It wasn't long before I learned that some people have different points of view, and a few just don't care for politics or politicians.

But overall, reception was positive. Most folks were glad to be asked for their votes. As the campaign got fully underway, I was able to juggle a job,

---

* "Humility," *New World Dictionary*, 2e.

a campaign, and a preschool daughter. I even had time to attend some charity events. It was at one of these that I met a lobbyist who asked if I was "the woman running for the legislature." I said I was, and he asked a few questions. Then he asked where I stood on the issue of abortion.

I told him I was pro-life.

"Well," he said, "you're young, and you might want to have more children. What would happen if you were to get pregnant during your campaign? You'd have to have an abortion, or no one would vote for you. You'd be ineffective pregnant."

I was stunned, but I quickly replied that if that happened, I would simply go ahead with the campaign and have my child.

"Well," the lobbyist said, "you need to rethink your position."

A few weeks later, I began to feel ill. I thought it was a touch of the flu. My doctor assured me my symptoms would pass—In six months! Unbeknownst to me, I was already pregnant when the lobbyist made his cynical inquiry. My child was due in late summer, during the interval between the primary and the November general election. How could I continue this campaign?

Abortion was not an option for me. I opposed it then, and I oppose it now. So I prayed and kept knocking on those doors. As primary election day approached, I was eight months along and definitely, visibly pregnant. It was interesting to see the reactions of voters as I rang their doorbells and presented them with my campaign brochure and my ever-expanding self as a candidate for the legislature. I was asked to step into many homes to rest my swollen feet and have much-needed refreshments.

I won the primary. My son, Price, arrived; and forty-five days later, I won the general election as the proud mother of a one-and-a-half-month-old baby boy and a three-year-old daughter. I was a state legislator!

I served two terms in the Oklahoma House of Representatives, and I had success in passing a number of bills that I thought were good for the state and for my district. As I neared the end of my second term, several people approached me to consider running for lieutenant governor. The incumbent lieutenant governor was stepping aside to run for governor. No Republican had ever been elected lieutenant governor in Oklahoma; neither had a woman. I decided to run; and, through a tough primary with a total of nine opponents, I was elected to Oklahoma's second-highest office. I had simultaneously set two historic precedents.

How could it get any better? If there's one thing I've learned, it's that such thoughts often occur during the calm before the storm.

I had always considered myself to be "in control" of many aspects of my life. I had worked for years climbing the ladder of success and was used to solving problems for myself and just about anyone who would ask. That was why I loved my new role as lieutenant governor of the State of Oklahoma. I was helping people and making things happen.

After my successful campaign for a second term as lieutenant governor in 1998, I took stock. Even though my life looked good from the outside— the highest-elected woman in office in Oklahoma, a beautiful family, nice salary and perks, awards and accolades—my life inside was falling apart.

In a three-year period, which peaked at the beginning of my reelection campaign, my mother became very ill, and my husband and I were battling many personal issues. Our relationship had become destructive, and finally we divorced. I lost most of my material possessions, including home and furniture. I received no financial help or child support after fourteen years of marriage. Mother became bedridden, her husband died, and I was left to care for her as a single mom with a job that required a great deal of time and energy. I didn't think I would make it. How could life be so good, then go so bad?

Why was this happening? I wasn't a bad person. I'm a Christian and a conservative; Christian public officials are not supposed to divorce! I was furious with what had happened to me, what people had done to me . . . what I had done to myself. That was when I came face-to-face with the humbling truth: I am not in control, especially of other people. I can certainly do my part as God would have me do, but He has given all of us free will to choose the direction of our lives, with God or apart from God. I can tell you that without God, life is difficult. But, thank goodness, years before I had started a deep search for God, and I knew Him.

I knew through faith that the Bible is true and that God's promises are real, that I could trust Him when I felt out of control. I had no choice but to rest in the comfort of knowing that God would take care of all my needs and all that concerned me.

He did.

My connection with God has never been broken. As times grew tougher, that connection strengthened. No matter how difficult things were, I had that anchor to hold me, to keep me turned into the wind and ride out the waves. Without it, I might have been lost; with it, I prevailed.

I replaced my home. I bought new furniture. I started a new life, as a mother and as a public official. I learned that faith does not mean simply expecting terrific things; it also requires accepting things that are far less than terrific. I learned that restoration is possible—of faith, of confidence, of hope. In the end, I discovered that, when bad things happen to good people, we can choose to either be pitiful or powerful and that power comes, ironically, when we turn complete control over to God.

And the most valuable lesson I learned through it all was this: humility is not subservience. It's not self-pity. It is knowing and accepting our place in life, which may not always be where we want to be but which is always, unfailingly, where God wishes us to be. He always knows what's best for us.

Humility brings a special kind of freedom. When I turned loose of those things I could not control—mostly things involving other people—I was released from much negativity. I was free to stop feeling responsible for the failings or problems of others. I could focus on the many positives in my life: my faith, my family, my friends, my career. As I phased out unhealthy relationships with others, I developed a healthier relationship with myself.

In 2002, I won a third term as lieutenant governor. Today my children are thriving, and I enjoy a level of happiness far beyond what I used to consider contentment; it's deeper and more satisfying because it has the added dimension of perspective. I am a blessed woman, with a life that is purpose-driven. I have forgiven, and I have been forgiven. And that is truly humbling.

Tea without Sympathy

Pam Fleischaker

"Boy, haahhdy. You must be in some kind of culture shock."

This greeting was often my "howdy-do" when I moved to Oklahoma City from Washington, D.C., in the early eighties.

It was an Okie version of a "glad-to-have-ya-but-look-out-honey" kind of shake 'n' smile. I'd been warned. But I wasn't yet armed.

I was a young political activist and organizer in Washington, working against the war in Vietnam, supporting public financing of elections, helping women run for public office, and, most importantly to me, advocating that abortion remain legal.

I believed then, and believe now, that a woman is not free and autonomous unless she is able to determine if and when she wants to become a mother.

I believed that the 1973 U.S. Supreme Court decision making abortion legal, *Roe v. Wade*, was an important, liberating moment for American women. My colleagues in Washington agreed and were as outspoken about it as I was.

From the early days of this decision, there were those who opposed it, but they were not the newly energized or elected women activists I knew. Most opponents of legalizing abortion also opposed contraception or even teaching young people about sexuality and birth control.

People who worked with women and families knew that before abortion had become legal, many women had abortions anyway. Placing themselves in the hands of disreputable doctors, these women were often physically and emotionally damaged. Worse, scores of women attempted to self-abort, introducing terrible infections into their wombs. Many died.

"Those days are gone!" cried advocates for women's rights as *Roe* became the law of the land.

208

Planned Parenthood, a national organization helping women with contraception and prenatal care, would now be able to include discussing abortion as a legal option to unintended pregnancy.

And so, armed with experience and enthusiasm, certainty, and a naive notion of how *everyone* talked about abortion rights, I moved to Oklahoma nearly a decade later. I intended to maintain my level of political activism, aggressively working, advocating, and fighting for these rights. Whatever it took, I'd do it.

Within a few weeks, I was hired by Planned Parenthood's national political group to lobby Oklahoma's then-U.S. Senator David Boren, hoping he would oppose a measure introduced in the U.S. Senate to overturn *Roe*.

I would organize—with mailings, phone calls, and meetings—some of Boren's key supporters in Oklahoma who also supported abortion rights. My job was to encourage influential people and as many of Boren's constituents as possible to contact him and tell him of their opposition to this measure, reminding him of their support for legalized abortion.

I knew it wouldn't be easy. Boren was one of a handful of swing votes in the U.S. Senate. He was a moderate, intelligent man who hadn't committed himself on this issue. Persuadable, in other words. He was a cautious man, careful not to take controversial positions, and abortion rights were rapidly becoming controversial. I knew that, if he had enough "cover" from constituents whom he knew and respected, he would feel better about voting against this bill.

I was soon into the deliciously thick world of grassroots organizing in Oklahoma. I made lists, wrote letters for mass mailings, and began "vistin'" with influential Boren supporters.

When I met with these allies, I kept in check my sometimes-too-aggressive manner; I toned down my feminist rhetoric; I minded my P's 'n' Q's and cleaned up my act for more careful Sooners. Still, I believed—as did my co-workers at Planned Parenthood—that nothing was more important to a woman's freedom than that abortion remain legal.

From its founding in 1937, Planned Parenthood in Oklahoma City was the much-loved charity of many of the city's doyennes. These women were often well educated, committed to helping the underserved, and were charitable, both in their attitudes and with their pocketbooks. Many understood that their daughters and their friends (if not, indeed, themselves) might be faced with an unwanted pregnancy.

And of course, there were terrible stories of girls impregnated by railing, drunk fathers; desperate pregnant girls attempting to self-abort; and babies having babies. Oklahoma had then (and has today) a high teen pregnancy and unwed pregnancy rate.

These women knew that, as enlightened, able citizens, they had a responsibility to help, and they did. For them, for many women and families, legal—and therefore, safe—abortion was a tremendous relief.

For many decades, Planned Parenthood enjoyed a reputation of not just being socially acceptable, but being an organization whose goals— preventing unwanted pregnancies—"we must all defend," as one of its founders said.

A lot of that goodwill had been passed down into the eighties, but as high society in the city became more traditional, so had its Planned Parenthood advocates. Still, *Roe* had been the law of the land for nearly ten years.

I thought we were all on the same page. But nothing could have prepared me for what I would learn in Oklahoma one hot, summer afternoon.

One of my first visits was to the president of the Planned Parenthood volunteer governing board, a pretty, bright-eyed, sixtyish woman I had only just met. She graciously invited me to her home for tea. The leader of the clinic's volunteer donors, a known supporter of Boren's, a presumed leader in the fight for abortion rights, she would certainly be glad to help out, I reasoned. This was a good place to start.

So on a typically hot and humid summer day in Oklahoma, Mrs. President and I sipped pale, sugary iced tea and munched on a few hard cookies in her air-conditioned sunroom in a very tony neighborhood in the city.

Her home was large; her china was beautiful; her nails were done but not painted. She was dressed in quiet good taste, expensively, carefully; while not formally dressed, she was dressed up, if you know what I mean.

Not being a total dummy, I had dressed nicely, too, and appropriately, I thought. Not like the radical I felt I really was, but professionally attired. More significantly, I had all my papers and talking points in order and thought I could hold my own. After trading "where you come from," "tell me about your family" stories, we got down to business.

I explained the project. I told her how I thought we, representing Planned Parenthood, might approach the senator. The first step, I said, would be a letter—approved and signed by her, Our Leader—to all Planned Parenthood supporters in our area, telling them of this threatening (I should have said "pesky") legislation; how, if it passed, it would provide terrible obstacles (I should have said "difficulties") to women and their reproductive freedom; and how we needed them to help us lobby (I should have said "visit with") Mr. Boren.

She nodded.

I brought out a draft of this suggested letter and showed it to her. At this point and rather briskly, she crossed her legs at the ankles, straightened her back, put on her glasses, and began reading.

When she finished the letter, she set it on the wrought-iron tea table, folded her glasses on top of it, and sat back in her chair. Something had gone wrong; she was not smiling at me. Had the air conditioning broken? I wondered, feeling the heat rise.

"Well, dear," she said, letting me know what she thought of my age (very young), my station (lower than hers), and my wisdom (none) in one downward sweeping glance.

"This is fine, except for a few little things."

Wide-eyed, I asked, "Yes?"

"I can't sign a letter as 'Mrs.' anything. I will sign it with my first name."

"Of course!" I replied with relief. "I certainly respect your independence! I know you don't want to be seen just as someone's wife, but as your Own Woman. I would never use 'Mrs. Anything!'"

"Oh, I don't mind 'Mrs.'" she corrected me. "But my husband knows Senator Boren *personally*, and I wouldn't want him to have any trouble over this, something that's just a pastime of mine. Please don't use his name, just mine."

Boy, was it hot in that sunroom! I felt a little light-headed and confused.

Wasn't she Planned Parenthood's chief? Yet this was just her pastime? Whatever work she was doing to keep abortion safe and legal was trivial, she was telling me, compared with her husband's important relationship with the senator. I was beginning to have a slight tingling feeling in my fingertips, but I managed to find my voice.

"Oh, sure, Mrs., um, Sue . . . , of course." Frantically, I made some notes on the page near the signature.

"Also," she added, "I'd rather we not use *this* word."

She wiggled her finger in the direction of the letter.

"What word?" I asked.

"You know, this word *abortion*' It's so, well, so, *harsh*. Couldn't we find another word?"

"Another word for abortion?" I asked. My forehead was hot, but my fingers were actually cold. "The U.S. Supreme Court used the word *abortion*; it's the accepted word for a medical procedure," I said. "I'm not sure what other word there is."

If the Planned Parenthood president isn't willing to speak the word *abortion* out loud, I realized, we had further to go than I could have ever imagined.

We finished our tea and I left. Outside it was hotter and hazier, and my car was sizzling in the heat. But at least my fingers had thawed.

I rewrote the letter, using some mangled construction of the phrase *termination of pregnancy* instead of *abortion*. I toned down my language, omitting anything too aggressive, passionate, or bold. In other words, I slowly tiptoed up to and around what was becoming the hottest issue of the era.

Eventually, Sue signed her name and we went forward.

Some time later, we slid back into using the word *abortion* in our mailings.

Ultimately, the project worked, or Senator Boren's conscience worked; whichever, he voted against the proposed amendment, and it failed.

I stayed around Planned Parenthood for a long time, as a lobbyist and in public affairs, then on the board of directors myself. Sue and I nodded politely toward one another over the years.

I still believe, thirty-two years later, that abortion should remain legal and safe. But the climate today in America is very different. This medical procedure has been cast in moral and political tones, and even reasonable people are afraid to defend it. Threats are made, clinics are bombed, doctors are intimidated, women are unable to make these decisions for themselves and their families. In fact, there are few reliable doctors in Oklahoma who will perform an abortion. The rest are frightened. Planned

Parenthood clinics in many cities do offer abortion as a legal option to unwanted pregnancy, but not in Oklahoma.

Now, three decades later, abortion may again become illegal; Planned Parenthood in Oklahoma is still helping women and is still tiptoeing around abortion rights.

I should have seen it coming that day I was given tea but not sympathy by a woman who claimed to be an advocate of legal abortion. While you wouldn't want to depend on her in the trenches, Sue understood better than I which way the wind was blowing for women in the eighties in the Heartland.

Creations

To Live Conventionally and to Paint Wildly

Jean Richardson

None of my grandparents had an education. Neither did my parents. They were unfortunately caught between wars, depression, and rural poverty; and, even though they were able and ambitious, they never managed to go to college. One of my grandfathers inherited a sizable ranch, but he had a large family. My other grandfather was a wheat farmer who owned his land but saw it blow away in the nineteen thirties. My grandmothers were hard-working, childbearing women of the pioneer type. They didn't complain but seldom had much beauty or joy in their lives. Church was the main activity outside of the endless toil of meals and laundry. Neither of my sets of grandparents had indoor plumbing or electricity when I was a child.

My father tried to get an education. He saved money to attend Cameron College in Lawton and made it through one year. The worst year of the dust bowl hit just as he started his sophomore year, and it became impossible for him to continue. At home his family was in desperate circumstances. The cattle had no pasture. Dust drifted over the barbed-wire fences that kept the stock near the dried-up tanks and windmills. Dad helped his father haul water for the family and the animals. Finally, the family left Oklahoma and, using what little money remained, rented some irrigated land in Texas. It was there that he met my mother.

My parents met at the worst time of the Depression. Dad landed a job on an oil rig, and my mother thought it was her dream come true that she had a man with a salary. As a ranch girl, she hated the uncertainty about rain and prices; she hated the debt and worry she had seen in her growing-up years. They married and set up housekeeping at Dodson, Texas, which was just across the Red River from Hollis, Oklahoma. Mother tells of sitting alone in their little house and watching tumbleweeds hour after hour. She said it was the loneliest time of her life.

My birth in February of 1940 was legendary in family tales, for it came in a blinding snowstorm. It was an epic journey to get from Dodson to the little hospital at Hollis.

The timing of my entrance into the world could have been better. My parents were pretty isolated and pretty broke, and war was breaking out in Europe. My dad got his draft notice when I was less than a year old.

It was never easy for me to understand how an artist came out of the background that I had. I guess I would have to say that one great influence was the time I had to myself. I lived a life in my own mind. I was an only child and only grandchild for six years. I had no playmates and was left to wander in the pasture or along the unpaved road by our house. My mother was home, but I mainly remember things I created in my imagination. This freedom was wonderful, and I ache to know that children of today may never have that same opportunity.

Before I learned to read, my mother read aloud to me. We never read a child's book but chose the books that my mother wanted to read. I remember lying beside her as she read aloud, with tears flowing down her face, *The Yearling* by Margery Rawlings. We read Edna Ferber's *So Big* and *Cimarron*. This was all before I was six. Our lifeline was the library.

Once I could read, I used the library for myself. Each patron could have a maximum of ten books per week. I always checked out the limit and read every one. This went on for all my years of childhood.

In addition to the world of reading, I was soon introduced to another civic institution, the museum. When I was seven years old, I was enrolled in a child's art class at the Witte Museum in San Antonio. Our class had a live model wearing a grass skirt. We children painted on large sheets of manila paper with tempera paints. My life was never the same. I have painted ever since. In my childhood the biggest problem was getting art supplies. My parents had no idea what to buy, and they were not too happy with the mess art made in the house. They were a lot more thrilled at other things that I accomplished, such as memorizing the sixty-six books of the Bible, or getting straight As on my report card. But I pleased myself with my painting. I never wanted to do anything else. I was an artist.

Painting was the constant in my life. In the elementary-school years, I drew and painted with a passion and remember frustration only with finding materials. I used shirt cardboards, scraps of wood, and reams of paper. Tempera paints were my favorite, but I always ran out of white and yellow first and had to make do with the rest of the set until the next birthday or Christmas. I don't fault my parents for not being more generous with art supplies because my needs were a bottomless pit.

When I finally met a real artist in high school, I had come to have standards that were hard to meet. Miss Skinner was not exactly what a teenage girl would dream to be like. "Spinsterish" is what we used to call a woman of her type. How I would love to get to know her now that I can appreciate what her life must have been like. She was a watercolorist of the abstract John Marin school, but we never thought about what *she* did. Our art classes were a vibrant, active hive of artist endeavor. At last my problem of getting my hands on materials was solved. Miss Skinner let me have as much paper and paint as I wished.

By my teen years, I began to be noticed as an artist. High school competitions and student exhibitions gave me a place to star. I also did pen-and-ink sketches for the newspaper, designed sets for plays, and always decorated for the dances. My interests expanded to boys and clothes, but I definitely was first and foremost an artist.

I had long been an artist in my mind by the time I arrived on campus to study for a bachelor of fine arts degree at Wesleyan College. There I met not only a wider field intellectually, but I was thrown in with a lot of other artists. Now I had faculty critiques and peers looking over my work in the studio. It was exciting! In my college years I turned in a required ten drawings a week of hands and feet. I worked out on location some part of every week and put in three hours daily in the painting studio as well.

I could pick out the art students on campus. They didn't look like everybody else. They wore all black and smoked cigarettes. In that innocent world before sex and drugs and at the very beginning of rock and roll, I had to decide whether to live the "rebel artist's" lifestyle. Should I leave the boonies behind and head for Greenwich Village and the hip scene?

When I looked around me I thought my work was better than that of my more bohemian classmates. In fact, I could not see any correlation between looking or acting like an artist and the quality of art. Somewhere along in those college years I chose my path—right or wrong—to live conventionally and to paint wildly.

Although I had not lived in my parents' home since I had started college, I never had the experience of having an apartment or being on my own until I married upon graduation. I then taught art in a big city high school for a while before the inevitable happened. Girls today have no idea what reliable birth control means for planning a future. I loved my babies, but they were my fate rather than my choice. Now I was an adult in every sense of that word.

Before and after the babies came, I painted in hallways; on porches; in attics, basements, and dining rooms. I taught classes at the museum and found a little space there for some of my larger work. I used Masonite when I could not afford canvas. My double role became second nature.

When I consider my life story, I suppose the most unique part was that, for my generation, there was little expectation that a woman could have a career in art (or anything else for that matter) and have children as well. The fact that I did reasonably well at both things was an accomplishment for that day and time. I did not set out to be a pioneer in "having it all." I just refused to give up my art when I had a family.

In retrospect, maybe the maturing and discipline that come with parenting gave me qualities that were necessary to my art. You see, I think an artist has to be a practical person—she can't be just a dreamer. An artist must wield a brush and handle the pigments without making mud of the color or leaving a composition hanging. You must learn your craft; and then, and only then, can attention be given to what you have to say in your art. The "slogging through" part of being a parent coincided with the mastering of the craft in my painting. The story was written as we went along. There were no guidebooks.

When an artist becomes a mother, a lot of things change and some doors forever close. I no longer considered moving to Paris to study at the Sorbonne or making the art scene in New York. People began to look at me differently. They did not see an artist; they saw a mother. But I had no intention of giving up being an artist, and I did not. My painting continued. I was grateful for my gift and felt responsible for its use.

Some of my youthful ambitions were tempered by motherhood. In the long run, however, the years I spent painting at home were incredibly important. The isolation helped me develop a style of my own without any outside influences. Working in the midst of distractions gave me good habits. I learned to inhabit my own space without needing motivation or approval.

The long, hard, slow work of raising a child is exactly the long, hard, slow path of becoming a painter. There are no shortcuts. Patience and acceptance of limitations are needed for both tasks.

My dual life as an artist and a mother seems the most natural thing in the world to me. I never had a second thought about either role. My life has had some sadness, and it has not always been easy, but to give up being a mother or to abandon my art was forever out of the question.

As I have aged, the painting has grown easier; the parenting has not. The children are successful adults but they still call me about their life crises. My skills as a painter are honed and second nature by now; being a parent is still uncharted territory.

My children were pioneers in their own right, living with a mother like me, and, if asked, they might provide the following observations for those who find themselves in similar circumstances:

- When your mother is an artist, you grow up accustomed to having Mother home; but she is not really there. She says, "Uh-huh" or "Mmmmm," a lot. She is always busy painting.
- When your mother is an artist, you get forgotten a lot. She gets so lost in what she is doing that she forgets about Girl Scouts or the carpool.
- When your mother is an artist, things are very messy near where she paints. There are scraps of canvas, scattered sketches, paints and brushes spread everywhere. There are drips of paint on the floor. There are paintings leaning against all the walls, and sometimes you cannot walk across the room.
- When your mother is an artist, you should never, never put your hand in her purse. She has razor blades and mat knives in there.
- Your mother is never dressed like all the other mothers. If you forget your math book and she has to bring it to school, she looks different from all the other mothers. Her hands are not dirty; they just have paint on them. There are spots all over her shoes. She sometimes forgets that she has on her apron. It has grayish streaks across her stomach.

- When your mother is an artist, your house sometimes has funny smells. She sprays things; then she opens the doors and fans the air. Even the neighbors notice the woman who opens the doors several times a day and mysteriously waves and fans the air. Everyone on your street thinks you are weird.
- When your mother is an artist, she never leaves you with a cool sitter or goes to an office so you may watch TV. She is always there.
- When your mother is an artist, you have to go to a lot of art shows. You have to look cute, stand there, and make nice because it is important to her. Art shows last about three hours.
- Museums take a really, really long time when your mother is an artist. She is never satisfied to just look. She lectures about every picture in the place.
- When your mother is an artist, you spend a lot of time waiting in the car while she does a sketch of something. By age five or six, you have been to many interesting places such as pool halls, courthouses, and powwows. An artist is always looking for new inspiration.
- When your mother is an artist, school projects are easy. She already has everything you might need to make a poster, or build a replica of the human brain, or papier-mâché a pig or a volcano, or build your science project. She has huge sheets of cardboard at the ready. She is the only mother who has a power saw *and* a propane torch.
- Your mother lets children use every material except oil paint, which gets everywhere, or India ink, which won't come out.
- When your mother is an artist, you get to paint anytime you want, but it is no big deal to you. Your painting is never as good as hers even if she tries to say so.
- When your mother is an artist, your artwork at school looks different from that of all the other children. She has drilled it into you to fill every inch of the paper.
- When your mother is an artist, there are embarrassing books around your house. It is hard to explain to your friends why people have very few clothes on in the art books at home. The bathrooms at your house have some racy artwork. When new friends come over, they giggle.
- When your mother is an artist, dinner is sometimes late. She may have forgotten to go to the grocery store. If there is nothing to eat

except rice, she tells you this breakfast is educational. Most children in the world have only rice for breakfast, she says.

- When your mother is an artist, you don't get to bake cookies after school. You *do* get the greatest Halloween costumes. When it's your turn to decorate for homecoming float, it is great that your mother is an artist.
- When your mother is an artist, your telephone has orange fingerprints on it.
- When your mother is an artist, every person you meet asks you if you are artistic too. Even if you are, you say no.
- When your mother is an artist, she worries when it is time for braces on your teeth or when school tuition is due. She never knows how much money she will have. You learn that a regular career might have its good points. On the other hand, she doesn't have to wear panty hose or have performance reviews. She may go on vacation whenever she feels like it. Wait, her life *is* a vacation.
- When you tell people that your mother is an artist, they *always* say, "Oh, my aunt (or cousin or grandmother) is an artist." Then when they see her paintings they say, "Oh, your mother is a *real* artist."
- When your mother is an artist, you get to have the best artwork in your college dorm. If your friends do not like abstract work, you feel sorry for them. If, however, they are impressed, you know they have good taste.
- When your mother is an artist, you always have someone to help you choose the paint for your apartment. She doesn't like things that match.
- When your mother is an artist, you have some special advantages because you live with a person who loves what she does every day. There is a little neglect as well. Children of an artist are very self-reliant. Somehow a regular paycheck and a two-week vacation are never as appealing as they might otherwise have been.
- When your mother is an artist, she expects you to be as sure as she is that you will find the right thing to do with your life. She never had to figure out what to do with hers because she always knew.

Becoming Maria Tallchief

Maria Tallchief Paschen

I was born in Fairfax, Oklahoma, to an Osage Indian father and a Scots-Irish mother. Every summer when I was a little girl, we would go to Manitou Springs, Colorado. My father liked to play golf and thought summers were too hot in Oklahoma (this was before air conditioning). It was in the basement of the Broadmoor Hotel that I had my first dancing lesson. I was three-and-a-half years old.

Back home in Fairfax, there was an itinerant woman from Tulsa who came to town. Her name was Mrs. Sabin. She knew absolutely nothing about ballet, but she told my mother, "Now, Mrs. Tallchief, you are the society leader of Fairfax and your daughters should learn to dance." Mind you, my father was a drunkard who never worked a day in his life. Mother, however, was a determined pioneer woman who wanted more for her children. So my younger sister and I started studying dancing.

Mrs. Sabin was a nice lady; but, as I've said, she knew nothing about ballet. Before I had any training at the barre, she said to my mother, "You have to go and buy toe shoes for her." My mother would buy my toe shoes, of all things, two sizes too big so she wouldn't have to buy another pair for a few years. I have pictures of me with tears in my eyes, up on my toes at the age of four. Oh, how I ended up not having the worst toes in the world, I don't know. But I never questioned my mother. Whatever she said to do, I did.

We moved to Los Angeles when I was seven, where Mother had relatives in nearby Glendale and Daddy could play golf year-round. Mother asked the grocer and the staff of the local drugstore if they knew of a good dance teacher. They recommended Ernest Belcher. The first thing Mr. Belcher did was to look at me and say, "Get that girl off her toes; throw those shoes away immediately! She has to start learning the basics of classical ballet or she'll know nothing." And that's the way my formal training began, when I was seven.

I studied with Mr. Belcher for five years. When I was twelve, one of the other ballet mothers told Mother about a world-famous teacher, Madame Bronislava Nijinska, who had moved to California. Mother immediately took my sister and me over to her; when I met Madame Nijinska, I knew that dancing was what I wanted to do. She was the personification of ballet. She had beautiful green eyes. She told us, "You must be a ballerina not only in class. You must *live* it. When you are waiting for the bus, you are a ballerina. Even when you're asleep, you're a ballerina."

I continued to study ballet for five more years with Madame Nijinska and other teachers, like David Lichine and Madame Slavenska. When I was around fourteen or fifteen, Serge Denham, the head of Ballet Russe de Monte Carlo, saw me in class and said, "One day I would like her to join the Ballet Russe de Monte Carlo." At the time, I was a straight-A student at Beverly Hills High; and, in addition to dancing, I played the piano and was in a string quartet at the University of California, Los Angeles (UCLA). Madame Nijinska gave a performance at the Hollywood Bowl, and one of the ballets was Chopin's *Concerto*, which, coincidentally, I was playing on the piano at the same time. Syd Charisse and I were given the leading roles; it was very, very difficult, but it was an incredible opportunity.

When I graduated from high school, I planned to attend UCLA. I loved school, and was being rushed by sororities. But Daddy sat me down and said, "Now, look, I've paid all your life for your education, piano, and dance. Now you have to get a job." It never occurred to me to say, "But, Daddy, you've never worked a day in your life." So I went out to MGM and applied. I was in the chorus of *Presenting Lily Mars* with Judy Garland. I came home the day shooting ended, and Mother said, "Quick. We're going out to buy you a bag. You're leaving for New York City. You're going to see Mr. Denham at the Ballet Russe de Monte Carlo." I got a huge Fortnighter bag and left for New York.

I got lost trying to find Mr. Denham's office. When I finally arrived, I said, "Well, Mr. Denham, here I am."

"Who are you?" he said.

"I'm Betty Marie Tallchief," I said.

"I don't know you," he said. "I don't remember you at all."

"Oh, you saw me in . . . ," I reminded him.

He said, "We don't have any room."

I didn't know what to do. I was desperate and crying. The next day, a call suddenly came. "Pack your bags," I was told. "You're leaving for Canada. Ballet Russe is going and none of the Russians have passports." So I lugged my big Fortnighter to the train that night. I couldn't believe it. There I was, surrounded by Frederick Franklin and all the famous dancers. It was just unbelievable. And that's how I started my career with the Ballet Russe de Monte Carlo.

Later, it was Agnes de Mille who suggested I change my name. She was choreographing *Rodeo* at the time, and she gave me a small part.

She said, "You know, there's already one Betty in the Ballet Russe. Why don't you use your middle name, change it from Marie to Maria, and become Maria Tallchief?"

I called my mother and asked if that was all right. She said it was.

And so, Betty Marie Tallchief—a half-Osage, half Scots-Irish little girl from Oklahoma—became Maria Tallchief. I am so proud of my heritage, and I love Oklahoma, especially Fairfax, which is a very, very dear spot to me, where I still have many relatives.

I was blessed to have a mother determined to expose her children to the arts. It's so important for all children to be exposed to the arts, whether it's piano, dance, painting, or what have you. It helps them to dream. And once there is a dream to follow, one must find a good teacher, listen to what that teacher has to say, and work very hard.

That was how this little half-Osage, half Scots-Irish girl from Fairfax, Oklahoma, became a ballerina.

"Miss D" and My Piano

Betty Price

The arts have been a driving force in my life. They are my passion. They have strengthened me in times of personal tragedy, given me fulfillment, and provided me with a challenging and exciting career in public service. As executive director of the Oklahoma Arts Council, I have worked with Oklahoma governors, legislators, and dedicated individuals who believe as I do—that the arts are vital to the lives of every citizen, and especially to the lives of our most precious asset, our children.

I have traveled across Oklahoma in blizzards and heat waves to attend events where tax dollars for the arts were used, and I have never been disappointed. My personal goals and those of the Arts Council focus on providing matching grants that make outstanding arts and arts education programs happen in Oklahoma's largest cities and smallest rural communities.

Recently, I visited an elementary school arts festival. I met Claude Monet and Georgia O'Keefe, slightly shorter than I imagined, but very willing to share their life stories with me. I viewed a stunning exhibit of student art, watched a fifth-grade boy dance like a pro, and heard a petite second-grader belt out a song from *Annie*. She was poised and on-key. These children and their dedicated teachers brought tears to my eyes and renewed my vow to keep art and music in our schools for the sake of every child.

That visit took me back to my own childhood.

Born in Booneville, Arkansas, I was fortunate that the adults surrounding me believed the arts were essential to children. My upbringing included music, dance, and art. At age four, I was tap dancing solo on the stage of a theatre in El Paso, Texas, but my mother's dream that I might be the next Shirley Temple was not to be realized. However, I did become proficient in counting, so the experience wasn't totally wasted!

A piano was our family's prized possession and survived the move from El Paso to Muskogee, Oklahoma, when I was five. With a tight family budget, my parents sacrificed so their three children could have piano lessons with Muskogee's highly respected Miss Mary deGraffenreid, a spinster who was classically trained in piano, organ, and violin. To my parents, music was as essential to our education as were arithmetic and writing. "Miss D," as we secretly called her, was my taskmaster in piano and organ for ten years. She expected more of me than even my parents did. I feared her, but her expectations for and influence on me and my siblings are still present in our lives.

An avid sportsman, my dad loved the great outdoors, people, books, and politics. Every Sunday afternoon after church, my dad put us in the car, lit a cigar, and drove us into the country to view the beautiful landscape. I hated the cigar, but my eye was developing as an artist. The color and texture in the fields, mountains, and sky of eastern Oklahoma fascinated me.

Members of our family had many interests in common and our dinner table became a sounding board for our views, especially political. I challenged Dad often. I seldom won, but I have never wavered from my interest in politics. I have the greatest respect for people willing to serve in public office, and for the office itself, which enables leaders to make change for the good of individuals and society.

It was a given that after graduating from Muskogee Central High, I would enroll at Northeastern State University and, upon graduation, would begin a career as a public school music teacher. Fulfilling my parents' dream, I eventually taught in the Norman, Oklahoma, public school system and had my first opportunity to work with children in a real classroom. I was determined to bring them the joy and stimulation the arts had offered me, and I passionately believed that the arts would change their lives forever as they had mine.

Soon my husband, Norris, went into real estate, I started teaching in the Mid-Del schools, and we had children of our own. I taught piano and began painting for galleries as Lisa Ann, John Randall ("Randy"), and George Campbell ("Skip") were growing up. Many a day they went off to school with oil paint on their socks and undies because the laundry room was also my studio. Lisa played piano, Randy sang, Skip played drums, and Norris paid the bills. Life was good.

Early on, the children learned to tote campaign signs as our neighbor, attorney John Garrett ran for, and was later elected to, the state senate. He and his wife, Hazel, asked me to work for him at the Capitol, opening a door that brought my interest in education, politics, and art into perfect alignment for a career in public service.

The value of the arts must never be underestimated. A year after I began my work with the Oklahoma Arts Council, our family experienced the loss of our first son, Randy, who was injured in a car-motorcycle accident. I immersed myself in my work and my painting, which helped me survive the most tragic time of my life. Several years later, when our house burned, we realized that tangibles, other than baby pictures and home movies, could be replaced. And, with the help of family and friends, life and work went on.

The struggle to strengthen the arts in Oklahoma while competing for tax dollars is a daunting task, but the satisfaction of knowing we are building a cultural legacy for our children is what drives me. The enriching relationships formed with visionary council members, staff, and community arts leaders are especially rewarding. The opportunity for me to direct commissions of murals, art, and sculpture for the Capitol is enabling and meaningful beyond description.

The arts pay tribute to Oklahoma's history; our heroes and heroines come alive through the work of great artists. These role models surround the schoolchildren who visit the Capitol and learn about the five little girls of Indian heritage who became prima ballerinas, a quiet little Apache boy who became a great sculptor, and others who have achieved international fame.

Fulfillment in my work as a public servant is knowing that a future Maria Tallchief or Allan Houser could be that second-grader gazing for the first time at the splendor of Oklahoma art and artists. Government and the arts have given me the privilege of realizing my own childhood dreams.

Looking Back

Carolyn Hart

I was a child during World War II. Even as a small child, I understood that newspapers mattered in daily life, that they were the source of important information. The bigger and blacker the headlines, the more important the story. From that realization, it was an easy step to wanting to be a newspaper reporter when I grew up.

I worked on the student newspaper, *The Chief Justice,* at Taft Junior High School in Oklahoma City. I worked on *The Classen Life* at Classen High School in Oklahoma City. I majored in journalism at the University of Oklahoma. I was sure I would be the next Maggie Higgins, the famous correspondent for the *New York Herald Tribune.* Then I met a young law student. We married and I worked on the *Norman Transcript,* and later in public relations at the university, while he was in school. After his graduation and after we started a family, I decided not to go back to work on a newspaper.

But I missed writing. That was the first time I ever thought about writing fiction. I subscribed to *The Writer* magazine. Writing competitions were listed on a back page. Dodd, Mead and *Calling All Girls* magazine offered publication and a $1,000 prize for a mystery for girls aged eight to twelve. I grew up reading Nancy Drew. I loved Agatha Christie and Mary Roberts Rinehart. I decided to write a mystery for girls. *The Secret of the Cellars* won the contest and was published in 1964. My thirty-sixth novel, *Murder Walks the Plank,* was published in 2004. The thirty-seventh book, *Death of the Party,* was published in 2005 and my thirty-eighth, *Dead Days of Summer,* was published in 2006. The thirty-ninth, *Set Sail for Murder,* and fortieth, *Ghost at Work,* will be published in 2008. And, of course, I've just started a new book. . . .

So many books. The beginning went well. I sold two children's mysteries, three young-adult novels, and an adult suspense novel. That sounds like an easy coast to success. But the numbers do not tell of the years after these publications when I wrote book after book that did not sell. Once I wrote seven books in seven years and not a single one sold at that time.

Year after year, I wrote and failed. Anyone with sense would have realized the quest was doomed to failure. The truth, of course, is that writers are compelled to write. We write for readers, but, whether we are published or not, we must write.

By the spring of 1985, I felt I'd reached the end of the road as a writer. But, I suppose with hope—or desperation—springing eternal, I decided to try one more time. I decided to write the kind of book I loved reading, an old-fashioned mystery with likable characters. In fact, since I had no expectations that the book would sell, I ignored all the suggestions about what editors were looking for or what the market sought. The common wisdom then was that no editor was interested in a traditional mystery with a female sleuth set in America. Since no one was interested in a mystery but I love mysteries, I decided to write a mystery that was all about mysteries. I set the book in a mystery bookstore, and that way I could share with readers wonderful mysteries of both past and present.

I wrote *Death on Demand* in six weeks in the summer of 1985 and sent it off without any hope. After all, my previous seven books had been rejected. When I received word that the book had sold, I was astonished, yet still not very hopeful of my future as a writer. I'd written many books, seen them published, and watched them disappear without notice.

This time my luck turned. As it happened, I sent in that manuscript just as mystery publishing was being transformed. Previously, American publishers had primarily been interested in two kinds of books, the hard-boiled private eye book written by American men with male protagonists and the traditional mystery written by dead English ladies. The success of the first books written by American women that featured women private detectives persuaded American publishers that readers were interested in books by and about American women. That opened the door to writers such as myself.

I'm not sure of the moral of this story. If the attitude of publishing had not changed, *Death on Demand* would not have sold. Yet *Death on Demand* and the subsequent books in the series have now sold more than 2 million copies. It would have been the same book, sold or unsold. I know that I owe the sale of the book to the change in publishing. Yet I also owe the sale to the fact that I kept on writing, that I failed and failed and yet kept trying.

Why did I continue to write? One factor might be the reality of gender, particularly at that time. As a woman, I was accustomed to receiving less pay for the same work as men. I had no sense of entitlement. Women are exhorted to rail against discrimination and rightly so, yet I think women have faced the barriers and been steeled to try harder. That means we hold the philosophy "Don't give up. Don't ever give up." We never expect the path to be easy.

I had to write to be fulfilled, but I also believe it was the recognition that barriers were there to be surmounted that helped me continue.

I taught writing for a period; and, if I ever shared one helpful precept with students, I think it would be "You cannot succeed unless you are willing to fail." Whatever it is we want in life, if we want it with our hearts and souls, then we have to be willing to fail. Sometimes I fear that our culture is so obsessed with success, with winning, with climbing to the pinnacle that we do not understand or discuss or accept that most effort requires struggle, that sometimes even our best efforts will fail, that failure can be the next rung up to success.

Every book—and for those who do not write but attempt to achieve other dreams, every dream—seems a mountain too tall to climb. Any grand hope or dream or objective will bring moments when the task seems beyond us. We aren't good enough or clever enough or smart enough. But if we have a dream, our hearts know the way if we follow them. And when we lose out, when the door slams shut, we simply pick ourselves up and try another time.

I believe this. I believe that we have to follow the precept we were taught as children of the plains: "Keep on keeping on."

I have also learned through my many years as a writer that it is best to:

- Be kind. Kindness begets kindness. Those who are angry or jealous or mean-spirited may not respond to kindness, but most people— if you give them a chance, if you look into their eyes and hearts and offer your own—will smile if you smile at them. If you help others, they will help you. I've known many generous writers and editors and agents, booksellers and librarians and cherished readers. I have smiled at them, and they have smiled in return.

- Make it as perfect as you can. I am fairly disorganized: my office has the ragged appearance of a bird's nest; I don't worry if my clothes aren't fashionable, but I work at my books with the persistence of cat stalking its prey. I write and rewrite, I polish, I smooth. I make mistakes but I have always, every time, given my best effort.

- Care passionately about what you do. If you care, others will care. Enthusiasm is contagious. I care about mysteries. I think they are morally instructive and socially important, and I want the world to share my joy in books that celebrate goodness.

- Always set the bar higher for your next project. I attempt to make every book better than the last. When I wrote *Letter from Home*, my Oklahoma book, it was a departure from the kind of book I usually write. It was a risk, and I wasn't at all certain I could achieve my goal. Now I feel that it is perhaps the best book I will ever write. Yet I have an idea for still another different book; and, one of these days, I will try it.

- Remember that the joy is in the doing. I've always loved Rudyard Kipling's poem "When Earth's Last Picture Is Painted" and the final stanza in which he extols the artist working for the joy of the work. Once a book is done, I never look at it again unless I need to remind myself of information about previous characters. So it isn't the final product that satisfies. It is the creation, the effort, the thought, the craft.

- Heed the advice in the old Protestant hymn: "Work for the night is coming." Our work—whatever it is, whether maintaining a home or drafting a will or writing a book—gives meaning and purpose and joy to our lives. The days pass swiftly, and soon we shall work no more.

As I near the end of a career, I remember as a child taking the bus to the library in downtown Oklahoma City and my feeling of delight as I came home with an armful of books, ready to embark on faraway journeys and adventures. Now I have my own bookcase full of my books and the sense of delight remains that I was privileged to share adventures with so many readers.

– 30 –*

---

* Editors' note: -30- is the symbol used by journalists to signal the end of copy.

Education

Strength of a Tall Oak Tree

Sandy Garrett

"Tall oaks from little acorns grow!"—the slogan of Oklahoma's Great Expectations program—is, in a nutshell, the core belief of all teachers. We believe we can instill in children knowledge and skills and motivate, inspire, and challenge them to achieve excellence in their lives. Many teachers have motivated, inspired, and challenged me to become the woman I am today. But my first teachers were my parents.

My family members were active in politics and public service throughout my life. When I was born, my father was a state legislator from Adair County. This was during the time when the legislature met every other year. Since I was fortunate enough to have a stay-at-home mom, we were able to spend more time together as a family by moving to Oklahoma City for every legislative session.

So one year I would attend school in Stilwell in eastern Oklahoma, and the next year I'd be at Dewey Elementary School near the State Capitol. The two experiences could not have been more dissimilar: one school small and rural, the other large and urban. Here began my understanding of the Oklahoma educational experience. In Stilwell, I was free to ride my bike and roam the woods; in Oklahoma City, I walked on concrete sidewalks and made friends with city kids.

In Stilwell Dad drove a black Chevrolet to work each day and came home each evening to a hot meal on the table in a white frame house near the edge of town. My mother's life's work was at home, making our clothes, taking care of us, being ready with cookies and milk after school. It was kind of like *Ozzie and Harriet,* except in our case, Dad actually worked for a living!

Whether in Stilwell or Oklahoma City, there were dinner conversations and bedtime stories. My sister, brother, and I played outside with the neighbors, fought with each other, loved our parents, and competed for their attention. We did all the things brothers and sisters did then and that I hope they still do.

In the years spent in Oklahoma City, we lived near the Capitol because my mother did not drive. I walked to Dewey Elementary each day and did so feeling secure in the quiet neighborhood. Oklahoma City has changed a lot since then, but so has Stilwell.

When in Stilwell, I rode the bus to school. One of my most profound memories of riding the bus was on the first day of third grade, when I realized that my neighbor, "Charlie," didn't get on the bus that morning. I suddenly realized that in all the years I had known him (I had attended Sunday school with him almost every week), I had never ridden the bus to school with him. My mom explained that Charlie was different: he was mentally retarded and so he could not attend school with regular kids. Still today, I think of that every time a special education issue comes up. I never went to school with Charlie because it wasn't until 1975 that the door to public schools was opened for every child.

Like most young women in the 1950s and 1960s, when it came time to decide what to do after high school, there were basically three choices: homemaker, teacher, or nurse. I chose to become a teacher. I also became a wife and mother. And, having grown up in a politically active family, as an adult I became interested in public service and in state and local government. But it wasn't my role as mother, my job as a teacher, or my support of candidates and issues that prompted me to launch a campaign in 1990 for state superintendent of public instruction, a statewide office that had never been held by a woman. It was because of a big bird.

Let me explain.

Some say there are just two ways to get to the top of an oak tree: climb the tree or sit on an acorn and wait. But in my experience, there are actually three ways to get to the top of an oak tree.

1. If you climb the tree: You go step by step up the professional ladder, paying your dues along the way, working hard, and accomplishing goals you have set.

    As a first-grade teacher in Muskogee County, I focused on reading and inspiring poor children to dream beyond their means.

I remember what a shock it was to realize there were children in my class who came to school each day hungry or went home to an empty house. I climbed my tree: I did the best I could to give all of my students the skills they needed to succeed, I worked with other teachers, and I became active at the negotiating table. I was then promoted to coordinator for gifted programs at my school.

The next limb on that tree was to join the State Department of Education. There, I developed my expertise in rural schools and in using new technologies for distance learning. I worked with educators, administrators, telephone and fiber-optic experts, and many others to build a fiber-optic network so remote schools in the Panhandle could share teachers.

2. If you sit on an acorn: You have a great idea or proposal, you develop that idea, you gather people around you who believe in it, and you pursue it with all your might.

My acorn was using technology for distance learning and sharing limited resources among schools. It was apparent that the high-tech tree was really starting to grow! So, I bought one of the first personal computers; fortunately, it came with a carrying case. I lugged that forty-pound plastic box from home to work and back home again, developing and promoting our distance-learning projects. I traveled statewide, pitching the wonders of satellite downlinks and fiber optics—and, in the mid-1980s, they were still wonders. Finally, with the help of legislators, we obtained grants for funding this cutting-edge project. The development in the Panhandle was precedent-setting as the largest landmass in America at that time to connect schools via fiber optics in order to share educational resources. My focus was to bring more opportunities to small towns like the one in which I was raised. The project received state and national attention, and my tree grew more and more limbs and shiny new leaves.

3. If you get to know a really big bird: Even while you are climbing your tree and/or sitting on your acorn, there's a way to learn more and climb faster.

My big bird was Governor Henry Bellmon. In 1988, the work we had done with schools in the Panhandle came to our governor's attention at a time when he was searching for a cabinet secretary of education. It was of no real concern to him that I was a Democrat and he was a Republican. It didn't bother me either. Our working relationship was excellent: I not only admired him, I also learned a great deal from this tenured statesman.

Not long after I was hired, Governor Bellmon called a special session of the legislature to address a crisis in education: in particular, low teacher pay and lagging student achievement. Nine months later (which I don't think is a coincidence), the Education Reform Act of 1990 was born. And maybe it is also not coincidence that a "good old girls' club" came together to hammer out this legislation: Representative Carolyn Thompson (now Taylor), Senators Berniece Shedrick and Penny Williams, and me. Because I worked closely with Governor Bellmon and legislators on this landmark legislation and knew major changes would be needed at the State Department of Education to implement it, I was encouraged to run for the office of state superintendent of public instruction.

The campaign was difficult from the start, especially for someone, particularly a woman, who had never run for public office, nor aspired to do so. It was difficult in those days because people weren't in the habit of writing checks to a woman in a statewide race, especially for a position a woman had never held. The ones who did write those checks probably looked at it as a risky bet.

My primary opponent was a man with many years of experience at the State Department of Education working closely with school superintendents and principals. Even though women compose about two-thirds of the public-school workforce, almost all of the school leaders at the time were men. Still, in 1990, Oklahomans were willing to say good-bye to the "good old boys" and we won! In January 1991, I was inaugurated as the first woman state superintendent of public instruction. Admittedly, it has not been an easy job, but the experience has been worth it.

Personally, my greatest accomplishment has been having the privilege to raise a healthy, responsible young man, my son, Chuck Garrett. After all, in the words of Jacqueline Kennedy Onassis, "If you bungle raising your children, I don't think whatever else you do matters very much."

Professionally, I have been proud to serve the state of Oklahoma. As a classroom teacher, I was able to educate dozens of children each year; and, as state superintendent, I am able to advocate for thousands of children every day. I hope I have also served as an example to women that nothing is impossible if you tap into the strength and endurance of the tall oak tree.

How Quickly a Lifetime Passes

Lou Kerr

I have a friend who talks about the "magic of why": Why are the stars so bright? Why don't we go see a movie tonight? But I prefer the "magic of when." It makes me think of when I was a young girl. Trotting off to a school that was only a block away from our family home. Enjoying the fall days and the excitement of meeting new friends and seeing old ones. It seemed like a simpler time. When I was young, education and optimism abounded. The future was bright, and everything was possible.

I remember once when the cold days of winter caused our school to be closed; the north wind blew so furiously you were not sure the old house you lived in would be able to keep you safe and secure. You were a little scared until you looked around you and saw your older siblings listening to the soft sounds of your mother's voice reading about a black horse and a brave young hero. The fire was warm, and you somehow knew you were as happy as you would ever be, and the reading continued. If Mom got tired of reading, you knew you could pick up the book and continue the extraordinary journey you had been introduced to through books.

During the "magic of when" days, it seemed a safe time. There were no locks on the doors, and you knew your neighbors and their children, whom you looked forward to playing with when you could go outside to play. You were always outdoors. There was no television, only the radio where you would gather around each evening to hear the wonderful stories that sparked your imagination. The dinner table was where the events of the day were discussed and the judgments and punishment for poor choices were decided on.

The "magic of when" seemed a reasonable, optimistic time. There were no bars on the windows of our schools, and the only police on the school grounds were the junior police escorting us across a busy street or carrying the American flag to assemblies. Teachers inspired, like my first-grade teacher Miss Horn, who taught me to love reading.

During the "magic of when," the teacher taught. My third-grade teacher, Mrs. Hedrick, taught the most beautiful handwriting and great math skills. Mrs. Richter taught us about music, and we learned to appreciate every instrument in an orchestra. We learned about the woodwind section, the string section, the brass section, and the percussion section. We learned to listen for the sounds each section made; and through her inspiration, I grew into a lover of symphony music.

We learned to appreciate art from Miss Cornett. Miss Cornett was an inspiration to all her students even to those of us who had absolutely no artistic talent. But through her teaching, we learned to recognize the beauty of most art disciplines, including most of the classics. Books were once again an avenue to explore the beauty of the past and look forward to the future as new artists emerged.

It seems like only yesterday I was a young person entering Capitol Hill High School; I can remember I was both inspired and overwhelmed at the prospect. My life in high school was a mixture of pleasure and challenge. Even though I lived at home with seven other siblings, there was little-to-nothing left for me, so working was my only option for survival. In the summer of my freshman year, I worked at the public market in a little café where I was lucky to be befriended by an old gentleman who worked at the flower shop next door. When one of the women employees resigned from the flower shop, I was offered the job.

With no experience myself, I didn't think I could possibly do the job, so I talked my talented sister Betty (who I knew was much smarter, more creative, and needed a job) into taking the position. She took the job and was fabulous. She learned creative floral design, bookkeeping, and administrative skills. As the summer moved along, I realized I could not work in the café and continue going to school. I was once again offered a position at the flower shop. This time, with my sister's encouragement, I took the job; and for three years I worked as a floral designer and a bookkeeper alongside my sister Betty. There I learned the skills of simple accounting, which turned out to be one of my most important lessons. Years later, when I owned a dress shop and other businesses, the experience I garnered at the flower shop helped me to survive in the business world. It also prepared me to help other people better understand the business world.

I had a busy schedule: I went to school at Capitol Hill High from 7:25 A.M. to 11:00 A.M., then to work, and then to night school at Central High School (which is now the home of Southwestern Bell) from 6:00 P.M. until 9:00 P.M. In those days of "when," there was no state vo-tech system, so the high schools were the training grounds for the people who wanted to choose a trade. Capitol Hill had wonderful classes. The mechanical class was outstanding, as were the electrical and carpentry classes. I remember visiting a house on South Grand Boulevard that was completely built by the carpentry classes at Capitol Hill High.

I became involved in the Trade and Industrial Club and was its reporter. I wrote about the people in the classes I attended and about the T&I Club. To have my articles published in the *Oklahoman* and the *Capitol Hill Beacon* was fantastic. I was also elected "club sweetheart," a great honor and an exciting moment in my life. I still have my wool coat with the club insignia on it; it doesn't fit, but the memories it holds for me are precious.

My job qualified me to attend James Kelly Mudd's class, Diversified Occupations. He was a dedicated teacher and a truly special person. Mr. Mudd gave me confidence in myself and helped me to believe in who and what I could become. One valuable lesson he taught me was about public relations and getting along with other people without sacrificing my values. I put this knowledge to work when I attended L. H. Bingston's class. I always took him a Coke from the Coke machine that was in the vo-tech building. The funds from the machine supported activities for the T&I Club, so I figured everyone benefited from my efforts—the teacher, the club, and me. I am sure it was the public relations I learned from Mr. Mudd that earned me the A and not the Coke I always took to Mr. Bingston. Mr. Mudd arranged for me to take classes in journalism, which helped me to be a better class and club reporter. You never know how much an experience like that helps you until years later when you have to produce a mountain of reports or become the grant writer for one of your favorite organizations.

The teacher of the cosmetology class, Janet Spencer, was a friend to everyone, even those students from outside her classroom. She had time for students like me. She would invite students to her home to talk about extracurricular activities and projects she sponsored. Her home was neat and clean, with white lace panel curtains on the double-wide windows. I remember walking up to her big, welcoming porch, all white with a porch swing, so inviting and just waiting for someone to join in for an evening visit. She had a doorbell. I had never really seen a doorbell, let alone been able to walk up and touch one and hear it play music. It was tempting to stand there and keep pushing the bell to hear its melodious sounds, but work was ahead of us and our lives had to be lived and adventures explored.

I also joined the Pep Club. I did this mostly because I loved the teacher who was the sponsor for the club, Mr. Bingston (the teacher for whom I bought the Cokes). I admired him greatly and took several classes from him; one of those classes was economics. I credit him with introducing me to the joys and treachery of the stock market. I also was privileged to help him on his political campaigns when he ran for the Oklahoma legislature. He won after several tries, and the area around Capitol Hill can credit him with bringing Oklahoma City Community College to its present location.

I loved being part of the Knoberettes. Knoberettes was one of the two pep clubs for girls at Capitol Hill High. What fun it was to attend football games on Friday evenings. Capitol Hill was an outstanding force in high school football, winning many state championships. I also liked a certain football player, and it was certainly exciting to attend the games with the Pep Club because we always got to sit on the fifty yard line. Perhaps because of this experience, I now find myself nearly every Saturday afternoon during football season screaming and yelling in support of the University of Oklahoma football team.

Over the years, I've had the pleasure of serving many outstanding organizations. I've had the honor to work with Oklahoma State University for the last fourteen years, helping to develop an award-winning program in leadership for young women who strive to be successful in business and in life. I also serve on a women's leadership board at Harvard University, and I currently serve on the National Symphony Orchestra Board.

I still have a special spot in my heart for high school students, with their contagious energy and great opportunities, and I enjoy serving as chair of the Foundation of the Oklahoma School of Science and Math. I know that, if my achievements have a special meaning today, if I have accomplished anything worthwhile, it is due to my fabulous and loving family and friends and to their willingness to let me be a part of their organizations and lives. The wonderful years of my youth were certainly enhanced by the teachers who influenced my life. Those special teachers had a huge impact on my values and the decisions I have made over the years.

It was truly a golden era way back when. I have to ask if, twenty to thirty years from now, our students of today will be able to call this time in their lives the "magic of when"? Will they have the pleasure of reflecting, as I have done in this essay, and be able to recall these as days of wonder? Will they say, "I'm so glad I was there in the magical time of 'when'"? I certainly hope so.

Teaching Generations

Joyce Spivey Aldridge

I am a teacher. I am a third-generation teacher. Like my grandmother and mother before me, I have shared in the responsibility of guiding Oklahoma's young people in the fulfillment of their dreams.

Teaching is not a job for everyone, and yet, at one time or other, all of my immediate family were teachers in Oklahoma. My grandmother, Lucille Hulsey Cartwright, was the matriarch of our family of educators. In her fifty-some-odd years of teaching, she touched the lives of many people because of her gifted ability to teach a variety of subjects.

I believe she was most influential in her years as an English teacher. Through her efforts, generations of Oklahoma children learned to value literature, poetry, and grammar. She loved to read and was quite expressive when she read to a class, including mine. It was great fun to hear her read the stories of some of our greatest writers and "watch" the scenes unfold in my head. My imagination grew along with my appreciation for reading.

Although I never knew my grandmother to write a poem, she was passionate about poetry. At one time in her career, she required her students to memorize and recite to the class William Cullen Bryant's poem "Thanatopsis." At my grandmother's funeral service, I was amazed and humbled to hear one of her former students stand before the congregation and honor her once more with the reading of this poem. This student spoke of the first time she stood before the class and recited it before her peers and Mrs. Cartwright. Although almost fifty years had passed, this student shared memories of her classroom experience that seemed as vivid as if they had happened yesterday. That is testimony about an excellent teacher. The learning experience was so rich and gratifying that it has withstood the passage of time.

In contrast to the gentle, lyrical expressiveness my grandmother brought to literature and poetry, she was a warrior in her battle against poor grammar in both speech and written work. I am confident that Oklahoma has far fewer people ending a sentence with the word "at" because of my grandmother's diligent efforts. If you were to make the mistake and ask, "Where is it at?" she would promptly reply, "Between the 'a' and the 't.'"

My grandmother was my seventh-grade English teacher. She was dedicated to the idea that all of her students, including her less-than-interested granddaughter, would master the process of diagramming a sentence. I remember many days when I sat on my grandmother's couch to receive after-school tutoring. And although there were times I wanted to bury my *Keys to Good English* in the backyard, my grandmother's teaching methods saw me through.

Like my grandmother, my mother, Earlynn Cartwright Spivey, taught a variety of subjects, but I believe she was most influential in her work in music. Through her efforts, she brought a level of cultural awareness and personal confidence to some students who, without her, might not have gained either.

My mother was a performer at heart, and she shared her joy in performing with her students. In addition to learning how to read music, identify instruments and their sounds, and appreciate classical orchestrations—such as my personal favorite, Prokofiev's *Peter and the Wolf*—Mother's elementary-age students were guaranteed stage time. Whether it was the yearly Christmas concert or end-of-the-year play, my mother actively sought to provide many Oklahoma children with their only experience of live performance and theatre.

This experience grew as the children matured into junior high and high school students. In addition to smaller-scale musicals and modest operettas, my mother worked tirelessly to prepare her students for vocal contests. Participation in district, regional, and state music competitions took an inordinate amount of her time and energy. My mother would work to find the "right" vocal selections for each of her students; she made each one a personal rehearsal tape and provided after-school lessons for weeks in preparation for these competitions. She did all of this so that the students who might be gifted in a different way from many of their peers could achieve the same degree of recognition and personal success.

I attended a small high school in southern Oklahoma where basketball championships were yearly expectations. Through my mother's efforts, many more Oklahoma students discovered what it meant to be a champion, although in her case, they were all-state vocalists or members of an all-state choir. These experiences fostered a sense of pride and self-confidence in these students that lasted a lifetime. Many of Mother's students were awarded vocal scholarships to attend college, giving them opportunities that might not have been possible otherwise. Many of them have become music teachers, continuing the tradition of sharing and encouraging a love of music in their students. For many of my mother's students, their performance experiences ended with high school graduation, but each took with them memories of travel to places they might never have gone and of people they probably would otherwise never have met.

I was with my mother recently as she was in the checkout line at a local Wal-Mart. There, on the other side of the counter, was one of Mother's former students. As the clerk shared stories of her children's exploits in school, she commented on how she wished they could have the same experience with music as she had. She looked to me and explained that she had been painfully shy in high school; but with the encouragement of my mother, she had learned to express herself in a way she had never thought possible. Although my mother took her comments in stride, I recognized that she, like her mother before her, was another of Oklahoma's best resources: an excellent teacher.

In spite of my roots in teaching, I entered the classroom almost unwillingly. I had dreams of becoming a professional actress. I loved all things related to theatre. The sensations when audition notices were posted, the adrenalin rush when casting was announced, and the emotional thrill when I knew my work as an actress was "right" in its presentation to an audience. How could a job in teaching compare with that?

After seventeen years as a university theatre professor, there are days when I still wonder where and how my dreams of becoming one of the greatest on the American stage went awry. And then I go to class. I am greeted by students who, in their newly discovered passion for this craft, are hungry for someone to teach them how to dig deep inside themselves to find the strength and discipline necessary to succeed in the theatre world. In their desires to be the best, they consistently encourage me to better myself. They challenge me to ask the questions that inspire thoughtful answers; and, in their need to know more about theatre, they motivate me to discover more that I can share with them.

Together, students and teacher, we immerse ourselves in the very thing we love best: theatre. At that very moment when the classroom atmosphere is heightened by our excitement, I, once again, realize why I chose a career in teaching rather than in theatre. It is because I recognize that actors experience this moment of "epiphany" with their audiences less frequently than teachers who are graced with this feeling on a daily basis.

I am a teacher. I am a third-generation teacher. My grandmother and mother were my English and music teachers. More importantly, they were the teachers who taught me how best to teach. They illustrated compassion for students who needed the extra attention, strength of will for those who needed extra discipline, and great expectations for all who needed to reach for the stars.

Oklahoma education has come a long way since the time when children sat in handmade desks that were generally furnished by their parents, wrote on pine boards that were painted black, and learned from teachers who had completed a two-week training course. Yet one thing has remained constant. Women like Jennie McKeever, who in the summer of 1891 held classes in the shade of trees outside her home in Oklahoma City, and Anna Ward, who in 1889 taught her students in a tent in Kingfisher until a frame building became available, are examples of what we Oklahoma teachers do best. Oklahoma teachers teach wherever, however, and whenever there is a student waiting to be inspired by the gift of knowledge.

Oklahoma Spirit

A World Beyond Race

Vicki Miles-LaGrange

What were African Americans looking for when they came to Oklahoma Territory? They were looking for the same things as any other settler—a better life, freedom to explore possibilities, and an opportunity to succeed.

Oklahoma's Pulitzer Prize–winning author, Ralph Ellison, wrote in his essay "Going to the Territory" that the United States was a place where individuals had the ability to invent themselves without any limitations on possibilities. Ellison said that individuals with talent and courage can be found in unimaginable places, and when talent and courage are combined, they form productive and useful citizens.[*]

Ralph Ellison was talking about the territory of what is now Oklahoma and how it represented freedom, education, and possibility. This was despite those who, as early as Oklahoma's constitutional convention, legalized segregated schools and Jim Crow practices. Oklahoma symbolized a promise for all who wanted to believe it, but that promise has never been fully achieved for every Oklahoman.

Each of us is a product of our own environment and a product of our own experiences. I learned to negotiate different worlds at an early age. The issue of race probably played the biggest part in shaping my experiences and transforming my humanity. Still, as a child of tender years, because of the attitude of my parents, I had no idea that I was limited by anything other than my own imagination.

As a child, I always loved to travel from my home in Oklahoma City across the many miles and states of the Deep South to my grandparents'

---

[*] Ralph Ellison, "Going to the Territory," in *Going to the Territory* (New York: Random House, 1986).

home in Buford, Georgia. Today, with modern highways and interstates, we think very little about traveling across country. However, in the times of my memory, the roads were two-lane, twisting and winding over hills and through valleys. Roads were sheltered from sight by trees and vegetation, and anything might happen to a small black family traveling alone. Concerned about his family's safety, my father would call ahead to relatives to get the informal "Klan watch."

Now, in the first decade of the twenty-first century, it is almost fifty years since those cross-country treks of my childhood. In spite of that, probably no rational American can be comfortable with where we are as a nation on issues of intolerance, indifference, and prejudice. As a nation we have not yet fully exploited our extraordinary wealth of human talent. Nor have we captured the strength of America's diversity to the greatest extent possible:

> Daily reminders of the color of my skin, albeit subtle and seemingly insignificant, somehow force me to call upon my inner strength, my personal commitment to excellence, and my faith. My parents provided me the necessary ammunition to deflect the "isms" (racism, sexism, classism) through their quiet vigilance and broad vision. They taught me lessons in working hard, being honest, having integrity, not sweating the small stuff, and keeping my best foot forward. If nothing else, they always gave me enough hope for the future. More important, they taught me not to hate. Children are not born hating: it is a learned emotion.*

The legendary labor leader A. Philip Randolph said in a 1961 speech to the Negro American Labor Council, "men often hate each other because they fear each other; they fear each other because they do not know each other; they do not know each other because they cannot communicate; they cannot communicate because they are separated."

According to Ralph Ellison, "The uneducated and educated alike saw Oklahoma as a land of opportunity." It was an Oklahoma value. He describes the impact of an unsung Oklahoman, Dr. Inman E. Page, on his

---

* Vicki Miles-LaGrange, "Building Bridges," in *True to Ourselves, A Celebration of Women Making a Difference,* edited by Nancy Neuman, (San Francisco: Jossey-Bass, 2000), 218–19.

own life. Dr. Page was the first African American to graduate from Brown University in 1877:

> I met Dr. Page in what was first known as the Indian Territory, and then the Oklahoma Territory. Long before it became the State of Oklahoma the Territory had been a sanctuary for runaway slaves who sought there the protection of the Five Great Indian Nations. Dr. Page went to the Territory in 1898 to become president of what is now Langston University, and by the time he became the principal of my old school (Douglass High School) he was a man in his seventies. At that time, the state of Oklahoma had attracted many of the descendants of the freed slaves, who considered it a territory of hope and a place where they could create their own opportunities. It was a magnet for many individually who had found disappointment In the older areas of the country, white as well as black, but for Negroes it had a traditional association with freedom, which had entered their folklore.*

An opportunity for an education impacts our own ability to become a value-added individual to society. This can be accomplished collectively, I believe, when we interact; when we share; and when we exchange our respective, unique, and diverse experiences for the benefit of the common good. It is imperative that this interaction, this sharing, this exchange occur with some frequency wherever we are, whether in the academy, the workplace, or even in our social groups.

Hans Brisch, former Oklahoma chancellor of higher education, has described this type of socialization as "citizenship." Brisch notes that

> Citizenship by its very nature requires that we place a high value on the group, and that we learn how to get along with people of different races, genders, cultures, socioeconomic levels, physical abilities, and intellectual capacities. If we cannot inculcate the value of "unity in diversity" within the elementary and secondary school system, we shall never have another chance, because the school system is the

---

* Ellison, "Going to the Territory," 132.

best and only laboratory we have where all the children of all the people come together in one place.*

When there is a respect and an appreciation for those things that make us different, and at the same time, a celebration of those things we share in common, everyone wins.

I, too, am a product of my own experiences—molded by the dignity of work, the worth of character, and the value of education, much like many of the citizens of Oklahoma. For me, the value of education was something I saw, I felt, and I experienced. I inherited the value of education.[†]

My own paternal grandparents, Frank and Carrie Miles, hosted the opening of the first school for "Negroes" in Fairfax, Oklahoma, in their living room on September 1, 1929.[‡] Osage County hired its first black teacher, Mrs. Minnie V. Chinn of Pawhuska, Oklahoma, to teach grades one through eight. I still cherish the original writing of Grandma Carrie memorializing, in her "broken-correct" English, this significant event.

My Uncle Hycle was in the first eighth-grade graduating class of 1935. The second graduating class consisted of Roy Jones and my daddy, Charles Miles. The third graduating class included my other uncle, Ernest Miles, as well as Emma White, Adie Allen, Junior Johnson, Beulah Smallwood, and Jessie Brown.

Even though Grandma Carrie worked as a domestic for a prominent Osage County state senator and my grandpa was a preacher, they never once wavered on the value of an education for their sons as "a way out" or "a way up." They both believed in this so deeply that they sent two of their adolescent sons away from home so that they could continue their education. This was done at a time that was not so friendly for "colored" boys and to a place seemingly far beyond Fairfax, Oklahoma.

Among our family papers is a letter to Grandma Carrie, dated June 5, 1937, from Elmer Petree, superintendent of the Department of Public

---

* Hans Brisch, *The Agenda for Public Education in Oklahoma* (Oklahoma City: Oklahoma State Regents for Higher Education, 1988).

† Excerpts from paper presented by Vicki Miles-LaGrange upon receiving the E. T. Dunlap Medal & Lectureship Award (Durant: Southeastern Oklahoma State University, 2000).

‡ Carrie Miles, handwritten recorded history of the first black school in Fairfax, Oklahoma, September 1, 1929, unpublished manuscript on file with author.

Instruction of Osage County. The letter acknowledges and grants Grandma Carrie's sons a transfer to the Taft public schools in Muskogee County so they could complete junior high school. There were no schools in Fairfax for "colored" children beyond the eighth grade. Mr. Petree mentions in his letter that the county is paying only for transfer fees and not for "books, clothes, board or anything like that."*

The more deeply Grandma Carrie became rooted in her belief in the value of an education for her sons, the farther her sons were removed from their home, their roots, their native culture, and all that they knew. Sometimes that's what education does; it can take us far beyond our bounds of familiarity and comfort. Several years later, when the Miles boys had completed all the education available to them in Taft, Oklahoma, Grandma Carrie sent them farther away to Booker T. Washington High School in Tulsa, where my own father graduated on May 26, 1941.

The local newspaper, the *Fairfax Chief,* reported that, after high school graduation, my grandparents sent my daddy to "the great educational facility for colored boys and girls at Hampton, Virginia."† The article describes "the fine success that a local colored boy has attained." The relative poverty of the Miles family did not prevent them from continuing to nourish belief in the value of education, but it would prevent my daddy's return to his native Fairfax for nearly a decade.

By then my grandfather had died and the military draft of World War II brought my daddy's higher education to a screeching halt. After the war, however, he returned to Hampton Institute to graduate in 1951. The U.S. Navy would later send him to Georgia to train "colored" veterans in the welding trades. It was there that he met my mother, Mary Lou Greenard, who emerged from a similarly situated family—just humble folks, just ordinary folks, who also valued education for their children. They married in 1948 and soon returned to Daddy's native Oklahoma. The value of education continued to dominate their lives, and my daddy received a master's of industrial education from the University of Oklahoma on August 8, 1954, six years after the Sipuel decision in which the U.S. Supreme Court desegregated the

---

* Elmer Petrie, superintendent of public instruction, to Carrie Miles, June 5, 1937, letter on file with author.
† *Fairfax Chief,* June 10, 1943 (title and page of article unavailable).

University of Oklahoma College of Law.* Both my momma and daddy received their master's of education and master's of industrial education degrees, respectively, on June 5, 1955, from that same university. Daddy worked as a classroom teacher and an administrator in the Oklahoma City public schools, retiring after forty-one years as an educator.†

For my parents, for me, for hundreds of Oklahomans, higher education was a way out and a way up—the great equalizer. Thomas Jefferson knew what this meant when he said of public education, "[L]et us in education dream of an aristocracy of achievement rising out of a democracy of opportunity." Oklahoma's educational values, combined with the pursuit of excellence, remain at the core of upward mobility for many Oklahomans.

It is incumbent upon us, as education-interested Oklahomans, to believe that the strength of academia also lies in people who look different, who think differently, and who do things differently. We need different people in critical places to keep our institutions of learning, common or higher, viable and thriving. I long for the day that I can walk into any educational institution, common or higher, and see the world. I envision a world beyond race.

---

* Ada Lois Sipuel Fisher, *A Matter of Black and White: The Autobiography of Ada Louis Sipuel Fisher* (Norman: University of Oklahoma Press, 1996), 147.
† "Charles Clifford Miles: Longtime Educator Retires," *[Oklahoma City] Black Chronicle*, December 17, 1987, B-1.

Legacies

From Generation to Generation

Lynn Schusterman

If I will not be for me, who will be for me?
But if I am for myself alone, what am I?
If not now, when?
                    —Hillel, first century C.E.

I first learned about philanthropy when I was very young. Some of my earliest and fondest memories of my father involve the time I spent with him visiting and helping care for people that I remember calling the "little old ladies"—women who, I shudder to think, were probably no older than I am today!

My father never talked in terms of charity. He spoke only of improving lives and, in turn, making the world a better place for all of us. Time and again, he would say, "Each of us is worth only what we are willing to give to others."

My father was not a religious man and was unfamiliar with the litany of prescriptions in Jewish texts concerning the proper way for Jews to help people in need. He helped others not because of a specific ideology, but because it was the way he thought he should act. Thus, my initial approach to philanthropy was as uninformed by Jewish tradition as was my father's. His values and traditions naturally became my own, and my early sense of giving mirrored his.

This all changed when my family traveled to Israel in 1977. Those ten days transformed each of us. During and after that trip, our Jewishness and our cultural heritage became essential aspects of our lives rather than simply a means of self-identification. For me, Israel was a revelation that placed my father's philanthropic model within the distinctly Jewish context of *tikkun olam,* the imperative to repair the broken aspects of the world. In this model, an act of kindness is the means to an end rather than an end unto itself. This realization led me to view the fabric of my own identity in a much broader perspective. It provided me with a context in which to practice my philanthropy and to transmit new values to my children about both family and service.

If I will not be for me, who will be for me?

In Jewish law and tradition, the family is paramount. While the individual lies at the core of many other faiths, the family is the center of the Jewish universe. Beginning with Genesis, the master story of the Jewish faith is an epic about family and extended family. There are many religious laws regarding interfamilial relationships, regulations covering everything from the way families conduct themselves in public to how families should act in their most intimate relationships.

Jewish law dictates that if there is a choice between assisting members of your own family and helping citizens of your own town, your family takes precedence. If the choice is between your town and another city, your town takes precedence. The priority in Jewish law to ensure the well-being of those closest to us stems from the understanding that the Jews will not be able to fulfill their covenantal responsibility of *tikkun olam*—helping to repair the world—unless all Jews everywhere are self-sufficient. Only when people are independent and viable are they in a position to help others.

My family is the center of my personal life. They are a loving, supportive, and talented group. In many ways, our family is the reason my late husband, Charlie, and I worked so hard on behalf of so many charitable causes. Since Charlie's death, I have continued to push forward in an effort to make the world a little bit better for our children, our grandchildren, and the generations to follow.

My definition of family, however, extends far beyond those to whom we are directly related. Like many other members of the Jewish faith, I consider every Jew to be one of my own and someone with whom I have a genuine familial relationship. As a member of an extended family, I share a common heritage and future with my fellow Jews, and I recognize the special obligation I have toward them. Many years ago, Charlie and I established our family foundation because we knew we had to share our good fortune with those "family members" in need of help. The Jewish people and Jewish institutions became a primary focus of our philanthropic work.

Helping people help themselves is the cornerstone of our philanthropic agenda, an approach that is fully consistent with Jewish tradition. According to the medieval philosopher Rabbi Moses Maimonides, one of the greatest scholars in Jewish history, there are eight levels of charity (in Hebrew, *tzedakah*, from the word for justice). The lower forms include giving begrudgingly and dispensing less than one is able to give. The highest form of *tzedakah* is to help an individual help him or herself, by working closely with that person and assisting him or her to develop the necessary skills to become self-sufficient.

But if I am for myself alone, what am I?

The Jewish responsibility of *tikkun olam* is widely interpreted as calling for the care of all people, not just for those of the Jewish faith. The Jews have a long history of concern for—and commitment to—building a just society wherever Jews live. I believe we must do this work (*tikkun olam*) not only because our tradition decrees that we do so, but also because we must answer to the ideals that we have instilled in our children. We must affirm their desire to be a part of a community that accepts the challenge of changing the world.

For these and other reasons, our philanthropy and volunteerism support causes extending well beyond the Jewish community. We don't exist in a vacuum; we live within a larger world, one to which we owe a responsibility to help repair and perfect. To that end, our support of secular programs is as much an expression of our family values as are the contributions we make to Jewish causes. Judaism, like the proper exercise of philanthropy, demands nothing less than a total commitment to helping make the world a better place for everyone.

If not now, when?

I interpret Hillel's question to mean that it is never too soon to begin teaching your children about philanthropy or to start actively pursuing a family-oriented philosophy of giving back.

A family is a complex system. It is a dynamic structure that can be likened to a garden. If you wish to pass your values along to your children and their children, you must cultivate and maintain that which you want to bloom: you must plant the seed, fertilize the concept, nurture its growth, weed out the problems, and otherwise help the source of your attention to flower at maturity.

Neither a garden nor my job is ever done. Not only does each member of my family change in some fashion every day, but the critical issues of our time are growing increasingly complex, making it ever more difficult to practice effective philanthropy. Despite these mounting challenges, I truly believe that now is the time to act.

And taking action is more than simply writing a check. This is not to suggest that financial contributions are not important: they are critical. I mean only to encourage each and every one of us to do more than simply provide financial support to those causes we hold so dear. We need to become personally involved—for ourselves, for our families, and for those we are attempting to assist.

Some people say service to others is the rent we pay for space on this planet.

I think service to others is the down payment we make to assure a safe, secure home on earth for our children, our grandchildren, and people forever.

At the end of the day, families everywhere will be strengthened by our efforts.

. . .

One day, a man walking on the road saw Honi, the Circle Maker, planting a carob tree.

Puzzled, the man asked, "How long will it be before this tree will bear fruit?"

Replied Honi, "Seventy years."

The man then asked, "And do you believe you will be alive in another seventy years?"

Honi answered, "When I came into this world, there were carob trees with fruit ripe for picking. Just as my parents planted for me, so I will plant for my children."

Babylonian Talmud, Ta'anit 23a

Never a Dull Moment

Roxana Lorton

When I was a little girl, I dreamed about becoming the CEO of a company. This was before women's liberation so I was a bit of an oddity. It just never entered my mind that I could not do anything, or be anything, I wanted. I have my family to thank for this. My mother was a champion golfer who grew up on Long Island. Her father was a great golfer too, an avid sailboat racer, and investor in real estate. My mother taught me to be creative and to look at new ideas and new ways of doing things.

Daddy studied music in Paris and at the Julliard School. Early in his career he played the organ during silent movies in New York theatres and was part of the NBC Orchestra. My grandmother Rosita paraded on Wall Street for women's right to vote. I never felt limited by being a woman.

We moved to Tulsa when I was four years old. My father had received his PhD and was hired by the University of Tulsa to teach music to graduate students. I attended Lincoln Grade School in Tulsa where I played cello. Oh, how I wished I had picked a smaller instrument so that it would fit on my bike better!

When I was about ten years old, my best friend moved away from Tulsa. When I discovered that another girl about the same age had moved into my best friend's old house, I strapped on my roller skates, skated over to the house, rang the doorbell, and introduced myself by saying, "My best friend used to live in this house, but she moved away, so now you have to be my best friend."

I've always been like this: if plan A doesn't work, then plan B might. My new best friend, Danna Sue, and I did so many fun things together. Growing up was such an adventurous time! She once invited me to go on the opening drive of the Turner Turnpike, and we stayed in the bridal suite of the Skirvin Tower Hotel in Oklahoma City. Our room had a round bed, and we had Shirley Temples to drink; we thought we'd gone Hollywood!

Science and music were part of my everyday life when I was growing up. My father eventually became the head of the graduate music department at TU. So many interesting people came to our house for dinner during these years, and the conversations were always fascinating. One of my favorite visitors was Edward Teller, the physicist who was known as the "father of the atomic bomb." He would visit us when he traveled to Tulsa to consult with the Williams Research Company. We always had Hungarian goulash when he visited; and, after dinner, he and Daddy would play chess. (My father was the Oklahoma state chess champion eleven times!) My brother eventually became a chemical engineer and worked at the Lawrence Radiation Lab, where Edward Teller began his work in top-secret weaponry and bombs.

I love the memories of my childhood and know that this time helped to shape who I am today. In 1969 I had the experience of a lifetime when Bob Wood, my father-in-law and sports filmmaker, suggested that several of us go to Africa on a safari. I had never even shot a gun before so, six months before we left, Bob taught me how to shoot handguns as well as rifles. Five of us traveled to Kenya and camped out. I didn't want to kill anything; I just wanted to watch the wonderful animals. One night my husband, Bob, tried to shoot a leopard, but it was so dark that he mistakenly shot a smaller leopard than he intended. He asked me to shoot the remaining leopard which, even in the dark, we could see was very large. I eventually agreed but worried that, because of my lack of shooting experience, I wouldn't be successful. Somehow I rose to the occasion and shot that beautiful leopard, which turned out to set the record in the London Record Book as the largest leopard shot that year. I learned more on that six-week trip than in four years of college. It was so interesting to see how the animals interrelate with humans—some were far superior to humans!

My husband, Bob Lorton, publisher of the *Tulsa World*, and I have three children. Bob has always supported and encouraged me in all that I do. My son Bobby likes to tell people that, when he and his siblings were growing up, I was the one who was always in the thick of things. "It was Mother who blew by the rest of us," my daughter Tracy likes to recall about our four-wheeling days together.

I have been incredibly fortunate to become the CEO that I fantasized about becoming when I was a little girl. I served as the first woman board president of the Tulsa Philharmonic, was the president and chairwoman of the Tulsa Town Hall board, and was the president and chairwoman of the Gilcrease Museum board. As a CEO, I especially liked the challenge of assembling a group of talented people and inspiring them to work together and be productive. I like the interaction of people who are creative thinkers.

My father used to play the devil's advocate—taking the opposite viewpoint to see how people thought. He was notorious for doing this at the university in the faculty lounge and also at home. Needless to say, my mother was very intelligent and a very good listener! From my parents, I learned tolerance, how to listen, and the importance of remembering details, even minute details.

When faced with a "we can't do that" attitude, my answer is always the same: "Of course we can do it." But people have to be willing to stay the course and not give up, and they have to like to laugh. That's the way I've dealt with most situations in my life: face toward the future, a smile on my lips, and a plan of action. If one plan fails, go to the next.

When I think about how I'd like my life described in my obituary, this is what I envision:

As late University of Tulsa professor Darcy O'Brien said, "The phrase 'Never a dull moment' must have been coined to describe Roxana, who lavishes her humor and warmth like paprika. She has that rare and elusive quality, a genuine personal style, joyful and dazzling." Roxana Lorton is a woman who has tangoed at Maxim's in Paris, walked through monasteries in Tibet, explored the ocean floor, hunted game in Africa, sailed the Greek islands, trekked to Chaco with climatologist Iben Browning, dined with author James Michener and the man who discovered the Dead Sea Scrolls, and told television star Robin Leach that he ought to laugh more. This is also a woman who can carry on three conversations at one time and never miss a beat, likes Agatha Christie mysteries, gardens, does needlepoint, and taught her Hungarian Puli dogs to sing. She wants to be remembered with these statements: "She put a twinkle in their eye and their hearts" and "To the world, you may be one person, but to one person you may be the world."

The passive among us are redeemed by the active, the timid by those whose lives are propelled by the sense of adventure. . . . It is never too late!

Confessions of a Compassionate, God-Oriented, Incurable Do-Gooder, Don Quixote Nut

En Garde! I'm A-comin' as Fast as I Can

Eddie Faye Gates

Is there anyone on the planet Earth who has not heard of comedian Bill Cosby's remarks about the parental failure of black parents in inner-city ghettos? While Bill Cosby made some good points about how those parents should rein in their rap-singing, high-spending offspring, I believe that he made some mistakes too. In fact, I was so concerned that I sat down at my computer and wrote a "Chill Bill" response.*

Here is what I said: There is a reason why certain population groups are the predominant inhabitants of urban ghettos. It is called institutionalized, systemic racism! Granted, things have gotten better in the fifty years since the *Brown v. Board of Education* case that declared segregation unconstitutional, but we still have improvements to make. And some explanations.

There are legitimate reasons for transportation problems, lateness problems, loan problems, rent problems, diet problems, health problems, etc., among inner-city, poor populations. They are economic-related issues; and,

---

* My Edison High School students taught me the "chilling" technique. Whenever I became distraught over an issue and "went over the line," my students, sympathetic to my genuine love and concern for all humankind, would gently tell me to "chill out." They would tell me that things would eventually work out. They were right. Many things did work out, others are being worked out in the present era, and others will be worked out in the future.

266

when you combine economic problems with race issues, the problem is compounded.

Some members of excluded populations groups *do* manage to succeed and to bless and benefit themselves and all of humankind. There ought to be awards equivalent to the Pulitzer Prize and the Nobel Peace Prize that reward such persons for their talents and their persistence. During my research, I learned about people overcoming all kinds of adversity—slavery, prejudice, discrimination, segregation, racism, sexism, war, famine, genocide, poverty, health problems, environmental disasters, and a plethora of other seemingly impossible conditions. The "take no prisoners" philosophy of black American mothers, in particular, is one of the main reasons that so many blacks *did* break into the mainstream of America and *did* become part of a nation from which they received little support. I wish that there were as much focus on black Americans who *did* break through the barriers and *did* succeed as there is on those still struggling to get out of their poverty and exclusion, especially those locked in inner-city ghettos.

My mother is one of the people who has made a difference in this society, although, on the basis of society's standards, many would not think of her as successful. Vivian Minter Petit, my mother, should receive the "Most Outstanding Mother in the Universe Award." She is one of the smartest women that I have ever known. Her mind is like a steel trap; it latches onto information instantly. She could have been a wonderful doctor, lawyer, or teacher. But you wouldn't know that from looking at her "credentials." Her resume would read:

- *Has sixth-grade education*
- *Speaks "Ebonics"*
- *Comes from lowest-level economic status: sharecropper housing, minimal finances from subsistence farming, sharecropping farmwork, cotton-field work, maid work*

A casual assessment of Mother's resume might lead the observer to make some wrong assumptions about her. But you must see the whole picture, the *big* picture to know why my mother's resume reads the way that it does.

My autobiography, *Miz Lucy's Cookies: And Other Links in My Black Family Support System* is a tribute to my mother. I tell of how I worried the poor woman to death when I was four years old, asking what the words on oatmeal boxes, flour sacks, and other household products meant. And that woman, with only a sixth-grade education, taught me how to read. She lit a fire under me, and a love of learning jumped into my heart which remains to this day. So, when I started school at age five at the two-room Douglas Elementary School, I could already read and write. It wasn't long before I was so inspired by my teachers that I began to write poems and stories for my dolls and bears!

My mother is smarter than I will ever be. Mother and countless other black Americans were undereducated or miseducated, and yet they succeeded. They encouraged their offspring as more opportunities opened for black Americans.

I would also give a "Persistent Mother's Award" to the late mother of noted national treasure Dr. John Hope Franklin for the support and guidance she gave to her children during a period of extreme racist exclusion. In a recent *Oklahoma Eagle* newspaper article, Dr. Franklin tells of the pain he still feels when he remembers an incident of indignity (and danger) that he and his beloved mother experienced eighty-six years ago in Oklahoma when he was six years old. Though the Franklin family was a prominent, well-educated family, this did not exempt them from the injustices of racial segregation. Mrs. Franklin and her children lived in Rentiesville, Oklahoma, until her husband could get housing in Tulsa for them. One day, Mrs. Franklin decided to take the children by train to Tulsa to an area that she thought was "neutral"—an area thought to be safe for black families. The ninety-two-year-old renowned historian, Dr. Franklin, is still haunted by memories of the night he, his mother, and his siblings were put off the train in the dark countryside between Rentiesville and Tulsa. Why? Because they sat too near white passengers on the train.*

The mother of Dr. Charles Ogletree also deserves a "Persistent Mother's Award." Her life story, set in Deep South cotton fields and kitchens, is as

---

* Noted comedian and activist Dick Gregory, in a speech at the University of Tulsa a few years ago, spoke about this same type of exclusion. He asked, "What do you call a black American with a PhD degree?" His answer, "A 'nigger' with a PhD." Gregory pointed out that many dark-skinned blacks still have to fight the system today with ingenuity just as they did in the past—pretending to be servants to their light-skinned relatives and adopting a host of other survival strategies—just to get a piece of the American dream!

near a carbon copy of my mother's life as one would likely encounter. Dr. Ogletree, a Harvard University law professor, is the lead attorney in the federal reparations lawsuit filed in Tulsa in February 2001 on behalf of black survivors of the worst race riot in U.S. history, the Tulsa Race Riot of 1921.

My mother and Dr. Ogletree's mother brought out the best in their children and were influential in so many lives. They dared to stress that their children could succeed, even in economically depressed and rigidly racist environments. They demanded not only diplomas at elementary and high school levels but also demanded college degrees, even being so bold as to expect master's and even doctoral degrees! And we, their children, got them! When my daughter, Dianne Gates-Anderson, received her doctoral degree in environmental engineering from the University of California, Berkeley, she spoke on behalf of the Black Students Union at the graduation ceremony. She brought the audience to tears when she told them my mother's story and how her determination brought so many people into the American dream! Dianne's diploma now hangs on the wall in Mother's living room in Tulsa.

And let's not forget the influence of black males in their families. Black males have generally been given a bad rap in the child-rearing, nurturing realm. Some of it is deserved; but many, many black men have been, and continue to be, the best providers that they can be for their families. For instance, in my research on slavery, I found records showing black male slaves who worked in cotton fields from "can to can't" (from the time you could see in the morning until the time you couldn't see in the evening). Then they walked up to fifteen or twenty miles to other plantations where their wives and children had been sold so they could see their loved ones and do their nurturing. Then they walked back to their own plantations to be ready for the bell call to the fields before sunrise.

Over the years I have taught many students and have given many lectures. Regardless of my audience, my methodology is always the same: I express concern and respect for the group. This philosophy worked well with the students, black and white, rich and poor, I encountered at Edison High School in Tulsa. It worked especially well with those who came from some of Tulsa's most impoverished neighborhoods and lived in the worst, lowest-income housing projects. Those poor students, some of them gang members with their colors hidden in their pockets, in their backpacks, or in their lockers, treated me with utmost respect—something my friends feared they wouldn't do. And when I got through sharing my aspirations for their future, I told them they could overcome significant odds like I did. Some of them got out of their seats, hugged and kissed me, and thanked me for caring enough about them to share a message of courage with them. This is something they hadn't heard often enough.

Even when we don't have the "necessities of life," we can't give up. We have to do the best that we can with what we have. The tiny Preston, Oklahoma, house where I grew up had no running water, an outhouse, and other "substandard" features—at least substandard according to the standards of the dominant society. We eight Petit kids might have lacked the tangible things that society said were needed, but what we *did* have was more important than wealth and prosperity. We had two parents who loved us fiercely, who gave us all that they had to give us, and who encouraged us to excel. And that was enough. We thrived and we succeeded, despite the odds.

I have loved historical research since I was first introduced to it in the two-room schoolhouse in Preston. But it is hands-on interviewing that I like best and that has led to my success as an oral historian today. My first interview, when I was eleven years old, was with an ex-slave, the oldest person in Preston, an elderly man whom everyone called "Old Man Polk." How important I felt sitting on the porch of his modest little house, holding my Big Chief tablet on my lap, and learning what his life had been like during slavery. I was captivated.

I continued to enlarge my pool of people to interview as I grew older. I recorded the history of black and white cowboys, oil men, war veterans, people with an outlaw's history, and anyone else who had an interesting story to tell. The most interesting outlaw story I heard was about Charles "Pretty Boy" Floyd, who had hidden on the farm across from my childhood home when he was running from the law! When I was sixteen years old, I wrote my first letter to the editor. It was about the city of Okmulgee's neglect of its black citizens. Each year Greasy Creek flooded a black neighborhood, ruining rugs, floors, furniture, and clothes, yet nothing was ever done about it. My letter was published, and I was hooked on writing for publication ever since.

My experiences at Tuskegee Institute in Alabama were tremendous milestones in my development as an activist. It was there that I developed what I call the Gates FFF philosophy—my philosophy of life. The three Fs stand for Facts, Feet, Fire. I do my research. I stand by and prove my writings. I take no flak, no scams, no excuses.

Sometimes I have uncovered facts during my research which have made others uncomfortable. I was sometimes called "militant" or "aggressive," and during the time that we worked on the report for the Oklahoma Commission to Study the Tulsa Race Riot of 1921, I received hate telephone calls in which I was sometimes called "nigger," at other times "bitch." Occasionally I was called the ultimate insult: a "*nigger bitch.*" But I didn't let those calls bother me. I felt that I was working on a worthy cause and that God would take care of me. And God did!

Throughout my career, I have tried to tell the true story of the United States, warts and all. I have never espoused a "gotcha" approach—"Now you devils must pay for your injustice against my people"—rather, I am driven to tell the *true* story—the good, the bad, and the ugly—so that it might lead to dialogue, discussion, healing, and reconciliation. I think I have done that, and I will continue to do that as long as I live.

Getting and Giving

Geri Wisner-Foley

In 2004, I was asked to be the keynote speaker at the Oklahoma State Capitol for the Native American Day celebration, "One Voice, Stronger Than Before." Thinking about what to say, I considered happenings that had most influenced my life. I wanted to give good examples of how perseverance under adverse circumstances can transform a person into one who understands the strength necessary to accomplish challenging tasks.

I am the oldest of five children. My mother raised us while my father was either working or traveling. There was a period of time when we did not struggle financially, but most of my childhood was spent in poverty. It was during such times I learned various strategies for taking care of my brothers and sisters.

I learned to be successful at shoplifting packages of panties and socks for my little sisters, since those items were most in demand.

I worked at a nursing home on weekends during high school to help supplement my mother's income as the overnight cook at the I-40 truck stop.

I learned how to feed a family with Indian commodities and a weekly grocery budget of $5.

I also realized how a family could work together to make anything happen.

During my senior year of high school, I decided to run for homecoming queen. I had not thought of how I would find a dress for the event, but the idea of being the queen overtook me. Two nights before the football game and the homecoming queen announcement, my mother held a family meeting. It was no surprise that we lacked the money to purchase a dress for homecoming, nor did we know anyone with a dress to borrow. Cutoff notices in her hand, my mother explained that she had intended to pawn some shotguns in order to pay that month's electric bill. However, she wanted to propose a family vote to choose between paying the electric bill and purchasing a dress for homecoming. It was unanimous: I was getting a dress.

As we expected, the Friday afternoon of homecoming our electricity was turned off. A friend from town, Bill Fife, who happened to be the future principal chief of the Muscogee (Creek) Nation, found out about our situation and offered his home to my family so I could dress for the homecoming event.

The loudspeaker blared the names of the homecoming candidates as we walked onto the football field. I saw my family in the stands, cheering the loudest. The second runner-up was announced first, and I was happy for the banker's daughter who had won something. The first runner-up was the head cheerleader, and I was happy for her. When I heard my name announced as the homecoming queen, I looked at my family. They were jumping up and down, arms punching the air and mouths open wide, cheering. We had won! That night, as we all slept together in the living room to keep warm, I set the homecoming crown on the coffee table and placed a handful of candles around it. We fell asleep watching the crown sparkle in the candlelight.

After high school, I enlisted in the U.S. Marine Corps instead of going to college. As a member of the Corps, I could help my family by sending money home while I trained and traveled the world. My first job as a Marine was as a bandsman. I quickly became restless playing John Philip Sousa marches and began to volunteer for various training assignments. I had the opportunity to train with combat Marine units that were formed to examine the potential for women in traditionally male roles. These units proved that, under the right circumstances, women could perform equal to men in a survival environment or combat operation. I also shot competitively, using the M16 rifle and 9mm pistol, and proved that I could shoot just as well, if not better, than most of my fellow Marines.

In the Marine Corps, the ratio of men to women is approximately 25 to 1. This means that each woman's actions reflect on every female Marine. Although all Marines feel esprit de corps, it is a bit different for women. There is a fierce, gung-ho attitude in women Marines. In my experience, this competitive spirit sets some women against each other rather than encouraging the formation of alliances.

A few women are Marines because they want the benefits of the GI bill. Other women join because they are given the option to enlist or go to jail. For me, and many others, it was an opportunity to grow, travel, and become an aggressive killer prepared to defend the United States. This positive aggression has served me well again and again.

As a Marine, I traveled all over the world and observed various peoples and cultures. In Japan, Guam, and Korea, I saw many religious symbols, as well as shrines and temples frequented by the people. Seeing these things expanded my understanding of how people outside of the United States view their place in the world. In Saudi Arabia, Marines were briefed on the appropriate protocol relating to local religious beliefs. We were informed that we should not interfere with them and that we should show proper respect during religious observances.

I found it ironic that we were being taught to respect the culture and religious beliefs of the host country's people. I compared that teaching with the vastly different attitude of the U.S. federal government when it confronted American Indian people and their religious beliefs in the late nineteenth century. At that time, traditional ceremonies were outlawed, and medicine men were threatened with prison if they performed their traditional duties.

After leaving the Marine Corps, I returned to Oklahoma to get my education. There I met and married my husband. We soon became pregnant. During my pregnancy, I kept my full-time student status, worked part-time, exercised daily, and was hyper-conscious about eating healthful foods. I read books about pregnancy and childbirth and watched videos explaining the step-by-step process of delivery.

However, nothing prepared me for what was about to happen.

After twenty-six hours of hard labor, I gave birth to my beautiful son. I expected the nurses to swaddle him, cut the cord, and congratulate me on a job well done. Instead, they whisked him to an examination table across the room where he was surrounded by masked faces and gloved hands. I calmly but firmly told them to give me my baby, but I was ignored. My husband watched as our son was examined under a bright light. There were hushed voices and looks of concern. My husband began to call out our son's name: "Nokose [the Muscogee word for bear], Nokose, we are so glad you could finally join us. Nokose, we love you and have been waiting for you."

Suddenly, between the bodies of the nurses, I saw Nokose's head turn toward the sound of my husband's voice. I saw two little dark eyes look toward the familiar voice of his papa. We then saw that Nokose was missing parts of the fingers on his right hand, that the fingers on his left hand were webbed, and that both legs were severely clubbed, while his toes either did not form completely or were webbed.

But he was healthy. He was beautiful. He was mine.

We learned his condition was called amniotic band syndrome. During the next three years, we traveled to the Shriners Hospital for Children in Shreveport, Louisiana, for weekly therapy, a series of surgeries, and casts and braces. I had to be strong for Nokose and my husband. I also had to cope with the fact that my service in the first Gulf War may have led to my son's situation.

I sank into depression as a result of the blame I placed on myself for Nokose's condition. In time, my son proved to be the best therapy for me by teaching me how capable and resilient he was. Certainly, if he could deal with his difficulties, I could deal with them as well. Talking with other parents at the Shriners Hospital was another eye-opener because I realized how fortunate we were and how much worse Nokose's condition could have been. It took time for me not to feel sorry for my son or be mad at myself. These are feelings I continue to battle even now, over ten years later.

While preparing for graduation from Oklahoma State University in 2000, and thinking about what to do next, I was encouraged by my husband to keep going to school to find something that I could do to help other people. After deciding on law school, I took the exams and applied to the three schools in the state. While my LSAT scores were not high enough to place me in the elite category of students, they were good enough to have my application wait-listed at the University of Tulsa, which had an outstanding Indian law program.

As the start of the next semester crept closer, I kept waiting for some word. I received the "thanks but no thanks" letters from the University of Oklahoma and Oklahoma City University, and I realized TU was now my only hope.

Since I hadn't heard from them, I decided to go to the TU law school and see what my status was. After a wait, an administrator sifted through a pile of applications and found mine. I was led to the dean's office where they decided my fate right then and there. They let me in, largely on the strength of my life experiences and the stated intentions of my cover letter: to better the situation of my family; to help Indian people; and to serve as a role model for other young American Indian women, women of color, and women in general, who have to face daily challenges as they try to succeed in a world weighted toward men socially and professionally.

. . .

In 2004, as I considered what I would say in the Oklahoma State Capitol rotunda while my parents looked on and people of all ages and backgrounds listened, I thought back on these events of my life, how they have shaped who I am and how they have led me to understand that no challenge is too great to overcome if given proper perspective and disciplined attention.

Neither gender, race, nor age should be a barrier to setting and accomplishing the highest goals. Without grounding in family and tradition, and without dogged pursuit of education, one cannot expect to overcome the many obstacles that often ground the best-intended and best-planned flights.

My voice is stronger than before as a result of my experiences; and I believe I can now use that voice to help my family, my community, and those people who come to me for my legal expertise. Without my background, though, I'm not sure I would understand how fortunate I am. And without my traditional grounding, I'm not sure I would understand that I am responsible to give back to the world that has given me such opportunities.

Contributors

JOYCE SPIVEY ALDRIDGE is a third-generation Oklahoman on both sides of her family. She has a BA from Southeastern Oklahoma State University, an MA from Oklahoma State University, and a PhD from the University of Colorado at Boulder. She is an assistant professor at Oklahoma Baptist University in Shawnee, where she lives with her husband and two stupendous sons.

RILLA ASKEW, a native Oklahoman and two-time recipient of the Oklahoma Book Award, is the author of three novels and a collection of stories. Her work has been nominated for the PEN/Faulkner Award and the Dublin IMPAC Prize, has received the Western Heritage Award, and was selected for *Prize Stories 1993: The O. Henry Awards*. Her novel *Fire in Beulah*, which deals in part with the Tulsa Race Riot of 1921, received the Myers Book Award and the American Book Award in 2002.

CAROLE BURRAGE is a native Virginian and an Okie on her mother's side. She attended undergraduate and law school at the University of Oklahoma, where she met her husband, Sean. She has worked in the nonprofit sector, as a federal law clerk, and as an assistant professor at Rogers State University before recently "retiring" to devote more time to her family. She and Sean live in Claremore with their two terrific sons, Truman and Carter, and the world's best German shepherd, Gretel.

JULIE CARSON moved to Tulsa with her family at the age of fifteen from Kansas City, Missouri, though her family roots in the state go back many generations on her father's side. She has a BA in economics from Vanderbilt University and a law degree from the University of Tulsa. She currently resides in Claremore with her husband, former U.S. Congressman Brad Carson, and their son, Jack David. She is a member of the Oklahoma State Regents for Higher Education.

SHERRI COALE is a native Oklahoman. She was born and raised about thirty miles to the right side of the Red River, which, to this day, she crosses only when in need of shoes or players. Sherri is the head women's basketball coach at the University of Oklahoma. She holds a bachelor's degree from Oklahoma Christian University, a master's degree from the University of Oklahoma, and her children's hands on a daily basis.

ALTHEA CONSTANCE (pseudonym) is a student at an Oklahoma university.

EMILY DIAL-DRIVER is a professor in the Department of Communications and Fine Arts at Rogers State University, having also been a waitress, hatcheck girl, assistant director of a Girl Scout camp, dietary interviewer on a national preschool nutrition survey, and captain in the U.S. Army Ordnance Corps. Reared as a traveling Army brat and a rancher's grandkid, she was born in Oklahoma but hardly lived in the state until she returned to college. She thinks of southwestern Oklahoma as the place where climate and foliage are correct: red dirt, brown grass, trees with thorns. She lives in Claremore with a husband and a large black dog. She has one child on each coast.

PAIGE DOUGLAS (pseudonym) is a student at an Oklahoma university.

SALLY EMMONS-FEATHERSTON is a self-described adopted Oklahoman who now proudly considers Oklahoma home. Of Choctaw and Cherokee descent, she is an associate professor of English at Rogers State University and teaches a variety of writing and literature courses. When she is not teaching, she serves as managing editor of RSU's literary and artistic journal, the *Cooweescoowee*. In her "free" time she teaches aerobics in spandex, watches (but isn't one of the) *Desperate Housewives*, and chases her three-year-old son, who one day wants to be an airplane pilot, race-car driver, artist, and cook.

MARY FALLIN is only the second women elected to Congress from Oklahoma. She began making political history in 1994 when she was elected Oklahoma's first woman and first Republican lieutenant governor. Prior to being elected lieutenant governor, she served four years in the Oklahoma House of Representatives.

PAM FLEISCHAKER is a freelance writer and the author of *American Woman, Lost & Found in Oklahoma*, a collection of her columns from more than a decade of writing for the *Oklahoma Gazette*, a weekly newspaper in Oklahoma City. She has been a political and media consultant for presidential, senatorial, and congressional candidates and for national women's organizations. She is an active participant in Oklahoma City's nonprofit community. She is married to David Fleischaker, secretary of energy for the State of Oklahoma; has two nearly perfect children; and lives in Oklahoma City.

SALLY FREEMAN FRASIER is originally from Arkansas but married a Tulsan and has firmly planted her roots in Oklahoma. She graduated from the University of Tulsa; taught first grade; is an active community volunteer; raised two productive, successful children with her husband, Jim; and has two beautiful granddaughters. These precious new Tulsans give her reason to continue pursuing her passion for public policy.

KALYN FREE is a member of the Choctaw Nation of Oklahoma and the founder and president of INDN's List (Indigenous Democratic Network), a national organization that recruits, trains, and helps elect American Indians to all levels of public office. Active in public service and the recipient of too many awards to mention, Kalyn was the first woman elected district attorney of Pittsburg and Haskell counties. Kalyn is most passionate about working toward a body politic that reflects the beautiful diversity of our country in both ethnicity and gender.

OTIE ANN FRIED is currently a partner in the lobbying firm of Fried, Kilpatrick and Guinn. She, her husband Jim, and their son, Bryan, all work together representing various clients at the Capitol. When the legislature is not in session, she can often be found at her home in Maine, where her days are spent painting; working in her gardens; and playing with her two dogs, Ike and Mamie.

SANDY GARRETT is an "Okie from Muskogee." She is the first woman elected Oklahoma's state superintendent of public instruction. Now in her fourth term of office, she has served longer than any woman elected statewide. She holds undergraduate and graduate degrees, having studied at Northeastern State University, the University of Oklahoma, and the Kennedy School of Government at Harvard. She is the mother of one married son, Chuck Garrett.

EDDIE FAYE GATES has gone from barefoot, cotton-picking share-cropper's daughter to author of three popular books about the black experience in the United States and the world. She gives lectures and hosts book signings all over the country, the Caribbean area, Europe, Africa, and the Middle East. She has co-hosted book talks on C-Span television and was recently featured in *Essence* magazine and in several issues of *Jet* for her work with Tulsa's 1921 Race Riot victims.

TWILA GIBBENS-RICKMAN was raised in Oklahoma public schools and graduated from Colorado College and Southern Methodist University. After nine years of serving churches in west Texas, she and her husband, Mark, came back to Oklahoma nineteen years ago to serve churches in Holdenville, Claremore, and now Tulsa. She presently pastors St. Paul's United Methodist Church in Tulsa. Much of her ministry is involved with youth, with her church's hospitality to homeless, and with interfaith dialogue.

JEAN GUMERSON received honors beyond counting, including the naming of a plaza at the Presbyterian Foundation Research Park as the Jean G. Gumerson Plaza. Involved with the arts and with fund-raising, she was engaged with—among other entities—the symphony, national mental health, congressional campaigns, art museums, Children's Medical Research, Inc., and the Presbyterian Health Foundation.

JOY HARJO, born in Tulsa, is a multitalented artist and a member of the Mvskoke/Creek Nation. She is an internationally known poet, performer, writer, and musician. She has garnered many national awards for her poetry and music, including such local awards as the Arrell Gibson Lifetime Achievement Award, Oklahoma Book Awards, and the American Indian Festival of Words Author Award from the Tulsa City County Library. To date she has published seven books of acclaimed poetry and two music CDs that feature her saxophone and voice. She is the Joseph M. Russo Professor of Creative Writing at the University of New Mexico in Albuquerque, where she teaches every fall semester. The rest of the year she lives in Honolulu, Hawai'i, when she is not traveling. She is a member of the Tallahassee Wygogye Ceremonial Grounds.

CAROLYN HART is the author of forty mystery novels, with almost three million books in print. She has been nominated nine times for the Agatha Award for Best Novel, winning three times. She writes the Death on Demand, Henrie O, and Bailey Ruth Raeburn series. *Letter from Home*, a stand-alone novel set in Oklahoma, was a Pulitzer Prize nominee and Agatha winner. She is a journalism graduate of the University of Oklahoma. She lives in Oklahoma City with her husband, Phil.

BECKI HAWKINS is a retired registered nurse. In 1986 she began writing a weekly article titled "Beyond Statistics" for a local newspaper and continued doing so for nearly ten years. Each week she shared lessons she'd learned from her patients as a nurse and then as a hospice chaplain. She lives with her husband and best friend, John, between Claremore and Pryor. Presently she stays busy with volunteer work, writing, and speaking—and helping out with her two teenage grandsons who continue her education in Life Lessons!

KIM HENRY is the First Lady of Oklahoma. She earned a bachelor of science degree in secondary education from the University of Oklahoma and spent ten years in the classroom. Kim is married to Brad Henry, and she took a leading role in his successful campaigns for governor of Oklahoma. They have three beautiful daughters. Kim is active in the Muscular Dystrophy Association. She is on the board of directors of the Close-Up Foundation, the Jasmine Moran Children's Museum, the Oklahoma Medical Research Foundation, and the Oklahoma Academy of State Goals.

Kim is on the board of trustees of the Sarkey's Foundation and the Oklahoma Foundation for Excellence. She also serves on the National Task Force on Early Childhood Education for Hispanics.

PAM HENRY had a thirty-one-year career, primarily in television journalism. She was inducted into the Oklahoma Journalism Hall of Fame in 2004. In retirement, she serves as chair of the Oklahoma City Mayor's Committee on Disability Concerns, on the board of Goodwill, and on the Governor's Committee on Hiring People with Disabilities. A graduate of the University of Oklahoma, she lives in Oklahoma City. She was the last national polio poster child for the March of Dimes in 1959.

SANDY INGRAHAM is an Oklahoman by choice, living in the state all of her adult life. She has two BAs, a master's degree, and a juris doctorate, all from universities in Oklahoma. She practices law and maintains an active role as a social-policy consultant, operating out of an office in rural Lincoln County at the end of a mile-long dirt road.

SUE IVESON (pseudonym) is a student at an Oklahoma university.

JANE JAYROE (GAMBLE) was Miss America in 1967. She was a prime-time television news anchor in Oklahoma City and in Dallas/Fort Worth. Jane was named cabinet secretary of tourism by Governor Frank Keating and served as director of the Oklahoma Department of Tourism and Recreation. She was the first woman to be president of the Oklahoma Academy. A graduate of Oklahoma City University, with a master's from Tulsa University, Jane is a dedicated volunteer for OCU and serves on the Oklahoma City Community Foundation and the Oklahoma Centennial Commission. With author Bob Burke, she has written a book, *More Grace Than Glamour: My Years as Miss America and Beyond*. She is married to Gerald Gamble and is mother to one son and "Mimi" to two grandchildren.

LOU KERR was born and raised in Oklahoma. She earned her bachelor's degree from Oklahoma City University and was also awarded an honorary doctorate from OCU. She is president and chair of the Kerr Foundation,

Inc., and chair of the Centennial Commission for 2007. She stays involved in many local, national, and international philanthropic endeavors and has won numerous awards for her work.

NANCY LEONARD is proud to be an Oklahoman and has great respect for the state's rich and unique cultural heritage. She is the former executive director of Leadership Oklahoma and the current vice chair of the Oklahoma Centennial Commission. Nancy lives with her husband, Tim, on seventeen acres in northeast Oklahoma City. Nancy has three wonderful children and six very special grandchildren.

BILLIE LETTS, born in Tulsa, has lived in Oklahoma most of her life. She retired from Southeastern Oklahoma State University where she taught English. She is the author of three novels: *Where the Heart Is, The Honk and Holler Opening Soon,* and *Shoot the Moon.*

ROXANA LORTON has three married children, two girls and one boy; eight grandchildren, five boys and three girls; and a BA in journalism with a minor in art from the University of Tulsa. She is the current chair of the Oklahoma Heritage Association, serves on the council of the Kennedy Center National Committee for the Performing Arts in Washington D.C.; sits on the boards of the Philbrook and Gilcrease Museums; and is a trustee of the University of Tulsa and the Tulsa Town Hall. She has honors too many to list.

CLAUDIA LOVELACE, a native of Hemet, California, graduated from Oklahoma City University in 2002 with a bachelor's degree in religion and recently completed a master's degree in divinity at Perkins Theological Seminary. A United Methodist minister, Claudia is also a licensed practical nurse and has been a counselor in an alcohol and drug treatment center. She is currently a member of the following honor societies: Phi Etta Sigma, Alpha Sigma Lambda, and Theta Alpha Kappa. She was elected to Who's Who among Students in American Universities and Colleges.

WILMA MANKILLER is an author and activist and the first female to be elected to the position of principal chief of the Cherokee Nation. She has received more than eighteen honorary doctorates and many other awards, including the Presidential Medal of Freedom. She lives in Mankiller Flats in rural Adair County with her husband, Charlie Soap. They have five children and ten grandchildren.

ANITA MAY served as executive director of the Oklahoma Humanities Council from 1976 until her retirement in 2006. She has an MA and a PhD in history from the University of Pittsburgh and has taught in Oklahoma and Texas universities. She hopes to spend her retirement pursuing research in history, teaching, consulting, traveling with her husband, and spending time with their grandchildren.

LOUISA MCCUNE-ELMORE is editor in chief of *Oklahoma Today*. A graduate of San Francisco State University, she was born and raised in Enid. Before joining the magazine in 1997, she worked for *George, Worth*, and *Harper's Magazine*. She is the founder and organizer of the Sallie McFarland Rucks Reader Series at Wilson School in Oklahoma City. She lives in Oklahoma City with her husband, Chad Elmore; their son, Mac; three dogs; and one cat.

VICKI MILES-LAGRANGE was born in Oklahoma City to parents who emphasized the importance of lifelong learning, the value of a good education, and giving back to the community. She received a BA from Vassar College, cum laude, and a JD from Howard University School of Law, where she was an editor of the *Howard Law Journal*. She was an intern for the late U.S. Speaker Carl Albert. After working for the Justice Department, she returned to Oklahoma City, joining the Oklahoma City district attorney's office. She then became the first African American female elected to the Oklahoma State Senate, chairing the Senate Judiciary Committee and sponsoring legislation on law and justice issues, women, children, families, and minorities. She was appointed to the U.S. District Court of Oklahoma, Western Division, in 1994 by President Bill Clinton, becoming the first African American judge on the Tenth Circuit. She has also had significant experience in international rule of law and human rights as a member of the International Judicial Relations Committee of the U.S. Judicial Conference. Her civic and professional honors include induction into the Oklahoma Women's Hall of Fame, the Child Advocates Hall of Fame, and the Oklahoma African-American Hall of Fame. She has won the Oklahoma Bar Association's Women Trailblazer Award, the Oklahoma Bar Association's Courageous Lawyer Award, and the Oklahoma Public School Foundation Humanitarian Award. She was named the *Journal Record* 2004 Woman of the Year. She received an honorary doctor of laws from Oklahoma City University. Judge Miles-LaGrange has a daughter and son-in-law, Johnna and Jimmy, and a granddaughter, Cheyenne.

JOAN CRENSHAW NESBITT grew up in Nowata, where she spent four years performing with the Nowata High School Clown Troupe. Juggling and entertaining demanding audiences of all ages are skills she continues to put to good use as a wife, mother, and vice president for institutional advancement at the University of Tulsa, her alma mater.

ELIZABETH WOODS PENNINGTON is the pseudonym for a woman who might be a politician, a news reporter, a university professor, a beauty pageant winner, or the woman who lives two houses down from you. She holds a PhD.

LESLIE PENROSE, pastor of the Community of Hope United Church of Christ in Tulsa and adjunct professor of practical theology at Phillips Seminary, is involved in community service and in writing and speaking on building communities of justice and diversity.

BETTY PRICE became executive director of the Oklahoma Arts Council in 1983. She is a passionate advocate for public arts funding in order to make the arts accessible to all Oklahomans. She has been a guiding force in the commissioning of public art at the State Capitol in collaboration with the Capitol Preservation Commission, and she was an advisor for the Capitol dome. Betty serves on numerous boards and commissions, including the Centennial Commission, the American Indian Cultural Center, and the Mid-America Arts Alliance. Among her many honors, she is a member of the Oklahoma Women's Hall of Fame and was recognized as the 2006 Red Earth Ambassador. In 2000, she was named State Arts Agency Director of the Year by the National Assembly of State Arts Agencies. Betty attended Muskogee public schools, graduated from Northeastern State University, Tahlequah, and began her career as a public school music teacher. As an artist, she has been represented by Norman Wilks Gallery. She and her husband, Norris, have two children and two grandchildren.

JEAN RICHARDSON is an artist whose distinctive paintings are seen in galleries and collections across the country and in Europe. Born in Hollis in 1940, she aspired to be an artist with her first painting lessons at the age of seven. She graduated with a major in painting from Wesleyan College and in later years attended the Art Students League in New York. *Turning toward Home: The Art of Jean Richardson* was published in 1998. With a studio overlooking a lake, she lives with her husband outside of Oklahoma City. They have seven children, fourteen grandchildren, and an exuberant Weimaraner puppy.

ANNE ROBERTS is a two-career household of one. She holds bachelor's and master's degrees in music from the University of Oklahoma and sings with theatrical productions, orchestras, churches, and colleges throughout Oklahoma. She serves as the executive director of the Oklahoma Institute for Child Advocacy, working to improve the lives of Oklahoma's children and youth. She lives in Norman.

CINDY SIMON ROSENTHAL is an Oklahoma transplant who has flourished in red dirt for the past twenty-one years. She serves as mayor of Norman, Oklahoma, and as director and curator of the Carl Albert Congressional Research and Studies Center at the University of Oklahoma. She is the author of *When Women Lead* and *Women Transforming Congress*.

CINDY ROSS is a fifth-generation Oklahoman. Her great-great-grandfather settled in the Wakita area during the Cherokee Strip Land Run in 1893. Cindy's career in Oklahoma higher education spans twenty-eight years in various roles. She currently serves as president of Cameron University. She has three degrees, including a doctorate from Oklahoma State University. Cindy and Dale, her husband of thirty-six years, live in Lawton. They have two children, Garrett and Jordan.

SUSAN SAVAGE currently serves as Oklahoma's secretary of state following her appointment in 2003 by Governor Brad Henry. Prior to her position with the State of Oklahoma, Susan served as Tulsa's first woman and longest-serving mayor from 1992 to 2002. She has also been a faculty member at the University of Oklahoma College of Architecture. Susan has received local, regional, and national recognition and honors for her public service in urban planning, criminal justice, environmental stewardship, and human rights issues.

LYNN SCHUSTERMAN learned about philanthropy from her father at a very young age. Through his words and deeds, he instilled in Lynn a deep sense of responsibility to help people help themselves. Today, through the eponymous foundation she founded with her late husband, Lynn continues the family tradition of pursuing *tzedakah* (justice) and engaging in *tikkum olam* (the repairing of the world). With a special emphasis in the areas of education, child development, and community service in and around Tulsa, the Charles and Lynn Schusterman Family Foundation provides assistance to nonsectarian charitable organizations dedicated to enhancing the quality of life throughout Oklahoma. The foundation is also dedicated to helping the Jewish people flourish by supporting programs throughout the world that spread the joy of Jewish living, giving, and learning. Long recognized as one of Oklahoma's most distinguished citizens, Lynn was inducted into the Tulsa Hall of Fame in 2000, into the Oklahoma Women's Hall of Fame in 2003, and into the Oklahoma Hall of Fame in 2006. Lynn is also an internationally renowned figure in the Jewish community and maintains a second home in Israel in her beloved city of Jerusalem. She has three adult children and six granddaughters. To those who know her best, Lynn is a passionate advocate for causes dear to her and a leader who acts quickly and decisively. In the office at her home are two pillows with needlepoint stitching that say it all about Lynn. One reads, "Life Is Not a Dress Rehearsal," and the other says, "Eat Dessert First; Life Is Short."

MARIA TALLCHIEF PASCHEN has been called "the most technically accomplished ballerina ever produced in America" (*Women of the Hall*, 1996). Born in Oklahoma, she studied with Bronislava Nijinska and danced with the Ballet Russe de Monte Carlo. She danced many works by choreographer George Balanchine, and together Balanchine and Maria formed what was to become the New York City Ballet. Prima ballerina with that company, Maria was also artistic director for the Chicago City Ballet.

CAROLYN ANNE TAYLOR is a fifth-generation Oklahoman. Her great-great-grandfather participated in the Oklahoma Land Run. She was born and raised in Norman and represented her hometown in the Oklahoma House of Representatives from 1984 to 1992. She received bachelor's and master's degrees from the University of Oklahoma and a doctorate from Oklahoma State University. Currently she is a professor at Rogers State University in Claremore, where she lives with her husband, Stratton, and their two children, Carson and Abbey Anne.

KATHY TAYLOR was elected the thirty-eighth mayor of Tulsa in April 2006. She formerly served as Governor Henry's secretary of commerce and tourism, having oversight of Commerce, Tourism, Workforce Development, and the Oklahoma Employment Security Commission. She is an attorney and has served on the boards of directors of publicly traded companies such as Sonic Industries and Bank of Oklahoma. She is active in education, arts, and women's issues. She is proud to have raised a strong daughter, Elizabeth Frame, who helped get her elected mayor. Elizabeth has just begun law school at the University of Oklahoma.

SUSAN URBACH grew up in Minnesota, came to Oklahoma to study music, and has stayed here ever since. She has her bachelor's and master's degrees in music from Oklahoma City University. She is the regional director of the Oklahoma Small Business Development Center with the University of Central Oklahoma. She lives in Norman and is owned by two cats. If you have cats in your household, you'll know what she means.

GERI WISNER-FOLEY is a citizen of the Muscogee (Creek) Nation, a former U.S. Marine who served during Desert Storm, and the mother of a twelve-year-old. She is attorney general for the Absentee Shawnee Tribe of Oklahoma, prosecutor for the Iowa Nation, the Muscogee (Creek) Nation's ambassador to the United Nations, and a partner with Legal Advocates for Indian Country, LLP. Geri has a juris doctorate and a Native American law certificate from the University of Tulsa College of Law. She is a member of the Hvtce Cvpv Baptist church and is a member of the Tallahassee Wvkokye Ceremonial Grounds, as well as the Muscogee Nation Honor Guard.

About the Foundation

The Women's Foundation of Oklahoma is the state's leading funder of change for women and girls. The foundation raises money to support an endowment that provides a reliable, permanent source of grants to invest in the economic self-sufficiency of women and brighter futures for girls. Unlike other nonprofit organizations, the Women's Foundation of Oklahoma is an endowed fund of the Communities Foundation of Oklahoma, with the potential to effect change statewide in all communities—metropolitan and rural. It is the only statewide initiative focused solely on lasting change for women and girls.